GALDÓS STUDIES

GALDÓS STUDIES

EDITED BY
J. E. VAREY

TAMESIS BOOKS LIMITED

LONDON

Colección Támesis
SERIE A - MONOGRAFÍAS, IX

SBN   900411   11   2

Depósito Legal: M. 9.806 - 1970

Printed in Spain by Talleres Gráficos de EDICIONES CASTILLA, S. A.
Maestro Alonso, 23 - Madrid

for
TAMESIS BOOKS LIMITED
LONDON

CONTENTS

CONTENTS

EDITOR'S FOREWORD

The original suggestion for a book of essays on the novels of Pérez Galdós was first put forward in 1966. The majority of the contributions were in typescript by 1967, but for various reasons —not the least important being the inability of the editor to keep pace with his fellow contributors— the publication has been delayed until now. I am much indebted to my colleagues for the patience and forebearance which they have displayed.

J. E. V.

ABBREVIATIONS

AEA	*Anuario de Estudios Atlánticos*, Las Palmas, Canarias.
AG	*Anales galdosianos*.
AION	*Annali dell'Istituto Universitario Orientali*, Naples.
Arch	*Archivum*, Oviedo.
As	*Asomante*, Puerto Rico.
AUP	*Annales de l'Université de Paris*.
BBMP	*Boletín de la Biblioteca Menéndez y Pelayo*, Santander.
BH	*Bulletin Hispanique*.
BHS	*Bulletin of Hispanic Studies*.
BICC	*Boletín del Instituto Caro y Cuervo*.
BRABLB	*Boletín de la Real Academia de Buenas Letras de Barcelona*.
BSS	*Bulletin of Spanish Studies*.
CA	*Cuadernos Americanos*.
CHA	*Cuadernos Hispano-Americanos*, Madrid.
Cla	*Clavileño*, Madrid.
HBalt	*Hispania*, Baltimore and Wisconsin.
Hispl	*Hispanófila*, Madrid and Illinois.
HR	*Hispanic Review*.
In	*Insula*, Madrid.
LT	*La Torre*, Río Piedras, Puerto Rico.
MLF	*Modern Language Forum*, Los Angeles.
MLN	*Modern Language Notes*.
MLR	*Modern Language Review*.
MP	*Modern Philology*.
NRFH	*Nueva Revista de Filología Hispánica*, México.
PMLA	*Publications of the Modern Language Association of America*.
PQ	*The Philological Quarterly*.
PSA	*Papeles de Son Armadans*, Madrid-Palma de Mallorca.
RF	*Romanische Forschungen*.
RHi	*Revue Hispanique*.
RHM	*Revista Hispánica Moderna*, New York.
RLC	*Revue de Littérature Comparée*.
RLit	*Revista de Literatura*, Madrid.
RNC	*Revista Nacional de Cultura*, Caracas.

RO	*Revista de Occidente*, Madrid.
RoN	*Romance Notes.*
RPh	*Romance Philology.*
RR	*Romanic Review.*
RUBA	*Revista de la Universidad de Buenos Aires.*
S	*Symposium.*

J. E. VAREY

Galdós in the Light of Recent Criticism

It was not to be expected that the novels of Benito Pérez Galdós should have pleased the *avant-garde* writers and critics of the 1920s. Valle-Inclán's jibe at «Don Benito, el garbancero» in *Luces de Bohemia (Opera omnia,* vol. XIX [Madrid, 1924], 82) reflected a point of view that came to be widely, if uncritically, held. In years when the lyric predominated — to such an extent that Pedro Salinas could declare that «el signo del siglo XX es el signo lírico» *(Literatura española siglo XX,* 2.ª ed. [México, 1949], 34), Galdós's novels could be superficially discussed as stodgy, or, in the words of José Bergamín, as «la gloriosa escombrera nacional» («Galdós redimuerto», *El Heraldo* [Madrid], 5 January 1933). The tone of his novels, their scope, and above all their sheer bulk seemed out of place. Antonio Espina recognised the need in 1923 for a revaluation of Galdós's position:

> Los demás escritores de su época están ya situados y casi historiados en la opinión vigente. Galdós no. Parece que se tiene miedo a mirarle cara a cara, a romper su cristal, quizá por no romper al mismo tiempo el amable recuerdo que su lectura nos produjo en la adolescencia. Incluso se llega a quererle idolizar, creando sobre la frágil base de la amistad y el buen deseo una superstición mítica. Y fuerza es confesarlo. Galdós no es un Dickens ni siquiera un Balzac que justifiquen —disculpen— la exageración del culto y la deformación del mito.

For Espina, Galdós revealed «la falta de ese centro de gravedad intelectual que se llama sentido crítico, o, con más exactitud, autocrítico». He represented nothing more than an «enorme medianía». (Book review of Galdós's *Fisonomías sociales,* in *Revista de Occidente,* I [1923], 114-117).

1

The literary critics of this period, who might perhaps have been expected to reflect a more detached point of view, found Galdós difficult to evaluate. The superficial judgement of Hurtado and Palencia in their *Historia de la literatura española,* 2nd. ed. (Madrid, 1925), 1020, appears at first sight to be based exclusively on *Doña Perfecta:*

> Su mérito principal es el poder extraordinario de observación; brilla más en la pintura de caracteres y descripciones de tipos y lugares (sobre todo de la clase media y baja) que en la acción y movimiento de las pasiones. Sus tipos característicos son : uno, simpático, que representa el progreso, la luz, el agrado (el ingeniero joven); otro, antipático, símbolo del obscurantismo, tal como lo entiende Galdós (el sacerdote): ambos están admirablemente contrapuestos en *Doña Perfecta.* Idealista a veces en su representación del mundo, es frío, y no tiene llama lírica. Sus concepciones trascendentales lo elevan en inventiva sobre todos nuestros novelistas. Es benigno con los desgraciados, cuya vida de inopias y miserias refleja exactamente : por eso su horizonte es triste. Si no es rígidamente correcto, su lenguaje es familiar y expresivo; su diálogo, suelto; su estilo, natural y castizo... Su obra, en frase de Maura, será «la historia íntima de los españoles que vivieron durante la centuria décimonona».

Galdós is thus a cold, sad writer, devoid of poetry; yet his work is a faithful representation of nineteenth-century Spain. Aubrey Bell, in his *Contemporary Spanish Literature* (London, 1926), acknowledges that Galdós's attitude evolves, and absolves him of the charge of coldness :

> It is usual to class Galdós among the realists, although a good deal of his writing is not strictly based on reality. In his first period the influence of the Naturalistic school led him into an excessive or one-sided display of details... Later a cloudy symbolism and allegory manifested themselves, and a certain narrowness of outlook is evident throughout, without, however, the defect of insincerity or coldness (53-54).

Bell concludes his criticism of Galdós's writings with the following startling thought :

> Many of Galdós's novels are rather bundles of charming shreds and delicious patches than individual works of art (61).

2

It is a little difficult to equate Benito Pérez Galdós with the juvenile lead of *The Mikado,* and this type of critical reference to Galdós's style and to the form of his novels is indicative of the unease with which most critics approached these aspects of his work. L. B. Walton, by contrast, in his pioneer study, *Pérez Galdós and the Spanish Novel of the Nineteenth Century* (London, Toronto and New York, 1927), viewed Galdós primarily in an historical context, as a precursor of the so-called Generation of 1898, diagnosing Spain's malady, a preoccupation which, in the eyes of Walton, prevented him from being a truly universal author:

> In conclusion —he writes— it would, perhaps be extravagant to claim for Galdós a place beside Balzac, Dickens, Tolstoy or Dostoievsky in the hierarchy of European letters (234).

These three critics, then, share a common view of Galdós as the realist writer —at times verging close to the horrid brink of Naturalism— sane, clear-eyed, compassionate, long-winded, unartistic, not deeply interested in aesthetic problems, and, above all, as the faithful delineator of Spanish society in the second half of the nineteenth century.

* * *

The revival of interest in Galdós began to be felt during the Spanish Civil War. Evidently Galdós had always had his followers; Vicente Aleixandre relates that

> almorzando un día en una tabernita madrileña con Federico Garca Lorca, nos descubrimos ambos admiradores apasionados de Galdós ¡en aquella época! y amigos «vividos» y sin falla, desde chicos, de Jacinta, de la Peri, de Orozco, del León de Albrit («Revisión de Galdós», *In,* VII, núm. 82 [1952], 3).

The years of the Republic and the Civil War were to summon up a new Galdós, the novelist and champion of the *pueblo,* and this attitude, preserved and developed in Spanish America, is evident in the symposium of 1943 published by *Atenea,* the review of the Universidad de Concepción:

Cuando era necesario una idea o una figuración de la España del siglo pasado, sólo en Galdós se encontraba la médula, el pensamiento, la vida del pueblo, sus idas y venidas, sus pensamientos, sus inquietudes, sus amores y sus tragedias. Galdós hizo revivir en la serie formidable de sus *Episodios* y en la serie de sus novelas, toda el alma múltiple, austera o jovial, o trágica de ese gran pueblo, al cual debe la historia, desde sus años más remotos etapas intensas de luchas y de grandezas («Puntos de vista. El centenario de Pérez Galdós», *Atenea*, XX, núm. 215 [1943], 89).

The centenary of Galdós's birth, which occurred in 1943, did indeed suggest the need for a re-examination of critical attitudes.

Another important symposium was published in año XII, vol. XXIV (1943), nos. 139-141 of *Cursos y conferencias (Revista del Colegio Libre de Estudios Superiores)*. Roberto F. Giusti, «Prefacio. La obra galdosiana», 3-12, explains why Galdós's works fell into disfavour and suggests that a revaluation is necessary. Rafael Alberti, in «Un Episodio Nacional: *Gerona*», 13-14, shows how the Civil War had given a new immediacy to the historical novels:

Para los que por desgracia y fortuna hemos vivido el sitio de una ciudad, durante todas sus fases, en medio de una guerra profundamente popular y de independencia como lo fue también la que sostuvimos los republicanos de España desde julio de 1936 hasta marzo del 39, los Episodios Nacionales de Galdós —sobre todo los diez primeros, y de ellos «El 2 de Mayo», «Zaragoza» y más aún este de «Gerona» que nos ocupa— tenían que volver con ímpetu a nosotros, después de ciertos años de descenso de la obra galdosiana, como alimento necesario, como espejo donde reconocernos y sacar fuerza de nuestra propia imagen.

In «Nueva estimativa de las novelas de Galdós», 25-37, Guillermo de Torre underlines the necessity of applying to Galdós «una nueva escala de valores, otra estimativa, harto diferente de la que establecieron los coetáneos del autor». The critic stresses the importance of the later works and, above all, of *Fortunata y Jacinta*, «que forma el eje del sistema novelesco galdosiano». The almost totally neglected plays are considered by Jacinto Grau in «El teatro de Galdós», 39-55, his criticism being centred on *Realidad* and *Los condenados*. José María Monner Sans writes on «Galdós y la generación de 1898», 57-85, and discusses the changing attitudes of various writers to Galdós. María Teresa

4

León's, «Una mujer de Galdós que no está en sus novelas», 89-97, is novelised biography, purporting to discuss the relationship between Pérez Galdós and Sisita. In «Galdós y el Romanticismo», 99-111, Alejandro Casona discusses

> cuáles son las características del romanticismo que se conservan vigentes en la obra del maestro: y sobre todo, cómo estos fermentos idealistas van adquiriendo a través de él una nueva personalidad y un tratamiento de maduración hasta incorporarse a la nueva tendencia realista.

In «El sentido popular de Galdós», 113-128, Angel Ossorio is concerned largely with the political and social ideas of the novelist. Ricardo Baeza deals superficially with *Fortunata y Jacinta,* 129-138. Clearly many of the lectures given at this congress and recorded in the journal were of the utmost significance in their day, and it is of interest to note the way in which practising dramatists, poets and novelists turn to Galdós with renewed affection.

A fresh critical appraisal was already evident in the introduction which Angel del Río wrote for an edition of *Torquemada en la hoguera* published as early as 1931 (reprinted in *Estudios galdosianos* [Zaragoza, 1953], 91-129), but it is in «Aspectos del pensamiento moral de Galdós» (first published in *CA,* núm. 6 [1943]; reprinted in *Estudios galdosianos,* 9-37) that it becomes explicit. Whilst not denying to Galdós the title of «el más fiel cronista de la realidad española del siglo XIX», del Río comments that.

> algunas de sus facultades artísticas de mayor rango, entre ellas el humor de su fantasía y la serenidad de su espíritu al enfrentarse con la dramática coyuntura de una España escindida en permanente discordia civil, no se han subrayado suficientemente aunque hayan sido señaladas en ocasiones. Esa serenidad suya, fundada en un sentido liberal, religioso y humano de la vida, encierra para nosotros hondas enseñanzas, al punto que si otras razones de índole puramente artística no lo justificaran, haría casi imperativo el retorno a Galdós (10).

The true greatness of Galdós is to be found, according to this critic, in those very aspects which seemed to the readers of the 1920s to deny universality to his work:

> Es posible que pueda empezarse a ver la grandeza indudable de Galdós precisamente en la aparente intrascendencia de su obra:

5

en haber mostrado en todos sus personajes su común humanidad y en haber desdeñado los primores de estilo, sin pretender
dar a la palabra un valor poético por sí misma (13).

Angel del Río sees religion as the fundamental theme of Galdós's
literary production, a theme which develops and deepens, «desplazán-
dose de lo político y social hacia la conciencia íntima del personaje».
Whilst this is a natural development in his writing, it nevertheless
reflects «las tendencias neoespiritualistas de fin de siglo» (31). Galdós
emerges from this examination as a much more up-to-date writer, his
later works in particular, with their emphasis on the non-rational,
having affinities with existential writing.

Guillermo de Torre, writing in the same year, sets Galdós in an
historical perspective and defends him against those critics who attacked
his literary style («Itinerario de Galdós», *Sur,* XII, núm. 104 [1943], 72-
85. He admits that Galdós's style is very colloquial but points out
that, apart from its value as a social record, this manner of writing is
a literary innovation, allowing as it does the use of internal mono-
logues, and permitting «frecuentes aciertos de visión y plásticos hallaz-
gos de imágenes» (76). Galdós, for Guillermo de Torre, is a writer who
is far from prosaic. «Su materia novelesca es prosaica, como arrancada
directamente, en vivo, de la realidad, pero su traducción artística es
poética.» But not in the lyrical vein of the 1920s. Galdós is an epic
poet in prose, and his creations attain symbolic values:

No importa que los más de estos personajes se muevan en medios mezquinos, condicionados por lo mediocre de la época.
El caso es que muchos de los caracteres galdosianos cobran soberana fuerza plástica y permanecen como símbolos decisivos
de virtudes o maldades, rigurosamente individualizados (79).

1943 saw also the publication of Joaquín Casalduero's full-length
study, *Vida y obra de Galdós (1843-1920)* (Buenos Aires, Losada, 1943;
reprinted in an enlarged form by Editorial Gredos, Madrid, 1951; further
enlarged in subsequent editions). Casalduero's work is an attempt to
see Galdós whole, to relate his biography to his writings, and to deal
not only with the *novelas* —on the whole the main preoccupation of
the critics up to this time— but also with the *Episodios Nacionales* and
Galdós's theatre. In the space of a comparatively few pages, his work
summed up the major themes and established the continuity of Galdós's
preoccupations and form. Inevitably the personal interests of the critic

are reflected in his judgements, and Casalduero's vision imposes a strict pattern upon Galdós's evolution which, with its constant emphasis on literary currents, does not do justice to the author's artistic free-will, nor to his ironic tone and multi-faceted humour. (See Angel del Río's review of the first edition, in *RHM,* XI [1945], 52-56; reprinted in *Estudios galdosianos,* 137-143).

More than 25 years have passed since that centenary date, and the critical position of Galdós studies has been revolutionised. Articles and full-length studies have proliferated; the number of Ph.D. dissertations has grown from a trickle to a steady stream; a book-length bibliography has appeared; and *galdosistas* — a significant coinage in itself — thanks to the initiative of a group of American scholars, now have their own very welcome journal. Even though a comparison with the present state of, say, Balzac or Dickens studies reveals only too clearly how long is the road yet to be travelled, nevertheless much, in terms of quantity, has been accomplished. The purpose of the present study is to examine the critical output of the last quarter of a century and summarise the broad trends which have emerged, and to attempt at the same time to point out the most profitable targets for the immediate future. In the short space of an introductory essay it is not possible — nor would it be appropriate — to mention all the works of criticism which have appeared in this space of time. Those which, to the present writer, appear most significant or symptomatic have been singled out for comment, and the choice is to that extent idiosyncratic; the reader who wishes to examine the whole field of recent criticism should consult Theodore A. Sackett's *Pérez Galdós. An Annotated Bibliography* (Alburquerque, 1968) and, since all bibliographies, once printed, are inevitably out-of-date, annual bibliographies such as that of the *Year's Work in Modern Language Studies* should be regularly consulted. In Vol. III (1968) of *Anales galdosianos* there appears a very useful Galdós bibliography for the years 1966-1967; it is the stated intention of the editors that this is to appear annually in future. The editors further state that this bibliography should be considered as the continuation of a bibliography prepared by Manuel Hernández Suárez, dealing with the period up to and including 1965; this volume is announced for early publication in Las Palmas de Gran Canaria. This publication and the new annual bibliography will undoubtedly strengthen the critical foundations of Galdós studies.

* * *

The standard biography of Galdós is still that of H. Chonon Berkowitz, *Pérez Galdós. Spanish Liberal Crusader* (Madison, 1948), a somewhat disappointing work which, although full of factual information and written with the cooperation of Galdós's daughter, fails to bring the novelist to life. Galdós will always be a challenge to the biographer; retiring, not given to self-advertisment, even his own *Memorias* are singularly unrevealing. That other material is to hand is shown by studies such as those of José Pérez Vidal, *Galdós en Canarias (1843-1962)* (Madrid, 1952); and José Simón Cabarga's informative article, «Santander en la biografía y bibliografía de Galdós», *BBMP,* XXXVI (1960), 363-395. Autobiographical elements in a major novel are noted by Walter T. Pattison, «*El amigo Manso* and *el amigo Galdós*», *AG,* II (1967), 135-153. Galdós's personal life will probably always remain at least to some extent an enigma, but it should be possible for diligent research to uncover more information about the publishing of his works and his relationships with publishers and printers; his relationships with the actor-managers who put on his plays; his political career; his travels in Spain and abroad; his reading habits; his friendships and acquaintances. Such studies would help to give depth and body to the outline sketch which is all we have at the moment of Galdós's elusive personality.

* * *

If we turn to consider the situation of Galdós's printed works, we find it no more encouraging. The edition most commonly used and referred to is the six volume so-called *Obras completas,* published by Aguilar and edited by Federico Carlos Sáinz de Robles (first edition, Madrid, 1941-1942; many subsequent reprintings). The edition has serious defects: it is unscholarly; it is plagued with printing errors; and it does not take into account variants and revisions due to the pen of Galdós himself. As W. H. Shoemaker points out in his review of the *Obras completas,* in *HR,* XII (1944), 258-264:

> This is not a critical edition in the meaning held by modern scholarship. Sáinz nowhere discusses the text, the editions or printings copied or used as a basic text or in any other way; editorial problems do not seem to have existed or at least he did not choose to discuss them.

The short-comings of this edition were dramatically revealed by C. A. Jones in an article entitled «Galdós's Second Thoughts on *Doña Perfecta*», *MLR,* LIV (1959), 570-573, which pointed out that there are two versions of the novel, with radically different endings. The version with which we are familiar, and which appears in the Aguilar edition, was published by La Guirnalda in December, 1876. But there exists an earlier version, published in serial form in the *Revista de España* (and later, in June 1876, in book form by Noguera), which is cruder in conception and much more black-and-white than the later version. Joaquín Casalduero, «*La Fontana de Oro* de Pérez Galdós», *Ateneo,* núm. 88 (1955), and, more recently, Florian Smieja, in «An Alternative Ending of *La Fontana de Oro*», *MLR,* LXI (1966), 426-433, have drawn attention to similar indecisions on the part of the author in the earlier novel. The first edition (Madrid, La Guirnalda, 1870), has one ending; the second (Madrid, Noguera, 1871), another; and in the third edition (Madrid, La Guirnalda, 1885), Galdós reverts to his earlier ending. José F. Montesinos, *Galdós,* I (Madrid, 1968), discusses in some detail the large number of variants to be found in the various editions of the early works, such as *La Fontana de Oro* and *El audaz.* There is clearly a need for variant-reading editions of Galdós's novels, and, in particular, of the earlier works; meanwhile critics should, where possible, carefully check the edition they are using against the *princeps.* A further defect of the Aguilar edition is obvious from a consideration of the two versions of *La loca de la casa,* one printed together with the novels, as though it were a *novela dialogada,* and the other with the plays. As Hal Carney has established in «The Two Versions of Galdós's *La loca de la casa*», *HBalt,* XLIV (1961), 438-440, both versions are plays; the longer was published before the first night, and the shorter is the acting version. The need for research into the circumstances of publication of Galdosian texts is here clearly established.

Nor are the *Obras completas* in any sense complete. In 1923-1930 Alberto Ghiraldo published the so-called *Obras inéditas,* a misnomer, for most of the contents were hitherto uncollected newspaper articles. The genesis of the series is recounted by Ghiraldo in an article entitled «Don Benito Pérez Galdós», *Atenea,* XX (1943), 165-177. Sáinz de Robles utilised some, but not all, of these volumes in the Aguilar edition. In 1957 Pérez Vidal reprinted, under the title of *Madrid* (Madrid, 1957), various early articles originally published in

La Nación. W. H. Shoemaker reprinted other articles from *La Ilustración de Madrid,* under the title of *Crónica de la quincena* (Princeton, 1948), and Pérez Vidal has also reprinted and studied Galdós's musical criticism : *Galdós, crítico musical* (Madrid-Las Palmas, 1956). More recently Shoemaker has edited those prologues of Galdós not to be found in the Aguilar edition: *Los prólogos de Galdós* (México, 1962), and in «Galdós y *La Nación»*, *HispI,* núm. 25 (1965), 21-50, he presents a carefully drawn up check-list of the 131 articles which Galdós contributed to that newspaper from 1865 to 1868, noting the articles already published by Ghiraldo and Pérez Vidal and adding a large number which had hitherto escaped critical attention. Leo J. Hoar Jr., in *Benito Pérez Galdós y la «Revista del movimiento intelectual de Europa» (Madrid, 1865-1867)* (Madrid, 1968), an *anejo* of *Anales galdosianos,* examines Galdós's connections with that newspaper and republishes 40 articles which appeared in 1865-1867. Further minor writings no doubt remain uncollected : the sketch entitled *Aquél* was first published in *Los españoles de ogaño* (Madrid, 1872), II, 266-274, and more recently in Correa Calderón's *Costumbristas españoles* (Madrid, 1951), II, 535-539, but it has not been printed in either the *Obras completas* or the *Obras inéditas* (see Vernon A. Chamberlin, «The Riddle in Galdós's 'Lost' Sketch. *Aquél»*, *S,* XV [1961], 62-66). In 1956 José Pérez Vidal published «Una industria que vive de la muerte», *AEA,* núm. 2 (1956), 473-507. A sketch entitled «El Toboso» has appeared in *AG,* III (1968), 151-161.

The correspondence of Galdós has been the subject of much recent investigation. Individual letters have appeared from time to time: e.g., the letter to Alice H. Bushee published by Ada M. Coe in *HR,* XIV (1946), 340-342 (and further discussed by Robert J. Weber, *HR,* XXXI [1963], 348-349). In 1943 E. Varela Hervías published *Cartas de Pérez Galdós a Mesonero Romanos* (Madrid, 1943); José María de Cossío published letters of Pereda to Galdós in Vol. XLVIII of the *Antología de escritores y artistas montañeses* (Santander, 1957); and Alfonso Armas Ayala, in «Galdós editor», *As,* XIX (1963), 37-51, edited a series of letters from Galdós to Miguel H. de la Cámara. More recently, W. H. Shoemaker has studied and edited «Una amistad literaria : La correspondencia epistolar entre Galdós y Narciso Oller», *BRABLB,* XXX (1963-1964), 247-306 ; G. J. G. Cheyne has published letters «From Galdós to Costa in 1901», *AG,* III (1968), 95-98; and Robert Ricard «Cartas de Ricardo Ruiz Orsatti a Galdós acerca de Marruecos (1901-1910)»,

AG, III (1968), 99-117. Alfonso de Armas Ayala has recently studied the relationship between Galdós and León y Castillo, *Homenaje al Profesor Alarcos García* (Valladolid, 1965-1967), II, 169-181. Marcos Guimerá Peraza's *Maura y Galdós* (Las Palmas de Gran Canaria, 1967), is based on their correspondence and on other documents. Perhaps the most important of such publications appeared in 1964, the *Cartas a Galdós* edited by Soledad Ortega (Madrid, 1964), based on the contents of a suitcase full of letters which Galdós himself had remitted to the care of Ramón Pérez de Ayala; the editor prints those letters which she judges to be of most interest, and lists those which are as yet unpublished. One of the most assiduous collectors of Galdós's correspondence has been Joseph Schraibman. He has published «Cartas inéditas de Manuel Tolosa Latour a Don Benito Pérez Galdós», *In,* XVI, núm. 179 (1961), 3; see also *Revista del Museo Canario,* núms. 77-84 (1961-1962); «Cartas inéditas de Galdós», *S,* XVI (1962), 115-121; various letters of Pérez de Ayala, *Hispl,* núm. 17 (1963); «An Unpublished Letter from Galdós to Ricardo Palma», *HR,* XXXII (1964), 65-68. More recently, in collaboration with Sebastián de la Nuez, Schraibman has given us, in *Cartas del Archivo de Galdós* (Madrid, 1967), a check-list of the «archivo particular» of the novelist preserved in the Casa-Museo of Las Palmas. This check-list largely complements that of Soledad Ortega, and in the volume itself the editors print selected letters. They also announce a project, headed by Alfonso Armas, which has as its aim the collection and eventual publication of the letters from Galdós which evoked or replied to the letters of his correspondents.

It is clear from what has been said that a great deal remains to be done before full and reliable texts of Galdós's writings are available. Because of the lack of textual studies and the paucity of the material available, very little work has been done on the process of authorship, or on the transmission of Galdós's texts. One of the most interesting publications of the last few years is Robert J. Weber's study, *The «Miau» Manuscript of Benito Pérez Galdós. A Critical Study,* Univ. of California Pub. in Mod. Philol., vol. 72 (Berkeley and Los Angeles, 1964). As Weber points out in his preface, «in no study of Galdós's creative process has a manuscript been examined in detail» (iii), an omission which he proceeds to make good by studying the two different manuscript versions of *Miau* (dated 26 December 1887 and 2 February 1888), together with the changes made by the author in proof. «My emphasis», says Weber, «is upon novelistic technique, the ways in which Galdós developed structure and theme, and the effects of the various textual changes upon theme and structure» (iii). Weber's study is thus of the greatest importance; in it we are able to see for the first time Galdós at work, and to appreciate the various methods by which he sought to achieve his effects. More recently the same critic has examined «Galdós's Preliminary Sketches for *Torquemada y San Pedro», BHS,* XLIV (1967), 16-27, basing himself on three outline sketches relating to the characters of Valentín, Fidela and Torquemada preserved in the Casa-Museo. It is to be hoped that other Galdós manuscripts, known to be in existence, will be subjected to a similar scrutiny, the results of which should influence critical interpretations as well as providing valuable textual evidence.

Until such labours have been undertaken, until scholars have diligently examined the remaining literary reviews and newspapers of Galdós's day, until the correspondence —both letters despatched and letters received— has been brought together, it will not be possible to contemplate a true *Complete Works.* The task is immense, not only because of the amount of material involved, but because of the paucity of bibliographical tools, the lack of similar investigations into the correspondence of Galdós's contemporaries, the disappearance of theatrical archives, and for many other reasons. Perhaps we shall have to be content in the first place with competent editions of the novels and plays; a series of volumes, the shorter novels each in one volume and the longer novels in two, three or four (as in the original editions), with variant readings, critical apparatus and notes on the transmission of the text, clearly printed on good paper, is long overdue.

* * *

The identification of sources has long been a favourite game of the academic, and the *Episodios nacionales* of Galdós provide very suitable material. It is interesting to note that the very first publication of Marcel Bataillon was on «Les Sources historiques de *Zaragoza», BH,* XXIII (1921), 129-141, and this field of study has been largely developed by French scholars, notably Jean Sarrailh («Quelques Sources du *Cádiz* de Galdós», *BH,* XXIII [1921], 33-48), G. Boussagol («Sources et composition de *Zumalacárregui», BH,* XXVI [1924], 241-264) and Robert Ricard. Ricard has published some very stimulating articles on *Aita Tettauen* («Note sur la genèse de l'*Aita Tettauen* de Galdós»,

BH, XXXVII [1935], 473-477) and on «Structure et inspiration de *Carlos VI en La Rápita»*, *BH,* LXVII (1955), 70-83.   C. Vázquez Arjona has published various studies of the historical background of several *Episodios:* «Cotejo histórico de cinco *Episodios nacionales* de Benito Pérez Galdós», *RHi,* LXVIII (1926), 321-550; «Un *Episodio nacional* de Benito Pérez Galdós, *El 19 de marzo y el 2 de mayo* (cotejo histórico)», *BH,* XXXIII (1931), 116-139; «Un *Episodio nacional* de Galdós, *Bailén* (cotejo histórico)», *BSS,* IX (1932), 116-123.   Alfred Rodríguez has studied the relationship between *Romeo and Juliet* and *Zaragoza* in «Shakespeare, Galdós y *Zaragoza»*, *CHA,* núm. 166 (1963), 89-98; and in «Galdós's Use of the Classics in *Zaragoza»*, *MLN,* LXXIX (1964), 211-213, the same critic turns to reflections of Horace, Virgil and the *Aeneid* in this *episodio*.   Hans Hinterhäuser, in his study of *Los «Episodios Nacionales» de Benito Pérez Galdós* (German edition, Hamburg, 1961; Spanish translation, Madrid, 1963), has examined the historical novels in the light of their use of sources, concluding that

> Galdós, en cuanto historiador, se documentaba con mucho más detenimiento de lo que hasta ahora se había creído: a las fuentes convencionales se suman en los últimos *Episodios* reflejos de su vida juvenil; y a ello he podido añadir muchas huellas —aun probablemente no todas— de inspiración pictórica (370).

The search for sources for Galdós's inspiration has been much facilitated by Berkowitz's publication of *La biblioteca de Benito Pérez Galdós* (Las Palmas de Gran Canaria, 1951), a useful list of Galdós's library, at present housed in the Casa-Museo of Las Palmas, Great Canary. Berkowitz lists 3.940 volumes, and his analytical tables show clearly their distribution.   Many of these works have marginalia, slips of paper, turned down corners, or other indications of Galdós's interests. It is to be hoped, for instance, that an examination now being undertaken of the 28 works on medicine may well throw light on Galdós's use of unusual mental states, hallucinations and dreams.

Work on the sources of Galdós's novels predates considerably the centenary of 1943.   In 1932 George Portnoff published two articles on the influence of Tolstoy on Galdós: «The Beginning of the New Idealism in the Works of Tolstoy and Galdós», *RR,* XXIII (1932), 33-37; and «The Influence of Tolstoy's *Ana Karenina* on Galdós's *Realidad»*, *HBalt,* XV (1932), 203-214.   This important field was further explored by Casalduero in 1937, in his «*Ana Karénina* y *Realidad*», *BH,* XXXIX (1937), 375-396. More recently, Mrs V. C. Colin has studied *Nazarín* and *Halma* in relation to Tolstoy's influence, in «A Note on Tolstoy and Galdós», *AG,* II (1967), 155-168, and a further study from the same critic appears in the present volume. The influence of English writers on Galdós, although a critical commonplace, has never been thoroughly investigated, and in particular the evaluation of the influence of Dickens on the Spanish author is by no means complete, despite Effie L. Erickson's «The Influence of Charles Dickens on the Novels of Benito Pérez Galdós», *HBalt,* XIX (1936), 421-430. Similarly, the debt of Galdós to Balzac has not been examined with the required degree of critical exactness; brief studies are to be found in Carlos Ollero, «Galdós y Balzac», *In,* VII, núm. 82 (1952), 9-10, and Francisco C. Lacosta, «Galdós y Balzac», *CHA,* nos. 224-225 (1968), 345-374. Turning to classical authors, Gerald Gillespie has recently studied the reflections of «Cervantine consciousness» and themes: «Reality and Fiction in the Novels of Galdós», *AG,* I (1966), 11-31, whilst J. Chalmers Herman's «*Don Quijote*» and the Novels of Pérez Galdós (Ada, Oklahoma, 1955), suggests influences on a wider scale.

Various recent articles pinpoint, or suggest, a literary source for a scene or even a phrase. Stephen Gilman has studied «Las referencias clásicas de *Doña Perfecta:* tema y estructura de la novela», *NRFH* III (1949), 353-362; among them, the burlesque etymology Urbs Augusta > Orbajosa, the tío Licurgo, don Inocencio's quotations from Horace and Virgil, don Cayetano's interest in classical antiquities. They are shown to be largely ironical in intention, and the critic endeavours to demonstrate through them «la razón del fracaso de *Doña Perfecta* como novela» (359); it falls, he considers, somewhere between the true tragedy and the study of the imperfections of Pepe Rey. José Fradejas Lebrero, in «Para las fuentes de Galdós», *RLit,* IV (1953), 319-344, compares *Misericordia* with Francisco Cutanda's *Doña Francisca, el portento de la caridad* (Madrid, 1869). Shoemaker has published «Galdós's *La de los tristes destinos* and its Shakespearean Connections», *MLN,* LXXI (1956), 114-119, relating the title of the novel to a line from *Richard III,* by way of Antonio Aparisi. In «Galdós's Classical Scene in *La de Bringas*», *HR,* XXVII (1959), 423-434, he endeavours to link the confrontation of Rosalía and Refugio, towards the end of the novel, with Act III of the *Asinaria* of Plautus. In «Galdós devant Flaubert et Alphonse Daudet», *AUP,* XXVIII (1958), 449-459 (reprinted on several occasions), Robert Ricard establishes points of comparison between Galdós and the two French novelists. Munroe Z. Hafter in «*Le Crime de Sylvestre Bonnard,* A Possible Source for *El amigo Manso*», *S*, XVII (1963), 123-129, compares the ironic portraits of the heroes of the two novels. Louise S. Blanco has written recently on the «Origin and History of the Plot of *Marianela*», *HBalt*, XLVII (1965), 463-467; and Otis H. Green notes parallels between the same novel and *Don Quijote:* «Two Deaths: Don Quijote and Marianela», *AG*, II (1967), 131-133.

More ambitious and more stimulating than any of these articles is Walter T. Pattison's *Benito Pérez Galdós and the Creative Process* (Minneapolis, 1954). Pattison starts from the premise that many elements of the two novels he studies, *Gloria* and *Marianela,*

> do not depend upon creative imagination but can be traced back to real-life people or places or again to literary sources; many ideas which we might at first believe original with Galdós find frequent expression in the magazines he read.

The critic's intention is

> to show some reason why and how this material was assembled into artistic form —why, for example, the author was impelled to write on religion in *Gloria,* how and why he looked for certain types of material, and how the associative bonds between these materials led him to recombine them in a new, original form (3-4).

Galdós himself states that *Gloria* was the result of a sudden flash of inspiration (a neo-Romantic evaluation of the creative process, reminiscent of Bécquer's *hilo de luz*), but Pattison demonstrates how his reading, his travels in the north of Spain, conversation with friends and the general climate of opinion are all reflected in the novel. (The letters of Pereda to Galdós published by Soledad Ortega in *Cartas a Galdós* enable yet more of the creative process to be laid bare, and form a valuable adjunct to Pattison's study.) All this disparate material is present in the mind of Galdós, and then, apparently instantaneously, the connection between the various parts becomes clear:

> The moment of crystallization took place. Out of the mass of material, consciously and subconsciously remembered, there flashed into place the elements necessary to make the first part of the novel. After two weeks of frenzied writing, it was down on paper (113).

15

This kind of study is stimulating, and Pattison's book, itself an important step forward, makes it clear that we need to know very much more about the climate of ideas in the second half of the nineteenth century in Spain before we can hope to appreciate Galdós's creative process, or arrive at a clear understanding of his novels. To the works of Pierre Jobit, J. B. Trend and Juan López Morillas on the *krausistas*, to those of C. M. Hennessey and Raymond Carr on the political state of Spain, we need to add sociological, economic and ideological studies if Galdós is ever to be seen in clear focus. The influence of the *krausistas* on the development of Galdós's thought has been discussed by Juan López Morillas in «Galdós y el krausismo. *La familia de León Roch*», *RO,* 2.ª época, VI, núm. 60 (1968), 331-357; by Sherman Eoff in *The Modern Spanish Novel* (New York, 1961); by Denah Lida, «Sobre el *krausismo* de Galdós», *AG,* II (1967), 1-27; and by Pattison. W. H. Shoemaker's «Sol y sombra de Giner en Galdós», *Homenaje al Prof. Rodríguez Moñino* (Madrid, 1966), II, 213-225, studies various reviews and letters which passed between the two writers, concerning Galdós's novels from *La Fontana de Oro* to *El doctor Centeno.* The influence of Comte is the subject of Joaquín Casalduero's «Auguste Comte and *Marianela*», *Smith College Studies in Modern Languages,* XXI (1939-1940), 10-25, and is further considered by C. A. Jones in «Galdós's *Marianela* and the Approach to Reality», *MLR,* LVI (1961), 515-519. Other philosophical movements and currents of thought —the influence of Hegel, Kant and Schopenhauer, and the impact of Darwinism and positivism in Spain— are considered in such general studies as Casalduero's *Vida y obra de Galdós,* Eoff's *The Novels of Pérez Galdós,* and the same writer's *The Modern Spanish Novel.* Critics such as Josette Blanquat, in «Au temps d'*Electra* (Documents galdosiens)», *BH,* LXVIII (1966), 253-308, and «Galdós et la France en 1901», *RLC,* XLII (1968), 321-345, and E. Inman Fox, in «Galdós's *Electra:* A Detailed Study of its Historical Significance and the Polemic between Martínez Ruiz and Maeztu», *AG,* I (1966), 131-141, are progressing in this same direction, and it is clear from such studies that have been made that Galdós is a novelist who must be seen against the background of his own times before we can appreciate his aims and evaluate his success. As Sherman Eoff writes in «Galdós in Nineteenth-Century Perspective», *AG,* I (1966), 3-9, «the student of Galdós is obliged to become a student of the nineteenth century».

Carlos Blanco Aguinaga pointed out in his review of Pattison's book, *NRFH,* IX (1955), 292-298, that the study is not so much of the «creative process» as of «fuentes ambientales, clima espiritual de una época a partir del cual el *genio* crea. Donde termina el libro de Pattison, empieza la creación». In other words, once the task begun by Pattison and carried forward by other critics has been successfully accomplished, the results of the investigations must be married to the fruits of stylistic studies such as Weber's on *Miau.*

* * *

The influence of Galdós on his contemporaries and successors is a field in which much remains to be done. Ricardo Gullón's *Galdós, novelista moderno* (Madrid, 1960), developing from the introduction to his edition of *Miau* (Madrid, 1957), is particularly interesting for the attempt to suggest a parallel between *Miau, Les Employés* of Balzac and Kafka's *The Trial.* The latter comparison is somewhat far-fetched, but its very existence shows that modern critics are no longer content to see Galdós as the *costumbrista par excellence* —that is to say, the most accomplished exponent of an art-form which flourished in the early part of the nineteenth century— but as a precursor of the non-realistic novel of the twentieth century. Casalduero's valuable study «Baroja y Galdós», *RHM,* XXXI (1965), 112-117, does not seek to

> unamunizar a Galdós, ni verlo a través de Baroja o Valle-Inclán, ya que eso nos impediría captar el forcejeo final del novelista por estar de acuerdo con el presente de sus últimos años que se le escapaba.

Nevertheless, argues the critic,

> es imprescindible aprehender el enlace de la generación del 98 con la visión galdosiana del mundo y de España. Asi no perderemos el sentido de continuidad de la cultura española.

Juan Ventura Agudiez, «Ganivet en las huellas de Galdós y Alarcón», *NRFH,* XVI (1962), 89-95, suggests that the Pío Cid novels reflect various themes and viewpoints in the work of Galdós, notably those expressed in *Angel Guerra.* Berkowitz linked Galdós with the so-called Generation of 1898 in an article published in 1942, *PQ,* XXI (1942), 107-120, whilst José Angeles dealt with the same topic in an article published twenty years later, *HBalt,* XLVI (1963), 265-273, concluding, by means of a set of rigid comparisons and contrasts, that

17

Galdós's influence on such writers as Unamuno, Azorín, Machado and Maeztu was negligible. A more positive influence is seen by Ricardo Gullón in «Cuestiones galdosianas», *CHA*, XXXIV, núm. 101 (1958), 237-254. José Angeles also deals in more detail with the differences of approach that characterise Baroja and Galdós, *RLit*, XXIII (1963), 49-64. Possible influences of Galdós on Ortega are studied by Ciriaco M. Arroyo, «Galdós y Ortega y Gasset: Historia de un silencio», *AG*, I (1966), 143-150. Emma Susana Speratti-Piñero links Galdós's *Doña Perfecta* with Lorca's *La casa de Bernarda Alba*, *RUBA*, IV (1959), 369-378; whilst David T. Sisto compares the same novel with Louis Bromfield's *A Good Woman*, *S*, XI (1957), 273-280; and Donald F. Brown establishes yet a further comparison with Manuel Gálvez's *Perdido en su noche*, *HBalt*, XLVII (1964), 282-287.

* * *

Other critics have followed more traditional lines, and the old labels are still being pinned on, defined and refined. Galdós as a realist is compared by Jaime Torres Bodet to Dostoyevsky and Stendhal, in *Tres inventores de la realidad; Stendhal, Dostoyevsky, Pérez Galdós* (México, 1955). Francisco Ayala, «Sobre el realismo en literatura con referencia a Galdós», *LT*, VII (1959), 91-121, attempts to define Galdós's own views on realism, linking his technique with that of seventeenth-century writers such as Quevedo, but his study lacks a firm historical basis and does not attempt to distinguish between the viewpoint of the realist and the naturalist. A more recent study, that of Salvador Bacarisse, «The Realism of Galdós: Some Reflections on Language and the Perception of Reality», *BHS*, XLII (1965), 239-250, shifts the critical emphasis, arguing that «realism can be defined in terms of the medium used to create the illusion, rather than in terms of the impression of *verosimilitud* it produces on readers». Sherman Eoff's «Galdós y los impedimentos del realismo», *HispI*, núm. 24 (1965), 25-34, gives a somewhat old-fashioned view of the writer: «Su realismo casual e inclusivo, sin tales acompañamientos de arte intelectual como intenso análisis psicológico ni sutilezas de estilo y técnica, presenta la apariencia de un arte inculto». Josette Blanquat has recently studied *El amigo Manso* in relation to naturalism, *BH*, LXIV bis (1962), 318-335, and sees the novel as a humorous attack by Galdós on the naturalists. Sherman Eoff, «A Galdosian Version of Picaresque Psychology», *MLF,* XXXVIII (1953), 1-12, declares *Lo prohibido* to be «anti-naturalistic in its thought content», and in its form, reflecting the novels of Cervantes. The impact of the theories of nauralism on *La desheredada* is amply considered by Eamonn Rodgers, *BHS,* XLV (1968), 285-298; Galdós lacks Zola's determinism and recognises that «the quality of this life is often influenced by romantic attitudes». Monroe Z. Hafter, analysing the some novel in «Galdós's Presentation of Isidora in *La desheredada*», *MP,* LX (1962), 22-30, sees the importance of naturalism in the work of Galdós as deriving from the attempt to break down «the generic forms of the novel». Anthony Zahareas, in «The Tragic Sense in *Fortunata y Jacinta*», *S,* XIX (1965), 38-49, considers that

> all the different relationships and the various levels of tragedy
> in the novel spell out the need to understand that the world,
> especially the inner world of man, is too complex to compre-
> hend. Because the novelist dramatizes this complexity and its
> tragic consequences, and because he forces the reader to grasp
> the particular dimensions of the individual's tragic situation,
> he succeeds in destroying the formulas of human relationships
> given by some philosophers and many naturalists.

The suggestion to be found in earlier critics that Galdós should be considered a naturalist solely because he described scenes of low life —as in *Misericordia*— is clearly erroneous. Recent articles on the figure of Almudena, the blind beggar, have clearly demonstrated that Galdós's own statement in the introduction to the Nelson edition of the novel (1913), which might lead the reader to suppose that the character is taken directly from life, needs considerable qualification. Galdós describes how he met and talked with a blind Moorish beggar: «De este modo adquirí este tipo interesantísimo, que los lectores de *Misericordia* han encontrado tan real. Toda la verdad del pintoresco Mordejai es obra de él mismo, pues poca parte tuve yo en la descripción de esta figura.» Perhaps we are intended to take the latter sentence *al pie de la letra,* for recent studies by Ricard («Sur le personnage d'Almudena dans *Misericordia*», *BH,* LXI [1959], 12-25; reprinted in *Galdós et ses romans* [Paris, 1961], 51-61) and Chamberlin («The Significance of the Name Almudena in Galdós's *Misericordia*», *HBalt,* XLVII [1964], 491-496) have demonstrated that, his physical description aside, Almudena is by no means an accurate picture of a blind Moorish beggar. He is intended to be an incarnation of the tolerance which Galdós sought in religion, a synthesis of Judaism, Mohammedanism and Christianity. Furthermore, Denah Lida has demonstrated, in «De Almudena y su lenguaje», *NRFH*, XV (1961), 297-308, that the strange language which Almudena uses can not be explained philologically in terms of his background as given in the novel, and is indeed a literary creation, and not an observed reality. Very clearly, Almudena is not a realistic or naturalistic portrait. The external features only are taken from life, and Galdós as *I am a Camera* —or *I am a Tape-Recorder*— is a gross over-simplification.

The most far-reaching study which has so far been attempted of the nature of Galdós's views on reality and the various ways in which he attempted to incorporate reality into his novels is that of Gustavo Correa, in *Realidad, ficción y símbolo en las novelas de Pérez Galdós. Ensayo de estética realista* (Bogotá, 1967). Correa plots the evolution which he diagnoses in the novelist's method of representing the external world and the inner workings of the human mind. Galdós moves from primarily socio-political problems in his first novels to an almost excessive concern for detail and fact in the novels of the Naturalist phase, thus defining the environment which, together with the factor of heredity, strongly influence without determining the life of the individual. In the later *novelas contemporáneas,* external reality is subordinated to the spiritual development of the principal characters. Correa deals in a very interesting manner with the planes of reality/fiction within the individual works, and with Galdós's artistic theory and practice; he studies the reflection of Romanticism in the novels, and his work includes also a consideration of the importance of Nature in Galdós's fiction.

In an interesting article, «Sobre la veta fantástica en la obra de Galdós», *Atlante,* I (1953), 78-86, 136-143, Carlos Clavería notes the way in which Galdós has been labelled a polemical writer (due to the success of the *novelas de la primera época)* and a *costumbrista,* and suggests that the vein of fantasy which characterises his novels has been unjustly neglected. The critic sees the origin of this fantasy in the late Romantic novel, the Spanish equivalent of the Gothic novel, and cites particularly Galdós's early tale, *La sombra.* At the other end of Galdós's long production, we have the last novels, *El caballero encantado* and *La razón de la sinrazón,* and the almost equally fantastic fourth and fifth series of the *Episodios nacionales.* Clearly these last productions of Galdós should be seen, not as the aberrations of a realist (as was the tendency of the critics of thirty years ago), but as one of the many reactions against the realistic novel which characterise the last years of the nineteenth and the beginning of the twentieth centuries. These novels should be equated with the Pío Cid novels of Ganivet, and with Unamuno's *Amor y pedagogía*.

The role of the fantastic in the novels springs in part from Galdós's interest in abnormal psychology, as Carlos Clavería notes in «Galdós y los demonios», *Homenaje a J. A. van Praag* (Amsterdam, 1956), 32-37. Whilst this interest is evident in the early novels and in the novels written under naturalist influence —as demonstrated by Marie-Claire Petit, «*La desheredada*, ou le Procès du rêve», *RoN*, IX (1968), 235-243— it was to fascinate the novelist throughout his career. It may be equated also with Galdós's use of dreams, hallucinations and other states when the rational faculties are no longer in control, a subject studied by Joseph Schraibman in *Dreams in the Novels of Galdós* (New York, 1960), a work which suffers from a failure to consider adequately each dream in relation to the theme of the novel in which it occurs. The conclusions are therefore obvious enough:

> The use of the dream technique afforded Galdós an opportunity to reveal openly the sex drives, frustrations, inadequacies and incompatibilities of the people in his books (182).

The book would also have gained from some consideration of Galdós's medical and psychological studies. Schraibman rightly insists that

> it is rather paradoxical that an artist endowed with the fanciful imagination of Galdós should be presented as a prime example of «Realism» by critics whose vision of realist practice includes a veneration of the photographic; i.e., very definite restriction placed upon the unusual, the bizarre, the contrived image. With the introduction of dreams into his novels, Galdós found a way to give free rein to his imaginative powers within the framework of true realism — for even in the most prosaic life the dream is imaginative, strange, almost poetic in its extraordinariness (183-184).

The study of this theme should be extended to include the fantasy elements in the novels, abnormal psychology, and the whole concept of an intuitive response to life which Galdós sets against the artificial and often hypocritical responses of society (compare Louise Nelson

21

3

Calley, «Galdós's Concept of Primitivism: A Romantic View of the Character of Fortunata», *HBalt,* XLIV [1961], 663-665; and the review article on Schraibman's book by Gerald Gillespie, «Dreams and Galdós», *AG,* I [1966], 107-115).

* * *

Studies dedicated specifically to Galdós's characterisation are not as prolific as might be expected. W. H. Shoemaker, in «Galdós's Literary Creativity: D. José Ido del Sagrario», *HR,* XIX (1951), 204-237, studies one of the more important of the recurring characters intended to give a sense of unity to the *novelas contemporáneas;* the critic stresses particularly the

> *jocoserio* nature of Galdós's attitude and style, evident in technical devices and practices, more deeply in the human harmony of the chord of comic humour and pathos, of mockery and sympathy, and from the very beginning in the name with which Galdós baptized his offspring.

Monroe Z. Hafter's «The Hero in Galdós's *La Fontana de Oro*», *MPh,* LVII (1959-1960), 37-43, is a stimulating study with wider implications for a study of Galdós's technique than the title conveys. Ricardo Gullón has studied «La invención del personaje en *El amigo Manso*», *In,* XIV, núm. 148 (1959), 1-2, and Renée Schimmel writes on «Algunos aspectos de la técnica de Galdós en la creación de Fortunata», *Arch,* VII (1957), 77-100. The Jew as a type in the works of Galdós has been the subject of several recent articles. The articles by Ricard, Chamberlin and Denah Lida on Almudena have already been noted, and Casalduero has written on the Jew from Daniel Morton to Almudena *(MLN,* LXXIX [1964], 181-187). Casalduero's article can profitably be compared to Chamberlin's study of «Galdós's Sephardic Types», *S,* XVII (1963), 85-100. A particular technique of characterisation is the subject of Mariano Baquero Goyanes's «Las caricaturas literarias de Galdós», *BBMP,* XXXVI (1960), 331-362, and his methods are closely compared with Quevedo, as well as with those of Dickens, Balzac and other contemporary writers.

* * *

In the past, Galdós's style has usually been labelled *castizo;* although it has been criticised as not always academically correct, his style has been said to be a faithful reflection of the period which he set out to depict. But more recent articles have looked beneath the surface realism of the novels, and this critical attitude is now to be seen also in studies of the style. Ricardo Gullón, «Lenguaje y técnica de Galdós», *CHA,* núm. 80 (1956), 38-61, writes that

> Galdós supera al realismo por el camino de la penetración poética en torno suyo... La poesía es también creación, invención, revelación de lo que el novelista quiere lograr : el descubrimiento del hombre en la sociedad, la épica lucha del individuo con el medio y —en el caso de Galdós— de un país consigo mismo... El lenguaje, ese lenguaje tan discutido y con frecuencia censurado, sirvió admirablemente a sus fines.

In a sensitive articles, «Vulgaridad y genio de Galdós». El estilo y la técnica de *Miau»*, *Arch,* VII (1957), 48-75, Antonio Sánchez Barbudo provides an acute analysis of Galdós's presentation of reality. The article contains also a useful study of Galdosian criticism up to the time of writing. The new approach to Galdós's style is exemplified by Stephen Gilman in «La palabra hablada y *Fortunata y Jacinta»*, *NRFH,* XV (1961), 542-560. The author underlines

> la riqueza idiomática casi inverosímil de Galdós, riqueza que llega a superar la del mismo Lope... Cada novela de Galdós constituye una *summa* del español del siglo XIX, una *summa* que no sólo registra cuanto hay de registrable, sino que también revitaliza la lengua, puesto que entrega ese tesoro al orden vivo del fluir temporal.

Graciela Andrade Alfieri and J. J. Alfieri have studied «El lenguaje familiar de Pérez Galdós», *Hispl,* núm. 22 (1964), 27-73, and have produced a lexicon of proverbs, *modismos, argot* and slang in *Fortunata y Jacinta.* Much more work on these lines is needed. The extent to which Galdós's slang or *argot* is genuine has yet to be systematically investigated; a starting-point is José de Onís's «La lengua popular madrileña en la obra de Pérez Galdós», *RHM,* XV (1949), 353-363. Gonzalo Sobejano has studied a specific, if restricted, field in «Galdós y el vocabulario de los amantes», *AG,* I (1966), 85-100. In «The Exordium of *Torquemada en la hoguera»*, *MLN,* LXXX (1965), 258-260, Pierre L. Ullman compares the opening of the novel to the proem of a *romance de ciego.* Critical notes have also begun to appear on particular words or phrases: Robert Ricard, «Trois mots du vocabulaire de Galdós: *cebolla, araña* et *barbero*», *AION Sezione Romanza,* V (1963), 173-175; Ricard, «La *loca de la casa*», *BH,* LXIV (1963), 65-66; S. G. Armistead, «The Canarian Background of Pérez Galdós's *echar los tiempos*», *RPh,* VII (1953), 190-192. Considering the problem historically, J. Chalmers Harman lists «Quotations and Locutions from *Don Quijote* in Galdós's Novels», *HBalt,* XXXVI (1953), 177-181. A more interesting —and more rewarding— approach is that of Chamberlin in his study of «The *muletilla:* An Important Facet of Galdós's Characterization Technique», *HR,* XXIX (1961), 296-309. Chamberlin argues that

> Galdós's utilization of the *muletilla* is a consistently realistic device —a verbalization consistent with the education, social status, environment and psychology of the character presented.

Chamberlin is particularly revealing in his analysis of the different *muletillas* used by Torquemada in the course of his career. Torquemada is clearly a key character in the Galdós corpus, and, as H. B. Hall's article in the present volume reveals, a full study of his developing language as he rises in the world of finance and government would be both fascinating and illuminating. In this type of approach the study of style and of characterization march side by side.

* * *

It is only in recent years that the use of symbolism and imagery in the novels of Galdós has come to be studied seriously. Casalduero's *Vida y obra de Galdós* proved illuminating in this respect, and further studies have developed this field, notably Chamberlin's «Galdós's Chromatic Symbolism Key in *Lo prohibido*», *HR,* XXXII (1964), 109-117, a study of the symbolism propounded by Galdós himself. Chamberlin's study is further extended in another article, «Galdós's Use of Yellow in Character Delineation», *PMLA,* LXXIX (1964), 158-163. Stephen Gilman, in «The Birth of Fortunata», *AG,* I (1966), 71-83, considers in detail the imagery associated with Fortunata in Part I of *Fortunata y Jacinta;* his views are considered by Carlos Blanco Aguinaga, «On *The Birth of Fortunata*», *AG,* III (1968), 13-24. The relationship of characters, incidents and plots to the heroes and myths of classical antiquity is considered by Gustavo Correa in «El simbolismo mítico en las novelas de Pérez Galdós», *BICC*, XVIII (1963), 428-444. The article by Carroll B. Johnson, «The Café in Galdós's *La Fontana de Oro*», *BHS*, XLII (1965), 112-117, takes a very different viewpoint, arguing convincingly that the detailed description given by Galdós of the café itself reveals an intimate relationship between setting, character and action. The choice of detail is highly significant, in that it gives —for instance— the impression that the café is a cheap fraud, all surface show; what may appear at first sight to be a merely humorous description of the deficiencies of the café is later revealed as having a definite thematic intention. Johnson is here commenting on one of the more significant aspects of Galdós's style : his ability to produce a realistic description or account which has at the same time symbolic overtones when considered in the perspective of the entire work. There is little doubt that this approach will provide a much deeper insight into Galdós's intentions and artistic method, once it has been systematically explored.

* * *

The structure of Galdós's novels has also been subjected recently to critical scrutiny. As we have seen, his contemporaries and the suceeding generation tended to see his novels as lacking in form, over-long, sprawling and spineless. Only recently have critics such as Charles A. Zamora come to realise that far from being shapeless, Galdós's novels have often a closely-knit structure. In «Tiempo cícli-co : estructura temporal en *Gloria* de Galdós», *HBalt*, XLVI (1963), 465-470, Zamora notes the way in which Galdós links the action of the novel to the calendar of the Church. In the first part of the novel Daniel Morton arrives at Ficóbriga on St John's Day (Saint John the Baptist, who «es el eslabón que une el Antiguo Testamento con el Nuevo»), but also Midsummer's Day — the day of pagan love. The first part ends on Saint James's day, the day of the patron saint of Spain, and on this day Daniel leaves and Rafael del Horro, the political Catholic, gains an electoral victory. The second part of the novel begins in Lent, the coming of Daniel coincides with Palm Sunday, and Gloria dies on Easter Saturday. These coincidences are clearly not casual, and suggest the need for a revaluation of Galdós as a constructor of novels. J. J. Alfieri has noted, in his study of various misers, that the author tends to present them as paired characters (*HBalt*, XLVI [1963], 722-729), but the most penetrating study of paired characters is that of Monroe Z. Hafter, «Ironic Reprise in Galdós's Novels», *PMLA*, LXXVI (1961), 233-239. Hafter studies pairs of characters who «complement one another, who react to and take on aspects of one another». His study of the characters of Fortunata and Jacinta in the light of this approach is of particular interest, and helps to explain the sub-title of the novel: «Historia de dos casadas». This is indeed a point of cardinal importance to the structure of Galdós's novels: paired characters often represent polarities, as was shown by Angel del Río in his study of *La loca de la casa*. The direct opposition of characters to be seen in *La Fontana de Oro* and *Doña Perfecta* is replaced in the later novels by the opposition of polarities which, in the course of the work, become fused together: Pepet-Victoria in *La loca de la casa;* Tormento-Caballero, in *Tormento*; Fortunata and Jacinta; among many others.

G. A. Davies has produced a rewarding study in «Galdós's *El amigo Manso:* An Experiment in Didactic Method», *BHS,* XXXIX (1962), 16-30. The critic sees the novel as

> an attempt to establish a concordance between the infinite, fluid society [which it describes] and the narrative structure of the novel.

He further remarks of the work that it is

> distinguished for the beauty of its construction: the ends are carefully tied up, the amount of irrelevance reduced to a minimum, the moments of crisis carefully distributed, the significance and balance of certain events given proper emphasis.

And the simple black-and-white technique of *Doña Perfecta* has given way to a much more complex approach, designed to present in terms of a novel an ideological argument concerning the *krausista* theories of education. This new form deliberately avoids the complete identification of characters and ideas which typified earlier novels, but does not for this reason lose in dramatic power. The same novel has also been studied by Robert H. Russell, «*El amigo Manso:* Galdós with a Mirror», *MLN,* LXXVIII (1963), 161-168. Agnes Moncy, «Enigmas de Galdós», *In,* XX, núm. 202 (1965), 1, 12, notes the differing struc-

26

tures of *Misericordia, Marianela, La de Bringas* and *Miau*. Frank Durand, «Two Problems in Galdós's *Tormento*», *MLN,* LXIX (1964), 513-525, considers the importance of José Ido's novel within the novel, and sees it as purposeful and effective. The «Significado y forma de *Misericordia*» is discussed by Joaquín Casalduero, *PMLA,* LIX (1944), 1104-1110 (reprinted in *Vida y obra de Galdós*). Suzanne Raphaël, in «Un extraño viaje de novios», *AG,* III (1968), 35-49, considers the structural importance of the honeymoon trip to Valencia of Juanito and Jacinta in Vol. I of *Fortunata y Jacinta*. Gonzalo Sobejano, «Forma literaria y sensibilidad social en *La incógnita y Realidad,* de Galdós», *RHM,* XXX (1964), 89-107, analyses the developments in technique represented by *La incógnita,* an epistolary novel; *Realidad* (1889), a novel in dramatic form; and *Realidad* (1892), Galdós's first mature play. The relationship between Galdós's novels and his own dramatic versions is clearly a field which merits further exploration.

The fullest study of the structure of Galdós's novels is Sherman Eoff's *The Novels of Pérez Galdós. The Concept of Life as Dynamic Process* (Saint Louis, 1954), an attempt to visualise Galdós's novels as «organic developments in which plot and characterization merge» (1). The approach is undoubtedly very rewarding, and Eoff is particularly valuable in that he sees Galdós not so much as a psychological novelist but as a «socio-psychological novelist or a literary social psychologist». Galdós is interested, Eoff states, «more in the formative influence of social relations, as regards the individual, than he is in the intricate workings of the mind» (3). This point of view may be somewhat debatable, but it is undoubtedly an important corrective to the attempt to see Galdós as interested solely in the delineation of psychological states. Unfortunately it is not always clear that the critic has fully understood Galdós's aims and, through a failure to appreciate the importance of symbols and imagery, he sometimes gets the wrong end of the stick, a notable example being his analysis of the ending of *La de Bringas*. (An excellent review of the volume has been published by Stephen Gilman in *RF, LXX* [1958], 455-465.) In spite of this and other misinterpretations, Eoff's study is important for the stress placed on Galdós as the creator of well-constructed novels, and particularly for the interplay between the individual and society, clearly one of Galdós's major preoccupations.

* * *

Various critics have taken to heart Casalduero's injunction that «Quizás sería conveniente que se hiciera un estudio de la obra galdosiana por temas» *(MLN, LXXIX* [1964], 181). Gustavo Correa, in his *El simbolismo religioso en las novelas de Pérez Galdós* (Madrid, 1962), deals with the religious aspects of the major novels, developing viewpoints presented by the critic in several earlier articles. His work is valuable in that it underlines one of Galdós's major preoccupations, and considers not only the thematic implications but also the presentation of the theme through vocabulary and image. Correa sets out to demonstrate that the development of religious symbolism to be found in the later novels is already implicit in the early works. At times his dissection of individual relationships is too black-and-white. Guillermina is by no means a complete angel, nor Mauricia *la dura* a devil. Clear-cut polarities of this type are avoided by Galdós in his later novels, although they do tend to appear —perhaps for reasons of compression or lack of technique— in the plays. The dissection of the theme of Angel Guerra by Correa needs the type of corrective provided by the article of Vera Colin which appears in the present volume. Galdós's presentation of religious themes, with special reference to *Angel Guerra,* is the subject of Francisco Ruiz Ramón's *Tres personajes galdosianos. Ensayo de aproximación a un mundo religioso y moral* (Madrid, 1964). The author studies the spiritual development of Angel Guerra, his treatment of Book I being particularly acute; further essays deal with the growing tolerance evident in Galdós's presentation of the clergy in the novel; and the character of the mysticism attributed to Leré. Robert Ricard has published in pamphlet form a valuable study entitled *L'Evolution spirituelle de Pérez Galdós* (Paris, n. d.).

The question of Galdós's attitude to the Church is examined superficially by Eugene Savaiano in «An Historical Justification of the Anticlericalism of Galdós and Alas», *The Municipal University of Wichita Bulletin,* XXVII (1952), 3-14. Studies of the religious theme and the theme of charity in the later novels have multiplied in recent years. Joaquín Casalduero's «Significado y forma de *Misericordia*», already noted, was a pioneer study in this field. E. J. Rodgers, «Religious Conflict and Didacticism in *Gloria*», *AG,* I (1966), 39-51, gives an excellent account of the theme of religious discord, which «has its origins in the clash between intolerance and certain attitudes which can be included in the term *latitudinarianism*». J. L.

Brooks dissected «The Character of Doña Guillermina Pacheco in Galdós's Novel, *Fortunata y Jacinta*», *BHS,* XXXVIII (1961), 86-94, concluding that the personage was not necessarily to be regarded as a perfect example of charity (an article unfortunately not taken into account by Correa in the above-mentioned study). The second volume of *Anales galdosianos,* 1967, includes a number of studies on the later novels, and in particular on the religious elements. Antonio Sánchez Barbudo, in «Torquemada y la muerte», 45-52, gives a summary account of this theme. Frank P. Bowman, «On the Definitions of Jesus in Modern Fiction», 53-66, considers the reasons why Galdós presents comparisons between Nazarín and Christ, a superficial study which suffers by comparison with Alexander A. Parker's «*Nazarín,* or the Passion of Our Lord Jesus Christ According to Galdós», 83-101. Ciriaco Morón Arroyo, «*Nazarín* y *Halma:* Sentido y unidad», 67-81, deals with the relationship between the two novels. Robert H. Russell, «The Christ Figure in *Misericordia:* A Monograph», 103-130, is concerned with the definition of true charity and selfless love in the novel, and the relationship of Benina to the figures of Nazarín and Halma.

Few of the studies so far discussed have attempted to assess Galdós's success as a humorous writer, even though this aspect of his work cannot fail to strike the reader and must have accounted in large measure for his success with his contemporaries. Michael Nimetz's *Humor in Galdós. A Study of the «Novelas contemporáneas»* (New Haven and London, 1968), is a detailed study of Galdós's concept of realism and his use of satire, irony, metaphor, caricature and type and the «humor of familiarity». Galdós's satire of romanticism is well considered, and aspects of style come under close critical analysis, a comparison between the style of the *novelas dialogadas* and plays with that of the novels proper being particularly revealing. The picture which emerges is of a much more human, and humane, Galdós than is to be found in the works of other contemporary critics, stressing particularly the sanity of the novelist's outlook. Nimetz also makes the interesting point that «as Spanish society reaches the point where it contracts more and more twentieth-century neuroses, readers will flock back to the *novelas contemporáneas* in ever-increasing numbers» (179).

Other themes which are worthy of further attention include that of money. Fernando Uriarte, in a brief article entitled «El comercio en la obra de Galdós», *Atenea,* XX (1943), 136-140, attempted to establish parallels between Galdós and Thomas Mann, as well as with Balzac. J. J. Alfieri writes on «The Double Image of Avarice in Galdós's Novels», *HBalt,* XLVI (1963), 722-729; and J. E. Varey, «Francisco Bringas: *nuestro buen Thiers*», *AG,* I (1966), 63-69, deals with attitudes to money in *La de Bringas.* Peter G. Earle, in «Torquemada: hombre-masa», *AG,* II (1967), 29-43, concludes that «en Torquemada no tenemos una simple víctima sino un monstruo de la civilización, elaborado y hasta idolatrado por toda una sociedad». But the subject of money is worthy of a wider study. The same may be said of the theme of education, briefly considered by Dorothy G. Park and Hilario Sáenz, in «Galdós's Ideas on Education», *HBalt,* XXVII (1944), 138-147, and alluded to by critics who have studied such novels as *La familia de León Roch* and *El amigo Manso.* But no overall study exists. A similar field might be found in Galdós's attitude to Spain, studied by Robert Kirsner in «Pérez Galdós's Vision of Spain in *Torquemada en la hoguera*», *BHS,* XXVII (1950), 229-235, and «Galdós's Attitude Towards Spain as Seen in the Characters of *Fortunata y Jacinta*», *PMLA,* LXVI (1951), 124-137, and by Gustavo Correa, «El sentido de lo hispánico en *El caballero encantado* de Pérez Galdós y la Generación del 98», *Thesaurus,* XVIII (1963), 14-28. Angel del Río has published «Notas sobre el tema de América en Galdós», *NRFH,* XV (1961), 279-296.

Clearly many such fields could be delimited; that some of them have been attempted can be seen from an examination of the files of *Dissertation Abstracts,* although such studies are not as completely in the public domain as the articles and books mentioned in the present survey. Those who attempt such studies should bear in mind the important point made by Joaquín Casalduero in *MLN,* LXXIX (1964), 181: a thematic study, writes the critic, «no se debe hacer en abstracto sino teniendo en cuenta la novela o la obra de teatro en que están incluidos y además —es muy importante— el momento en que fueron tratados». Once again we come back to the need to see the works of Galdós against a living background, against the development of the structure of society and the ideological clashes which characterise the second half of the nineteenth century.

* * *

The most ambitious survey to date of Galdós the novelist is that of José F. Montesinos, *Galdós.* Vols. I and II (Madrid, 1968) have so far appeared and the criticism extends, at the time of writing, chronologically as far as *Fortunata y Jacinta.* Montesinos calls his work «una guía de los lectores del novelista», but the study is more wide-ranging than this modest claim suggests. The first volume covers the early writings, the first two series of the *Episodios nacionales* and the *novelas de la primera época.* The works are set against a very valuable study of the influence of Romanticism in the early work, of *costumbrismo,* the novels of Balzac and the literary discussions in the Ateneo. The artistic development of Galdós in this period is also considered, from the «flagrantes inexperiencias» evident in *El audaz* (I, 74), to the much more mature and successful *La familia de León Roch.* Montesinos makes the interesting suggestion that the desperate urgency of *Doña Perfecta* and the loose ends of plot and characterisation may be due to its being published *por entregas,* a theory which might well be tested by reference to other works first published in this way. Volume II opens with an important essay on «La segunda manera». In his consideration of the earlier *novelas contemporáneas,* the critic reviews the development of Galdós's technique in this period and puts forward views on the construction of the novels. Throughout he stresses the humanity of Galdós's characterisation, a trait which he sees as part of the debt which Galdós owes to Cervantes. Clearly it is not possible at this stage to give a final comment on Montesinos's work. Many of the pages were written, he says, several years ago, and it is to be regretted that he does not put forward his detailed views on recent critical attitudes; clearly he is aware of contemporary trends in Galdós criticism, and he tells us that he deplores some aspects of it: «Disquisiciones de ese jaez pueden pecar de bizantinas si no tienen en cuenta la condición humana de las personas que en la novela animan o la de el mundo en que se ven instaladas» (II, 273). Nevertheless, we are offered in these two volumes a panoramic view of Galdós's novelistic production which goes far beyond the stated aim. A study of style is promised for a later volume, and this alone is sufficient to whet the reader's appetite for what is to come.

* * *

The *Episodios nacionales* have not attracted as much critical endeavour as the *novelas contemporáneas*. Reference has already been made to source studies and to other aspects of criticism. Carlos Vázquez Arjona, who has compared Galdós's historical view with that of professional historians and other writers, has also published an «Introducción al estudio de la primera serie de los *Episodios nacionales* de Pérez Galdós», *PMLA*, XLVIII (1933), 895-907. More detailed and more recent studies are those of Gabriel H. Lovett, «Some Observations on Galdós's *Juan Martín el Empecinado*», *MLN*, LXXXIV (1969), 196-207; Pablo Cabañas, «Comella visto por Galdós», *RLit*, XXIX (1966), 91-99; and the same critic's «Moratín en la obra de Galdós», *Actas del Segundo Congreso Internacional de Hispanistas* (Nijmegen, 1967), 217-266, both of which study the portraits which the novelist draws of eighteenth-century dramatists; and Antonio H. Obaid, «La Mancha en los *Episodios nacionales* de Galdós», *HBalt*, XLI (1958), 42-47, and «Sancho Panza en los *Episodios nacionales* de Galdós», *HBalt*, XLII (1959), 199-204. Gaspar Gómez de la Serna has published an unsympathetic —because uncomprehending— study of the genre in two parts, «El *Episodio nacional* como género literario. I — De la *épica* al *episodio,* pasando por la novela», and «II — Las dos Españas de Don Ramón María del Valle-Inclán», *Cla,* III, núm. 14 (1952), 21-32, and III, núm. 17 (1952), 17-32.

In 1961 appeared the first serious full-length study: Hans Hinterhäuser's *Die «Episodios Nacionales» von Benito Pérez Galdós* (Hamburg, 1961), later translated as *Los «Episodios Nacionales» de Benito Pérez Galdós* (Madrid, 1963). Beginning with an excellent analysis of previous criticism, the author then places Galdós's work in the context of the nineteenth-century European historical novel. He states his aim as follows: «Galdós como historiador, como educador político, como artista; es decir, los *Episodios nacionales* como mensaje político y como novela» (21). In other words, he does not concentrate solely on the history of sources or on checking the veracity of the historical viewpoint —although both of these are thoroughly examined— to the neglect of aesthetic criticism. In discussing the educative intention of the novelist, Hinterhäuser makes the point that Galdós is never the dispassionate observer when dealing with the political and social state of Spain; he adopts a definite view-point and his own prejudices are made sufficiently clear. The chapters on «los *Episodios* como novela» are most enlightening, studying the methods by which Galdós seeks to fuse history, fictional characters and language into a convincing artistic whole. Hinterhäuser shows a tendency to treat the five series as a whole, and perhaps does not allow sufficiently for the changes of emphasis in the final three series which undoubtedly owed much, not only to the added maturity of the author and to the changing political scene, but to the experience gained in writing the *novelas contemporáneas* which intervene chronologically. The whole problem of the relationship of the *Episodios* to the *novelas contemporáneas* —to some extent considered by Montesinos in *Galdós,* Vol. I— is an absorbing and complicated question. Hinterhäuser's study is lucidly written and temperately presented.

In Antonio Regalado García's *Benito Pérez Galdós y la novela histórica española: 1868-1912* (Madrid, 1966), the emphasis is largely on the ideological content of the *Episodios nacionales* and, in part, of the *novelas contemporáneas.* The author examines Galdós's own political position, which he sees as fluctuating and open to political pressures, and his historical convictions. The critic is particularly hard on the first series of the *Episodios:*

> La idea de la nacionalidad que flota en la primera serie de los *Episodios* no es tan pura e independiente como lo aparenta, por hallarse afectada de las influencias del contenido económico-social del sistema de la Restauración (74-75).

The study of the *novelas contemporáneas* is slight, and the critic concludes that:

> Toda la obra novelística de Galdós está orientada en favor del *Statu quo* de la Restauración y contra los dos mayores peligros que lo amenazaban, la revolución política y el cambio de la estructura social propugnado por las aspiraciones del cuarto estado, encarnadas en la ideología de socialistas y anarquistas (193).

It is for this reason that Regalado García charges Galdós with possessing what he calls a «cant mentality». The chapter on the *novelas contemporáneas* reveals the limitations of this critical approach when applied to the major novels; the critic does not allow for Galdós's irony and he makes the mistake of crediting the author with the views of his characters. It is for this reason that he can conclude that Nazarín and Halma «tratan prácticamente de retrasar con la caridad particular

33

el advenimiento de la justicia social» (304), and make this a charge against the author. It is the fourth series of the *Episodios* which Regalado García finds most satisfying:

> A través de los diversos personajes ficticios y reales que intervienen en la vida pública, da una idea del juego de la política y de las motivaciones económicas, psicológicas y sociales que la impulsaron (431).

At first sight, the critical approach evident in this volume is most promising, and the author reveals an enviable depth of knowledge in his assessment of the ideological and historical background of the period. However, his critical conclusions are clearly coloured by his own prejudices, and Galdós is castigated when he fails to live up to the ideals of the critic. Nevertheless, the study is to be recommended for the deep insights which it presents into the political development of Spain during the second half of the nineteenth century, and for the general and specific relationships established between literature and politics.

By comparison, Alfred Rodríguez's *An Introduction to the «Episodios nacionales» of Galdós* (New York, 1967), takes a more traditional viewpoint. Galdós is seen as the tolerant Liberal, endeavouring, in the first and second series, to present a «precise historical reconstruction» of events (101). There is more literary criticism than in Regalado García, but the author adds little that is new to our picture of the novelist. The same viewpoint is shared by Clara E. Lida, «Galdós y los *Episodios nacionales:* Una historia del liberalismo español», *AG,* III (1968), 61-67. Miguel Enguídanos has dedicated an article to the final series of the *Episodios,* «Mariclio, musa galdosiana», *PSA,* VI, número LXIII (1961), 235-249, further evidence of a growing interest in the later novels which can be seen also in the works of Regalado García and Gustavo Correa. Stephen Gilman has studied «Realism and the Epic in Galdós's *Zaragoza»*, *Estudios hispánicos. Homenaje a Archer M. Huntington* (Wellesley, Mass., 1952), 171-192. Galdós's view of history in his other novels is considered by Carlos Clavería, «El pensamiento histórico de Galdós», *RNC,* XIX, cxxi-cxxii (March-June 1957), 170-177, and has also been the subject of recent articles. Antonio Ruiz Salvador has written on «La función del trasfondo histórico en *La desheredada»*, *AG,* I (1966), 52-62, and Juan López Morillas has given us a penetrating study of one of the earlier novels, «Historia y novela en el Galdós primerizo: en torno a *La Fontana de Oro*», *RHM*, XXXI (1965), 273-285. Clearly this is an approach which merits further investigation.

* * *

The stress in Galdós studies has evidently shifted considerably in the quarter of a century which has passed since the 1943 centenary. The emphasis latterly has been on the analysis of structure, symbols, the study of language and the dissection of particular themes. It is very probable that José F. Montesinos's study of Galdós the novelist may be the last to appear on the heroic scale for several years. We are still in the process of breaking down Galdós's work into its constituent elements, and some time must elapse before a full and considered study of the novelist, which takes into account the results of the new criticism, emerges.

Before that is possible, much remains to be done. We need a more comprehensive and more sensitive biography. We need an edition of the novelist's correspondence, with letters and replies. We need a truly complete critical edition of the *Obras completas,* including all the journalistic writings as well as the novels, short stories, plays, and criticism. We need a deeper study of the element of fantasy in Galdós's novels; a study of the evolution of his ideas on charity; a study of the emergence of non-rational philosophical attitudes; a full study of his attitude to Romanticism. Galdós's plays still await their critic. These needs spring to mind, and there are others which will no doubt readily occur to students of the nineteenth-century Spanish novel. There is indeed much to be done; and the most urgent task of all is the collection of biographical and bibliographical data and the preparation of reliable variant-reading editions. Then, perhaps, we shall be able to judge whether Galdós fulfilled or did not fulfil the programme which he outlined in 1870; certainly we shall no longer see him as an arch-realist, who, in a moment of aberration, tossed off a few cloudy fantasies and whose novels are things —even delicious things— of shreds and patches.

Westfield College,
London.

NIGEL GLENDINNING

Psychology and Politics in the First Series of the 'Episodios nacionales'

Many general questions of approach to Galdós' historical novels have been clarified in recent years as a result of the penetrating work of Hans Hinterhäuser [1] and the less disciplined but suggestive discussions of Regalado García. [2] Yet some aspects of the *Episodios nacionales* remain relatively unexamined — more particularly the structure and the relation of structure to content in individual novels in the various series. Most of the detailed work on separate *Episodios* has been concentrated on historical sources, and where the first series is concerned Stephen Gilman's essay «Realism and the Epic in Galdós' *Zaragoza*» of 1952 is the only distinguished exception. [3] Since that article there has been little attempt to analyse story-telling processes or characterisation in individual *episodios,* or to relate these techniques to the wider political, social and moral implications of the novels. Above all, Galdós' concern with the psychological motivation of individuals, both historical and fictional, in these early novels has been inadequately discussed. For Hinterhäuser, psychology is simply an aspect of the aesthetics of the novel, [4] a minor factor in the technique of realism rather than something which contributes to the total mean-

---

[1] Hans Hinterhäuser, *Los «Episodios Nacionales» de Benito Pérez Galdós,* Madrid, 1963. The original German edition was published in 1961. All references in the current essay are to the Spanish edition, and the author's name followed by a number will refer to the pages of that edition.
[2] Antonio Regalado García, *Benito Pérez Galdós y la novela histórica española 1868-1912,* Madrid, 1966. The author's name and the page numbers only are given in subsequent notes.
[3] Cf. *Homenaje a Archer M. Huntington,* Wellesley, 1952, 171-92.
[4] Hinterhäuser, 298-9.

ing of the work, and for many critics, as Hinterhäuser points out, psychology appears to be virtually nonexistent in the *Episodios*.[5] Yet characterisation was thought to be an important element in Galdós' earliest historical novels by their first reviewers, and if we cannot now feel that the delineation of character makes a significant contribution to their realism —which José Alcalá Galiano thought to be the case in *La Fontana de Oro*[6]— this is largely the result of our different conception of realism in general and of psychological motivation in particular. Yet characterisation constitutes a non-historical element which is more directly relevant to the reader than period material and its full function deserves further examination. Psychology is more obviously central to Galdós' later work perhaps, but the part it plays in the early novels is not without significance.

In reality, there can be no doubt that character and motivation were major interests of Galdós as a novelist from the start. His first short novel, *La sombra,* published in 1870 but written earlier, takes as its central character a person who is a victim of an over-imaginative nature and an *idée fixe,* and who becomes increasingly dominated by his obsessions.[7] In *La Fontana de Oro,* Galdós' first historical novel, psychology is again important, but this time less as an end in itself than as a factor which helps to explain a political situation and patterns of social behaviour.[8] From one point of view *La Fontana de Oro* is plain-

---

[5] Hinterhäuser, 302-3. The most recent general study of the *Episodios*, «Galdós in the light of Georg Lukács' 'Historical Novel' », by Madeleine de Gorgorza Fletcher in *AG*, I, No. 1, asserts that the novelist identifies the lives of his characters «with the historical fate of the group they represent». This does not take into account the presence of psychological material in the novels and makes the novels conform to a particular politico-historical pattern by failing to consider many of the elements of the series.

[6] Cf. his review of the novel in the *Revista de España*, vol. XX, 148-58. Ramón Rodríguez Correa makes a similar point in passing in *Noticias literarias* of 1873 in *Revista de España*, vol. XXXIV, 570. Revilla speaks of «la verdad en la pintura de los caracteres» in the series (*Críticas 2.ª serie*, Burgos, 1885, 116).

[7] Joaquín Casalduero's essay on this novel makes some observations on this subject although it is mostly concerned with the early appearance of elements which recur in later works (cf. *AG*, I (1966), 33-38).

[8] J. López-Morillas has a useful study of the political significance of the novel entitled «Historia y novela en el Galdós primerizo: en torno a la *Fontana de Oro*», in *RHM*, XXXI (1965), 273-85. On the question of psychology Monroe Z. Hafter argues that Galdós «subordinated psychological motivations to his thesis», and used various narrative devices which made the hero «more typical and less personal» («The Hero in Galdós' *La Fontana de Oro*», in *MP*, LVII (1959-60), 37-43). The analysis of Lázaro however cannot be carried out satisfactorily without taking into account psychological motivations in other

4

ly concerned with the effects of political extremism and the violence and disunity which accompany it. But political attitudes are shown to stem from the character and upbringing of the individuals involved and not merely from their political circumstances or beliefs. Lázaro, for instance, is a liberal in part because his imaginative nature is moved and excited by the idea of freedom.[9] Logically his character also influences his approach to literature, and he ultimately accepts a moderate Romanticism although he has been brought up on Neoclassical rhetoric. He is not determined by his background, however, and is able to learn to control the wilder flights of his imagination. In the same way Clara, who might have suffered a personality disorder as a result of the rigid, joyless and anti-social upbringing Coletilla gave her had her character been less fundamentally generous, is enabled to express her love and concern for others in part because of her friendly contacts in childhood with Ana in Ateca.[10] Coletilla, on the other hand, was almost bound to be an Absolutist because he had been repressed in his early years and had been educated rigidly by monks.[11] His pas-

characters. Psychology, in fact, is part of the thesis. Professor López-Morillas also underestimates the importance of character, in the opinion of the present writer, when he asserts that «los personajes acaban siendo 'representaciones' simbólicas de esta opinión política o estotro fenómeno social» (op. cit., 274-5). The fact that Galdós himself considered Charles Dickens a realist in character delineation suggests that for him psychology was not inconsistent with representation, and that it was possible to be realistic on one level and symbolic on another at the same time. This seems to be the general trend of his arguments about the novel in his Observaciones sobre la novela contemporánea en España (Revista de España, Vol. XV, 162-172).

[9] Cf. especially Chapter 7. Galdós points to the egoism which underlies some of Lázaro's political aspirations as useful egoism because his aim is to serve others: «Egoísmo sublime, pero egoísmo al fin. Lázaro tenía ambición. ¿Pero qué clase de ambición? Esa que no se dirige sino al enaltecimiento moral del individuo... Lázaro aspiraba a la gloria; quería satisfacer una vanidad; cada hombre tiene su vanidad. La del joven aragonés consistía en cumplir una gran misión.»

[10] Cf. Chapter 6. «En esta comunicación de las dos jóvenes, Clara se desarrollaba moralmente con una rapidez desconocida. Para quien había pasado su juventud en compañía de un viejo excéntrico e insociable, aquellas franquezas inocentes y el cambio simultáneo de pensamientos, comunicados sin disimulo y en toda su hermosa sencillez natural, realizaron en el alma de la huérfana una revelación de sí misma, que fijó y fortaleció más su bello carácter.»

[11] Cf. Chapter 4. «Aquel hombre, que desde que tuvo uso de razón no vivió sino con la inteligencia, ni en su juventud experimentó los naturales sentimientos de amistad y afecto, estaba a los cuarenta años enardecido con una fuerte y violentísima pasión. Esta pasión era el amor al despotismo, el odio a toda tolerancia, a toda libertad... Su carácter era apasionado por naturaleza, aunque los asiduos estudios le habían comprimido y desfigurado... la escondida vehemencia de sentimientos de Elías se manifestó, y no en forma de amor, ni de avaricia, ni de ambición: se manifestó en forma de pasión política, de

sions were the same as Lázaro's only misdirected. The religious intolerance and avarice of the three Porreño sisters and the mysticism of Doña Paulita are other consequences of childhood repressions, and the life of «La Chacona» illustrates the ways in which uncontrolled egoism (as in the case of Coletilla) can lead to perverse behaviour patterns. [12]

The interest in tracing a somewhat oversimplified relationship between the psychological background of individuals and their political or social attitudes, linking upbringing and education with politics, reasserts itself clearly enough in *El audaz* and the early *novelas contemporáneas* concerned with the problem of religious tolerance: *Doña Perfecta, Gloria* and *La familia de León Roch*. In *El audaz* the conflict between Muriel's good moral qualities and liberal faith and his corrupt and temporising environment lead in the end to his tragic disintegration. But neither he nor those around him are wholly blameless, nor wholly to blame. Muriel's radical tenacity is a product of his special childhood experience as well as of his character, and the resignation and support for the *ancien régime* of many of those with whom he comes into contact is due in part to their religious beliefs and education.[13] Muriel is, initially, a model hero —idealised in much the same way as Gabriel was to be in the first series of *Episodios*— humble in origin, firm in his moral standards and without financial ambition. But while his «deseo muy grande de influir para que este país se trasforme por completo, y cambie parte de su antigua organización por otra más en armonía con la edad en que vivimos» [14] is admirable, some of his methods are not. In a different society or at another period Muriel might have been an influential and constructive person; but the

adhesión frenética a un sistema...» In the first edition and that of Leipzig, 1872, which I have consulted, his political career is even more closely linked with his education than in Chapter 4 in the last chapter: «Coletilla era faccioso, guerrillero, absolutista. Habíase educado con frailes, y perfeccionaba su buen instinto con el ejercicio laborioso de las camarillas reales.» (Ed. cit., 368).

[12]   Cf. Chapter 5.

[13]   *El audaz. Historia de un radical de antaño,* Madrid, 1871, 10: «Siendo niño tuvo que hacer esfuerzos de hombre y de héroe para sobrellevar la vida. Semejante escuela no podía menos de robustecer su voluntad para lo sucesivo, dándole una iniciativa de que carecen los que no conocen las enseñanzas de la contrariedad.» For resignation in others see Muriel's conversation with the monk (21; *OC*, IV, 238-239) and Don Buenaventura (138; *OC*, IV, 303). More critical comments on religious education occur when Alfonso is described (29; *OC*, IV, 243). «Tenía además una habilidad no común para todos los recados que exigieran astucia y agudeza de ingenio, revelando en esto la educación frailuna que había recibido.»

[14]   Ed. cit., 57; *OC*, IV, 258-259.

apathy he feels around him drives him to violence and disaster. Like Pepe Rey, Daniel Morton and León Roch in later novels, Muriel is perhaps a victim of other people's characters and attitudes as much as or more than of his own. The process is the opposite of that in *La sombra,* where the protagonist is a victim of his own obsessions even though those obsessions are also universal. In one sense all these early novels are about education and psychology as well as about politics and religion, concerned with the impact of individual character and behaviour on the social and political patterns of groups and *vice versa.* It is my contention that this is equally true of the *Episodios nacionales.* They too evince a deeper interest in psychology than is generally believed, and their relevance for Galdós' contemporaries turns in part on this interest.

Before proceeding further, however, it is necessary to clarify hypothetically Galdós' probable conception of psychology at the time of the publication of these early novels. The term «psychology» would almost certainly not have been used by the novelist, but he treats character in ways which suggest that he was aware of and interested in what we now call psychological motivation. His conception of character is not at all complex. Every individual has certain basic qualities —virtues and vices— and these determine character and events. In his article on the novel in the *Revista de España* in 1870 Galdós speaks of «los vicios y virtudes fundamentales que engendran los caracteres y determinan los sucesos». [15] But these basic qualities could clearly be modified in his view, to judge from *La Fontana de Oro,* by an individual's upbringing or contacts with other people, or by outside circumstances in general. The possibility of such modifications is implied in Chapter 16 of *La Fontana de Oro,* where Galdós explicitly suggests psychological explanations for the cruelty of the Porreño sisters to Clara. «No podemos explicarnos esto», he begins, «¿Era tal vez desahogo de espíritus reconcentrados por falta de trato con las gentes, por falta de amor y de los goces de la vida?» (Leipzig, 1872, p. 143). In later novels motivations are less directly stated as the omniscient narrator approach is modified or dropped, but they are none the less implicit in the conversations of characters themselves or in their actions.

---

[15] Benito Pérez Galdós, «Observaciones sobre la novela contemporánea en España», in *Revista de España,* Vol. XV, 1870, 169-70.

To the modern reader the Porreño sisters appear almost like caricatures and are essentially unrealistic. Yet Galdós thought that characters of the Dickens type with certain rather simple or exaggerated traits were perfectly true to life at the outset of his career as a novelist. Provided always that the traits in question were common virtues or vices of society their embodiment in a character was legitimate by Galdós' standards. For him, in fact, a character could be both «true» and a caricature —realistic and symbolic at one and the same time, like Agapito in Ruiz Aguilera's *Hasta los gatos quieren zapatos.* [16] Basically the approach is not unlike that of the Neoclassics when they sought to make characters «verosímil» yet universal, by combining in a single literary case the essential characteristics of a multiplicity of persons observable in real life.

In the 1870 article of the *Revista de España* Galdós explains the link between the individual and society as he sees it. All individuals inevitably contribute to the life of the society in which they find themselves and can «influir personalmente en la suerte de la sociedad». The portrayal of the virtues and vices of individuals is therefore an important element in the portrayal of society as a whole. A study of the psychology of an individual may help to explain collective as well as individual behaviour.

Conceivably Galdós was following Herbert Spencer here. It is true that he does not seem to consider the psychological interplay between the individual and his social environment as part of an evolutionary process as Spencer did. But he clearly shares the latter's belief in the importance of the «human faculties which take part as factors in social phenomena» and recognises the extent to which environment helps to form individual behaviour. He may well also have accepted Spencer's theory that inherited psychological peculiarities could be found in peoples as well as in people. Certainly he speaks in the prologue to his friend José Alcalá Galiano's *Estereoscopio social* (Madrid, 1872) of the «buenas porciones de extravío y aberración» which result from social fashion and routine patterns of behaviour as well as from the inevitable «vicios, irregularidades y extravagancias» attendant on human nature.

---

[16] Id. Vol. XV, 1870, 172. Useful comments on this article of Galdós are to be found in S. H. Eoff, «The formative period of Galdós' social-psychological perspective», *RR*, XLI (1950), 33-41; and José F. Montesinos, «Galdós en busca de la novela», in *In*, núm. 202, Septiembre 1963.

The novelist's description of both human and social aberrations helps the reader to understand the human condition and its need for improvement. But it is not the business of the writer himself, in Galdós' view, to administer the correctives. In his 1870 article he states that the novelist *describes* individuals and societies but does not try to amend them : «sólo se trata de decir lo que somos unos y otros, los buenos y los malos, diciéndolo siempre con arte». The same point is reiterated in the prologue to Alcalá Galiano's *Estereoscopio* (ed. cit., p. xxi). The artist does not actually correct vices, but experiences «un deseo vivísimo de decirlos, de hacerlos públicos».

Obviously by selecting both what he describes and the way in which he describes it, the novelist can seek to influence his society, and this is what Galdós appears to do in his early novels —and in his later ones too for that matter. He takes, in his historical novels, periods and behaviour patterns which have clear analogies with the Spain of his own times. Thus in *La Fontana de Oro* the situations of the 1820's which arose as a result of extremist and intolerant views in religion and politics, are relevant also to the revolutionary period of 1868. [17] But the characters in the novels are relevant too : in the cases of Lázaro and Clara we have object lessons in the ways in which egoistical leanings can be usefully channelled into the service of society. By choosing such characters as Lázaro and Clara, by contrasting them with others, and making *La Fontana de Oro* in part a love story (with or without a happy ending), Galdós presumably brought home the psychological, as well as the moral and political, implications of his story to a reasonably wide public.

Both in form and in content Galdós' first series of *Episodios* resembles the earlier historical novels. The central love interest is no doubt evidence of the author's continuing concern with situations of emotional tension and conflict. But the topics of love and war may also suggest that Galdós felt his novels to be relevant to a wider readership than they had previously enjoyed. Gabriel Araceli (in love with an aristocratic lady) and the Peninsular War could obviously command a larger public than Lázaro and Clara and the 1820's. Gabriel's rise in society from an inauspicious beginning as «pillete de playa», [18] is a suc-

---

[17] Cf. J. López-Morillas' article mentioned above.
[18] The phrase is Galdós' in his *Memorias de un desmemoriado, OC*, VI, 1660

cess story of a familiar and provenly popular pattern, and it would be surprising if Menéndez y Pelayo were not right (and Clarín wrong) about the appeal of the *Episodios,* which, Menéndez maintained, «han penetrado en los hogares más aristocráticos y en los más humildes, en las escuelas y en los talleres».[19] The Peninsular War, and the serial story, also had a popularity in Spain which Galdós certainly knew.[20] In publications of the «pliego suelto» type the Vidal press in Reus offered *Napoleón, emperador* in 1852,[21] and Santarén in Valladolid *La guerra de la independencia, Don Francisco Espoz y Mina* and *El cura Merino* (1863).[22] The same works had been in Santarén's lists in 1848,[23] and Carlist war material was also available in the four *pliegos* of *Vida del carlista Ramón Cabrera.*[24] José María Marés in Madrid —on whom Galdós is believed to have modelled Juan Bou in *La desheredada*[25]— poured forth similar works, including *Napoleón I, emperador de los franceses, El sitio y defensa de Zaragoza* and *Guerra de la independencia española,* alongside the abbreviated version of *Bertoldo, Bertoldino y Cacaseno,*[26] to which Camila turned for solace and instruction in *Lo prohibido.*[27]

Whatever Galdós' intention, it is clear that he had observations to make about Spanish society and the individuals in it in the first series of *Episodios* which a wide readership would appreciate. His hero belonged, as the Condesa points out in *Juan Martín el Empeci-*

---

[19] Cf. *Discursos leídos ante la Real Academia Española en las recepciones públicas del 7 y 21 de febrero de 1897,* 67-68, and Leopoldo Alas, *Galdós,* Madrid, 1912, 308-9. Menéndez y Pelayo's view is supported by Berkowitz's evidence in *Pérez Galdós, Spanish Liberal Crusader,* Madison, 1948, 99-102 and 128.

[20] Cf. his *Observaciones sobre la novela contemporánea en España,* in the *Revista de España,* Vol. XV, 164-5.

[21] Cf. the list at the end of *Historia del esforzado caballero Pierres de Provenza y la hermosa Magalona,* Reus, Juan Bautista Vidal, 1852.

[22] Cf. the list at the end of *Historia de Pablo y Virginia,* Valladolid, Imprenta de Fernando Santarén, 1863.

[23] Cf. the list at the end of *Extracto de la Historia de Pablo y Virginia,* etcétera, 1848.

[24] I have also seen a Santarén edition of the *Historia del cura Merino,* a work which covered the 1834 civil wars and the 1820 revolt as well as the Peninsular War period. It was dated 1860.

[25] Cf. Helen F. Grant, «Una 'Aleluya' erótica de Federico García Lorca y las aleluyas populares del siglo XIX», in *Actas del primer congreso internacional de hispanistas,* Oxford, 1964, 311 and note 9.

[26] Cf. the list at the end of *Historia de la Urraca Ladrona,* Madrid, 1864. The *Bertoldo* was also in Vidal lists in 1852, and there was a reprint of the work in 1873 according to the *Revista bibliográfica* of the *Revista de España,* vol. XXXVI, 432. Palau lists two editions that year and twenty-four editions in all between 1745 and 1880.

[27] Cf. Chapter 23, sections 1 and 4; Chapter 26, section 1.

nado, to a new and more socially useful class than the old aristocracy: one, what is more, to which all could aspire, since it was based on moral calibre and not on birth — «una aristocracia *de las almas,* cuya nobleza, aunque la ahoguen desgracias y privaciones, al fin ha de abrirse paso y llevar su dominio hasta las mismas esferas donde campean llenos de hinchazón los orgullosos» *(OC,* I, 1044). This «aristocracia de las almas» is not, of course, the virtuous aristocracy of which 16th, 17th and some 18th century moralists had written. It is an aristocracy which could be achieved by character rather than by Christian belief. Gabriel needed great willpower to attain success and overcome certain minor defects in his makeup. The significance of the central character, in fact, is psychological as well as social and political.

Appealing, then, through form and subject matter to a wide public, Galdós could create in the first series of *Episodios* a more influential depiction of the inter-relationship between personality and politics than he had achieved in *La Fontana de Oro* and *El audaz.* If the whole series constitutes a view of the forces which could unite or disunite Spain in the past, it also perhaps shows how individuals contributed to the making or marring of that union. It remains to be seen how far individual *Episodios* support such an interpretation.

In the first series there is a basic tension between the egoists, the greedy, the ambitious and the intolerant on the one hand, and the unselfish, unambitious and patriotic on the other. Put in other terms the basic conflict is not simply between France and Spain, or one political class and another, but between different kinds of individual who feel love, humanity and a desire for social order, or hate, self-seeking and a delight in social chaos. In part these tensions constitute the essence of popular literature of the «hero and villain», «cops and robbers» and «goodies and baddies» type. But the tensions also reflect the psychological, moral and political preoccupations of the novelist, and are used by him to describe in dramatic terms the problems of human society in general and Spanish society in particular.

In *Trafalgar,* the qualities of the individuals involved in the action are less obviously important than the action itself. But over against Gabriel himself and the Spanish patriots are set the bad moral qualities which appear to be more particularly serious in politicians, since their personal ambition, pride and greed can plunge whole countries into misery and strife. In Gabriel's child's eye view of world society, countries are islands, «y sin duda en todas ellas debe de haber hombres muy malos, que son los que arman las guerras para su provecho particular, bien porque son ambiciosos y quieren mandar, bien porque son avaros y anhelan ser ricos. Estos hombres malos son los que engañan a los demás, a todos estos infelices que van a pelear; y para que el engaño sea completo, les impulsan a odiar a otras naciones; siembran la discordia, fomentan la envidia, y aquí tienen ustedes el resultado» *(OC,* I, 253). Beyond Gabriel's naive analysis, however, Galdós shows (as he had earlier in *La Fontana de Oro)* that though political corruption may have roots in the character defects of rulers, it cannot spread without help from misguided or ineffectual individuals at other levels in society. Those who are normally morally weak can be used as unwitting instruments by perverse politicians. Such moral weakness, which can undermine the goodness of others, is seen in a number of characters in *Trafalgar,* and at more than one level in society. It is patent, for instance, in the self-concern of Don Alonso's Paca, who is incapable of seeing things «más que por el lado de su egoísmo» *(OC,* I, 261) and who cannot understand Alonso's willingness to serve in the ships. It is equally patent in the sailors who lose all sense of charity when their lives are in danger. [28]

In *La corte de Carlos IV,* the anti-social qualities of greed and egoism are principally examined in terms of the ruling class, yet self-seeking, which is identified as a national as well as an individual failing, leads Gabriel himself astray. [29] Later volumes tend to be less simple in their analysis, and the dividing line between good and evil in individuals is less firmly drawn. Characters with mixed motivation make these novels more convincing as well as more effective in dramatic terms, although both characterisation and psychology remain somewhat schematic by modern standards.

Particularly interesting in its examination of the motives and conduct of people at different levels of society is *Zaragoza.* Critics have tended

---

[28] Cf. Chapter 15. While Gabriel stays to help Marcial, others look after their own safety: «Para comprender esta inhumana crueldad es preciso haberse encontrado en trances tan terribles: el sentimiento y la caridad desaparecen ante el instinto de conservación que domina el ser por completo, asimilándole a veces a una fiera» *(OC,* I, 267).

[29] «Ya habrá observado el lector que, al suponerse amado por una mujer poderosa, mis primeras ideas versaron sobre mi engrandecimiento personal y el ansia de adquirir honores y destinos. En esto he reconocido después la sangre española.» *OC,* I, 308.

to see this novel as one in which the patriotic unity of the inhabitants is expressed in an idealised way. The obvious exception to the pattern of idealisation —Candiola— becomes in Gilman's terms the anti-hero who is a foil for the total-hero of the people. [30] Perhaps Galdós himself invited this patriotism-centred interpretation of the novel when he timed its first publication to coincide with the Dos de Mayo celebrations in 1874. [31] But there is much in the novel that is far from heroic, and it is not hard to find evidence of the anti-epic quality which Casalduero noted in the series as a whole. [32] The patterns of behaviour of characters in the novel are, in fact, rather more varied and complex than is usually thought.

The structure of *Zaragoza* itself reflects the anti-epic or unheroic. It progresses from the proud recollections of the triumphs of the first siege of the city to the collapse of the Spanish when the French re-enter Saragossa at the end. Within this general pattern the structure also throws into relief certain polarities beyond the surface struggle between Spanish and French: between aggression (war) and love (peace) for instance, public and private worlds, egoism and self-sacrifice, triumph and defeat. The tensions between these are traced through the siege and the lives of those who endure it. The form of the opening chapters invites the reader to make a series of contrasts. We start with public images —recollections of the heroism of the first siege and the roles of José de Montoria and others— before going on to explore the inner world of characters: their lives and motives and disintegration during the siege. After the major characters have been introduced in the first five chapters, the second attack of the French begins in Chapter 6 and from that point until Chapter 21 the narrative follows and ironically juxtaposes and contrasts love and hate on a personal level with love and hate on a national and international level, rising to a period of particular intensity in chapters 14-15, which cover the period from the 25th to the 27th January 1809 in great detail. The last ten chapters of the novel describe battles with the French and house-to-house fighting between the 27th January and the 21st February, again juxtaposing characters and their public and private circumstances and attitudes. An idyllic night when Ma-

---

[30] Cf. Hinterhäuser, 244.
[31] Cf. 'Revista bibliográfica del año 1874' in *Revista de España*, Vol. XLII, 1875, 275.
[32] Joaquín Casalduero, *Vida y obra de Galdós*, Madrid, 1951, 60-61.

riquilla and Agustín are lovingly together (Chapter 27) ends with the threat of mining operations, just as in Chapter 15 a night meeting between the lovers is rudely interrupted by a bombardment.

The pattern of contrasts is particularly important within and between characters. José de Montoria is not entirely ideal, even when we first see him, although he becomes a hero of the siege in a sense. If his lack of polite education is largely a virtue and his self-satisfaction seems justified, his lack of self-control is clearly a more significant defect than the oaths which he takes to be his own most serious failing. Furthermore his Aragonese obstinacy can be misguided, as is palpably the case when he expresses his determination that his son Agustín should enter the church at the end of Chapter 4. The character of his son is both a parallel and a contrast to that of Don José. Agustín has the same basic generosity of spirit as his father, but education has eliminated some of the coarseness. He has the tact to avoid hurting people.

The avaricious Candiola is an obvious foil for the generous Montorias. But neither he nor Don José are simply individuals: they are universals as well as particulars. Montoria is like «la generalidad de sus paisanos» *(OC,* I, 675); [33] and Candiola is cast in the mould of the typical greedy merchant, apparently like Shylock in physical appearance. [34] The novel also traces the way in which their basic qualities are mixed with others like love of family and ultimately have an effect on the lives of other individuals and society. On the private level Don José's deep love for his own kin is contrasted with Candiola's preference for money even above his daughter. On the social level Don José is patriotic, while Candiola betrays the city to the French.

The structure of the novel is obviously designed to parallel and contrast these central characters with one another and with other individuals and groups against the background of the second siege. On one level the novel follows known historical events. But from the first, juxtaposed patterns of behaviour and attitudes enable the reader to make comparisons and value judgements about moral qualities

---

[33] Don Roque also refers to him as a man all heart «como buen aragonés» *(OC,* I, 670).

[34] In Chapter 7 Gabriel states that if Candiola had had a beard he would compare him to «cierto mercader veneciano que conocí mucho después, viajando por el vastísimo continente de los libros». This could well refer to Shylock.

and motives as well as patriotism. *Sursum Corda's* boastful and ultimately boring account of exploits in Zaragoza during the first siege in Chapter 2 is followed in Chapter 3 by Don Roque's deceitful eulogy of Gabriel to Don José. Montoria's pride is, in turn, reflected in the repast he gives his guests, slightly reminiscent of that in Larra's *Castellano viejo*. As the novel progresses it becomes increasingly necessary constantly to revise our initial assumptions about characters. In Chapter 12, for instance, the story of Candiola's inhuman unconcern for two wounded soldiers who had knocked at his door and been refused admittance, precedes an inhuman action by José de Montoria who loses his self-control and brutally kicks Candiola when the latter has fallen unconscious to the ground; this second example of human cruelty is echoed shortly afterwards by the children who mistreat and persecute the defeated Candiola. These incidents form a chain of inhuman actions in responsible and irresponsible people, which make the reader realise that Montoria is not always better than Candiola and remind him that children, in particular circumstances, delight in cruelty. In consequence, Candiola's inhumanity can be seen less as an isolated case of moral perversity than as an example of a common human pattern of conduct.

In part, of course, it is war which brings out the inhumanity in people. It has much the same effect on them as avarice and egoism have on Candiola, as Galdós points out at every turn of the story, by comparing and contrasting his actions with those of others. In the two plots — love and the siege — avarice and egoism on the one hand and war on the other are seen to be equally responsible for frustrating love and creating human misery. Galdós gives the reader ample evidence of the way in which war has a psychological impact and perverts human behaviour. In Chapter 6, the defenders of the Convent of San José are jubilant over the decimation of their French attackers;[35] elsewhere the innocent, «que nunca hicieron mal a nadie»,[36] constantly suffer, now in groups and now, like Estalla, individually *(OC, I, 723)*; the humane pattern of behaviour is rejected time and time again, and

---

[35] «De este modo celebra el feroz soldado en la guerra la muerte de sus semejantes, y el que siente instintiva compasión al matar un conejo en una cacería, salta de júbilo viendo caer centenares de hombres robustos, jóvenes y alegres, que después de todo no han hecho mal a nadie.» *(OC, I, 682).* Cp. *OC, I, 683.*

[36] Cp. above Note 35 and the same phrase in Chapter 15, *OC, I, 709.*

brutal revenge and courageous effort become difficult to tell apart; [37] heroism is merely all that is left when the heart is ossified and the soul has lost its more beautiful properties; [38] ultimately, it becomes more logical for a man to climb up a pile of corpses to speak with someone in the upper storey of a house than to go inside and up the stairs (OC, I, 739). [39]

The perverted values of violence are frequently in this way expressed explicitly. But often in *Zaragoza* Galdós uses situations which make the same point less directly. Clergy and monks who leave their calling to help in the war exemplify the distortion of normal existence which war brings; and in Chapter 22 the battle in the Church of San Agustín gives Galdós an opportunity to describe the vilification of sacred things which accompanies hostilities, by dramatically juxtaposing the divine and the barbarous in the reredos and other parts of the church where soldiers are fighting (OC, I, 728-9). Ironic juxtaposition helps to draw attention to the cruel indifference of people to suffering in Chapter 24. Candiola's protests at the failure of people to help him recover his receipts, trapped in a box under a fallen beam, are naturally seen in an ironic light — the more so since Candiola's greater concern for his money than for his daughter at this point underlines

---

[37] «A los esfuerzos del valor se unían ferozmente las brutalidades de la venganza.» (OC, I, 714-5).

[38] «Los corazones estaban osificados, y las almas parecían haber perdido sus más hermosas facultades, no conservando más que el rudo heroísmo.» (OC, I, 739).

[39] The piles of corpses strongly recall scenes in Goya's *Desastres de la guerra* (plates 18, 22, 48 and 63). It is hard to accept Hinterhäuser's rather dogmatic view that Galdós was not inspired by this work, although he accepts the importance of Goya for Galdós in general (Hinterhäuser, 85). The horror and violence of the war captured in Goya's etchings certainly occur in a modified form in Galdós, so does the irony about heroism (Goya's Plate 39 for instance, «¡Grande hazaña, con muertos!»), the barbarism of the populous (Goya's Plate 28, «Populacho») and the shooting of prisoners (Plates 15 and 26). Some of the same historical scenes —Manuela Sancho or Agustina Aragón firing the gun (Plate 7), women participating in the fighting (Plates 4 and 5)— inevitably crop up in both Goya and Galdós, but that does not prove any connection in view of the common currency of these scenes. But given that the first edition of the *Desastres* had only appeared in 1863, it would be surprising if Galdós did not know of its existence. The central belief in the ability of war to turn men into beasts is certainly common to both Goya and Galdós. It is true that certain sorts of violence are absent from Galdós. These are clearly «atenuaciones» if not necessarily «artificios patrióticos» on the part of the novelist (cf. Regalado García, 51). But Galdós never disregards the brutality and the bitter suffering, and Regalado García's view that his approach is basically that of a patriotic history for children is a gross oversimplification.

his inhumanity, as do other of his actions. [40] At the same time the explicable neglect of Candiola is contrasted with the unjust and inhuman neglect of a small child who has lost his family in the same chapter. Another ironic juxtaposition occurs in connection with Montoria's attitude to Agustín's vocation in Chapter 26. He refuses to allow his son to take orders, because «yo no puedo quedarme sin sucesión directa» *(OC,* I, 743); and yet he has only just ordered him to go on fighting (despite the possibility of his death) for the honour of his country *(OC,* I, 739-40). Egoism, more or less reprehensible, in fact, is always on the point of breaking out.

In Montoria's case the egoism is, of course, less vicious than in that of Candiola because it arises under acute stress. It is, nevertheless, egoism, and as such contributes to the general sum of misery and human perversity in the book. In Montoria, however, egoism is frequently mitigated by generosity and patriotism. The main counterparts to egoism and inhumanity are love and tolerance, and these are also thrown into relief on occasion by being juxtaposed with their opposites. In Chapter 26, for example, Montoria's tolerant attitude to María is contrasted with the intolerant, suspicious and perverse views of a monk; later in the same chapter Montoria's tolerance and humanity are again in evidence when he protects Candiola against the mob who wish to throw him down a well. Montoria has not, however, acquired the ability to control himself, and later voices similar views about María to those expressed by the monk *(OC,* I, 755); he also orders the execution of Candiola. In contrast neither the good Agustín nor, in Chapter 30, Gabriel, are capable of killing in cold blood, although the latter finally forces himself to order Candiola's death — «somos estúpidos y vanos hasta en los momentos supremos» *(OC,* I, 757). With this, the reversal of order by war and human cruelty is compete : «La religión misma anda desatinada y medio loca. Generales, soldados, paisanos, frailes, mujeres, todos están confundidos. No hay clases ni sexos. Nadie manda ya, y la ciudad se defiende en la anarquía.» *(OC,* I, 757.)

Significantly the novel ends with the entry of the French after the second siege, not with the ultimate liberation of the city and Spanish

---

[40] Candiola also seeks help from a group of men who are carrying a dying man to hospital and even prays to the Virgen del Pilar for a miracle to help him recover his papers *(OC,* I, 736).

victory. Love, family life, order and concern for others give way to anarchy, egoism and greed in *Zaragoza*. Spain as a nation, capable of united action, seems far away despite appearances. And the parallels with the disunited society of Galdós' own times are both implicitly and explicitly stated. Explicitly in Chapter 30; implicitly in the way in which the violent clergy and the general public who delight in destruction would have reminded Galdós' contemporaries of the Carlist supporters and other disruptive and violent movements. The actor-like leadership of Palafox [41] also, no doubt, found echoes in the 1870's, and so, above all, did the propensity of Spaniards to anarchy. Side by side with patriotic fervour in *Zaragoza* Galdós gives his readers those qualities which were most likely to create a divided society in Spain — the divided society of his own or any times. The point that María makes about her father in Chapter 27 is surely significant: he might have been different if his neighbours had been humane in their attitudes towards him instead of persecuting him: «Yo creo que si los vecinos de la ciudad no le mortificaran, él sería más humano... Esta tarde ha sido maltratado otra vez en el claustro de San Francisco, y cuando se reunió conmigo en el Coso estaba colérico y juraba que se había de vengar» *(OC,* I, 746). In all but exceptional people inhumanity and violence can only breed greater inhumanity and vengefulness. Human nature and the patterns of human behaviour are as much to blame as war itself for the cruelty and destruction which accompany it.

In a more complex pattern Galdós follows a similar line of argument in *Juan Martín el Empecinado.* Once again parallels and contrasts between the egoists and the unselfish are drawn: between those who delight in war and use it for their own ends, and those who fight to

---

[41]   «Vanagloriábase [Palafox] de ser el impulsor de aquel gran movimiento. Como comprendía por instinto que parte del éxito era debido, más que a sus cualidades de general, a sus cualidades de actor, siempre se presentaba con todos sus arreos de gala...» *(OC,* I, 733). Galdós appears to take the basis of his view of Palafox from the Conde de Toreno's *Historia del levantamiento, guerra, y revolución de España,* Madrid, 1837, Vol. I, 269. His approach however is marginally more critical than that of the historian. I have not been able to consult Agustín Alcaide Ibieca's *Historia de los dos sitios que pusieron a Zaragoza en los años de 1808 y 1809 las tropas de Napoleón,* Madrid, 1830, and do not know what view is expressed of Palafox there. Marcel Bataillon proved that Alcaide was the main source for *Zaragoza* in his important article «Les sources historiques de *Zaragoza*» in *BH,* XXIII (1921), 129-141. There is perhaps slightly more common ground between Galdós and the Conde de Toreno than Bataillon suggests. In Chapter 9 for example Larripa, Betbezé and Simonó are in Toreno (Vol. II, 270); in 10 Renovales' defence of San José is in Toreno (II, 269-70); equally the material for chapter 18 is in Toreno (II, 273-5).

achieve peace for the good of others. But by comparison with *Zaragoza,* much more is made of the connection between the character and psychology of the individuals concerned and their attitudes and behaviour. Furthermore, the characters are revealed more gradually than was the case in *Zaragoza.* Indeed the first impression of the central characters is substantially modified subsequently — a technique similar to that employed by Galdós in Nomdedeu in *Gerona* and in some of the novels he wrote later in the 1870's, *Doña Perfecta* for example.

This process of gradual revelation of character is consistent with a central moral and psychological concern on the part of the novelist: seeking the reality behind the appearances and revealing the true motives behind behaviour. But it is also a process which allows Galdós to extend the range and variety of character and to express in a clearer way than in *Zaragoza* the paradoxical value of some bad characters in a war situation, illustrating the perverted standards of existence which accompany war. Thus, at the beginning of the novel, both Mosén Antón and Saturnino Albuín seem more dynamic and perceptive than their superior officers — the fat and somnolent Vicente Sardina and the apparently hopeless administrator and incompetent speller Juan Martín. Both Albuín and Mosén Antón are cut in an heroic mould; [42] but both are described in terms of animals rather than humans; increasingly so as the novel develops. [43] Gradually their moral shortcomings emerge: Mosén Antón's vaulting ambition, his envy and bestial pleasure in violence; Saturnino Albuín's greed for gain, first clearly revealed in the exchange between the two subalterns in Chapter 8. Ultimately their self-absorption is not merely a moral flaw in their characters, but also has its effect on others and leads to the break-up of the gue-

---

[42] Cf. *OC,* I, 964: «Trijueque... era un gigante, un coloso, la bestia heroica de la guerra, de fuerte espíritu y fortísimo cuerpo, de musculatura ciclópea, de energía salvaje, de brutal entereza...» For Albuín, see *OC,* I, 980: «Albuín era el hombre de acero... Su cuerpo en conjunto parecía templado al fuego y al agua, y modelado después por el martillo... Los codos del héroe, no inferior a Aquiles en el valor, se parecían a los de un escolar.»

[43] Mosén Antón is «monstruo apocalíptico» at the end of Chapter 3; is compared to a boar, a horse and a bird of prey in Chapter 4. In Chapter 8 he is «un macho de noria» and for the second time «monstruo del Apocalipsis»; also «un tigre que tomara humana forma». In Chapter 10 he is «hiena salvaje», and «el bravo animal, la bestia traidora más valiente que cien leones» in Chapter 14. Albuín is «perro soñoliento a quien la persona mordida insultara desde lejos» in Chapter 10, and in the following chapter he is «culebra sin veneno» and «animal vencido».

rrilla band. Albuín defects to the French in Chapter 13; Mosén Antón goes the same way in the next two chapters.

Moving in the opposite direction towards ever greater stature, Juan Martín and Vicente Sardina acquire first moral and subsequently military distinction as the novel develops. Their view of war is selfless and humane in contrast to that of «el Manco» and Mosén Antón. Both oppose the shooting of prisoners and suspected spies and the burning and sacking of villages; both want to finish the war as soon as possible in order to return to their normal peace-time occupations. As Vicente Sardina says in Chapter 9, he and Juan Martín did not seek «honores, ni grados ni riquezas», but only «la paz, la felicidad de la patria, la concordia entre todos los españoles, para que nos sea lícito volver a nuestra labranza y al trabajo honrado y humilde de los campos, que es la mayor y única delicia de la tierra» *(OC,* I, 988). So far as their military outlook is concerned, they recognise the strategic need for concerted action, unity and order in the guerrilla band, and strenuously oppose Albuín and his followers when revolt threatens. They are going to bring Mosén Antón to heel when attacked by the French in Chapter 15.

By the middle of the book the conflict between the two main opposing groups has reached its climax with the defection of Albuín (historical fact) [44] and that of Mosén Antón (fictional). In the defection, as in earlier actions, Albuín's and Mosén Antón's motives and behaviour are echoed by the group of ex-students, whose nick-names Viriato, Pelayo and El Cid are as ironic as the real names of Doña Perfecta and Don Inocencio. Like Albuín and Mosén Antón they see the war as an opportunity for self-advancement, [45] and betray the Spanish cause for gain. Their egoism, together with that of the two subalterns, leads to the defeat and the break-up of the band. At this half-way point in the novel Galdós switches the reader's attention to Gabriel and, to a lesser degree, El Empecinadillo and Santorcaz. But the sense of continuity is not lost. Unity is, however, preserved less on the plot level, in which Gabriel, the child and Mosén Antón provide tenuous links with the first half of the novel as the action moves from

---

[44] Cf. Conde de Toreno, *Historia del levantamiento, guerra y revolución de España,* Madrid, 1837, Libro XIX, Vol. V, 16-17. Other historical defections to the French from Juan Martín are noted by Toreno in Libro XV (IV, 181).

[45] Cf. Chapter 3. There are further indications of Pelayo's greed at the end of Chapter 26.

the Spanish to the French camp, than on the level of character and motivation. Gabriel's qualities under adverse conditions are similar to those of Vicente Sardina and Juan Martín. His patriotism is as unshakable as theirs and he refuses to collaborate with the French when pressed to do so in Chapter 17. Like them too, Gabriel is deeply humane, and his concern for his fellow creatures is reflected in his treatment of El Empecinadillo and Mosén Antón. In Chapter 23, Gabriel prefers to take the child with him when he escapes from the prison rather than risk stifling it in order to prevent its cries from being heard, and later he refuses to leave it in a garden, although tempted to do so. He shows his concern for the predicament of Mosén Antón in his conversation with the priest, reasoning with him, and attempting to show him the futility of his pride. Subsequently, in Chapter 25, Gabriel shows similar qualities to those of Juan Martín in the face of supreme crisis: «el poder invencible de la voluntad humana» *(OC,* I, 1036). Equally, in the second half of the novel, there are contrasts with Gabriel to parallel the earlier contrasts between Juan Martín and Vicente Sardina on the one hand and Mosén Antón and Albuín on the other. In addition to Mosén Antón himself, Santorcaz provides a particularly obvious foil for Gabriel. Like Gabriel, Santorcaz is a man of humble origins; but like Albuín he is an individual of violent and vengeful propensities, which his circumstances have exacerbated. [46] His treachery and inhumanity are contrasted with the loyal, human concern of Gabriel in Chapter 18. But, of course, his whole life and career is a parallel and contrast for that of Gabriel.

Once again, as in *Zaragoza* and also in *Gerona,* war leads to the overthrow of the normal order of things. In Chapter I, the drones assault the bee-hives, the rich beg, churches are blown up or used as warehouses. «Estaba supensa la Naturaleza, olvidado Dios» *(OC,* I, 960). El Empecinadillo, brought up by guerrilleros in wartime, seems to exemplify this perversion of order and human values in war. When Gabriel invites the child to pray, he blasphemes. But Galdós is as interested here, as in other novels, in tracing an evil situation back to its root causes. Part of the explanation lies clearly as it did in *Trafalgar,* in the greed of political rulers, particularly Napoleon. To some extent he is to blame for the war, and the mass of the people are victims of the vices of their leader, as the case of the French

---

[46] Cf. Chapter 18.

soldier Plobertín seems to imply. [47]   At the same time in *Juan Martín el Empecinado* as in *Zaragoza,* there are many ordinary people whose moral defects are accentuated in war.   They delight in the opportunity to fight and destroy; and Santorcaz, Albuín and Mosén Antón are obvious examples of this tendency.   War is worse than it need be because of men such as these, and others suffer because of their lack of moral fibre.   Their egoism and lack of concern for others will be as dangerous to society in peacetime. [48]

Juan Martín el Empecinado, unlike *Zaragoza,* ends more or less happily.   It offers greater hope for unity than did the earlier volume. The guerrilla band is re-formed; the self-less live on; the traitor Mosén Antón commits suicide.   But the novel has shown once again how social unity and disunity are to some extent connected with the attitudes of individuals and their outlook on life.

At this point it is necessary to ask whether Galdós may not have been simply idealising the attitudes that he wanted the public to respect — peace, unity, patriotism, humanity, will and effort — by idealising those characters which embody these principles.   This is a possibility which cannot be entirely dismissed.   The fact that Mosén Antón is identified with Judas Iscariot (by his constant oath «Me reviento con Judas» and by the manner of his dying), suggests that Juan Martín, like Lázaro and Clara in *La Fontana de Oro,* [49] is to be seen in part as a Christ-figure, an ideal as well as a reality.   But no character is wholly idealised or symbolical, and there are shades of degradation on the «evil» side too.   Mosén Antón is a more pathetic figure than Saturnino Albuín and his character defects are marginally less serious.   At the end he sees the error of his ways, yet his pride is such that he is incapable of seeking Juan Martín's pardon. The group of ex-students are still less psychologically disturbed than either Mosén Antón or Albuín, and their attitudes are more the result of thoughtless egoism than deep-rooted perversity: a general lack of

---

[47]   Cf. Chapter 21.   Plobertín blames the emperor when relating the death of his child: «Tiene la culpa el emperador..., ese ambicioso sin corazón» (*OC,* I, 1025).

[48]   Cf. Chapter 5 (narrator's analysis), and Vicente Sardina's comment on the love of war in some guerrilleros in Chapter 9, «lo cual me hace creer que aun después de vencidos los franceses, todavía tendremos para un ratito.» (*OC,* I, 988).

[49]   Both Lázaro and Clara have a *via crucis* in Chapters 22, 27 and 28.   In contrast religious terms are used ironically about Doña Paulita in Chapters 24, 25, 30 and 42.

concern for others and social sense. It is presumably in such minor characters as these that the real moral object lessons lie. Candiola in *Zaragoza,* Coletilla in *La Fontana de Oro,* Saturnino Albuín and Mosén Antón in *Juan Martín el Empecinado,* are hardened in their attitudes. Others can only recognise them as morally and socially dangerous, and try to change them. At times, indeed, some change can be brought about as in the case of Mosén Antón whose suicide is a sign of his awareness of his error. Different treatment might have altered Candiola; different education Coletilla; formal education may change El Empecinadillo. Characters in the *Episodios* are seldom, in fact, simply black or white. There is, no doubt, considerable simplification, as one would expect in a novel which was almost certainly designed to appeal to a wide readership, but it is not excessive. The wide readership is invited by the structure of the novels to compare and contrast human behaviour, and to understand some of the root causes of certain behaviour patterns; Galdós leads his readers to judge humanely and will not allow them to be too easily swayed. There is clearly vice but there is also ignorance to be combated. [50]

Ultimately, therefore, Galdós is doing much more in these historical novels than just tracing the political conflicts of his own times back to their origins in the past, [51] or finding a high point of Spanish nationalism and patriotic spirit to hold up as an example to his contemporaries, [52] or even analysing the Spanish national character. [53] He is also clearly creating individual human beings (and recreating historical personalities) with a variety of characters, and showing how their psychological make-up and consequent attitudes and behaviour affect the lives of those around them and are in turn affected by their circumstances. His constant use of parallels and contrasts between characters and actions shows that his central concern is with man and his moral, social and political circumstances. Regalado García's criticism of the inadequacy of the geographical circumstances of these novels is unjust because geography is mostly not the central concern. [54]

---

[50] When protesting against riots which appear to have neither political nor psychological motivation in one of his Crónicas in the *Revista de España* (Vol. XX, 633), Galdós sees them as the product of a class «envilecida por el vicio y *atrofiada por la ignorancia*».

[51] Hinterhäuser, 173 *et seq.*

[52] Hinterhäuser, 45 and 162 *et seq.*; Regalado García, 50.

[53] Hinterhäuser, 150 *et seq.*

[54] Regalado García, 53.

The political relevance of the novels for Galdós' contemporaries is as much a consequence of the novelist's interest in character as of his use of situations which recurred in Spanish history. Moral and psychological patterns also recur. It is obvious that the analysis of guerrillero activities in *Juan Martín el Empecinado* was relevant to the 1870's. The Peninsular War was, as Galdós suggests, «la gran academia del desorden» *(OC,* I, 976); Carlist guerrilla bands and their activities echoed the past. But individuals have to be personally interested in disorder in order to want to study it in an «academia». As Vicente Sardina points out in Chapter 9, there are those who so delight in war that they want «la guerra eterna, *porque así cuadra a su natural inquieto»* *(OC,* I, 988). Ultimately the reasons for divisions in Spanish society are not simply political, but also the greed, envy, ambition and violence of many individual members.

It is on this level of individual characters and motives that history and fiction meet in the *Episodios.* In the quartet of central personages in *Juan Martín el Empecinado* history and fiction are carefully balanced: the primarily historical Juan Martín and the largely fictional Sardina on one side; the completely fictional Mosén Antón and the partly historical Albuín on the other. [55] The approach recalls theatrical techniques of balancing characters, and paralleling and contrasting situations are also common devices in the theatre as in Cervantes. [56]

---

[55] There is no lack of material about Juan Martín in Galdós' main source book, the Conde de Toreno's *Historia...* (Madrid, 1837, 5 vols.). There is, however, only one reference to Vicente Sardina that I have been able to discover, and nothing to throw any light on his character or motives (cf. Libro XV, Vol. 4, 262). The references to Albuín's counter-Empecinado activity are in Toreno (Libro XIX, Vol. 5, 16-17), but Galdós is more specific about the area of Albuín's cowardice than the historian. The latter, describing el Manco's flight, notes that «no cabe por lo común valor muy firme en los traidores»; Galdós, in chapter 11 specifies the type of cowardice of Albuín in relation to his moral theme by saying that he was extraordinarily brave in battle but «carecía de valor *moral»* *(OC,* I, 997).

[56] The idea of using history analogically is also, of course, common practice in the theatre in the nineteenth century as at earlier periods. A number of examples from the middle of the century are perhaps worthy of mention. López de Ayala's *El conde de Castralla* was certainly thought to have political implications when it was banned shortly after the first performance in 1856. The *comuneros* revolt, with which it was partly concerned, had frequently been used by writers to attack political injustice. Yet Ayala's mob's critical comments on the aristocracy hardly amount to political doctrine, and the ending brings a marriage between noble and commoner of the type which foreshadows the later compromises of Galdós himself in *La loca de la casa* and *La de San Quintín.* More explicit perhaps is Tamayo's defence of traditional Spanish monarchy and religion (and love) in his *Locura de Amor* (1854), which seems to reflect the absolutist leanings of its author. More particularly its anti-foreign

But on the basis of dramatic principles it is possible not only to find precedents for Galdós' structural features but also a special significance in his use of historical characters. Aristotle, after all, advocated the use of historical characters in tragedy because they added to the sense of verisimilitude. Galdós, too, may have felt that they sharpened the sense of reality in the works, and by extension, underlined their relevance.

The concern for moral rectitude as well as for order and national unity, and peace and understanding between nations which is to be found in the *Episodios,* was perhaps more politically meaningful at the time when Galdós' novels appeared than recent critics have thought. [57] Regalado García has, in particular, argued that Galdós was incapable of seeing the reality around him and sought a Utopia where peace, order and progress would bring about the unity of his country without political struggle. [58] Such a view cannot, however, be supported from Galdós' political articles. In them Galdós, like other liberal contributors

---

sentiments had relevance to the designs on the throne of the Montpensier faction in the 1850's. Some historical novels of the same period also had political significance. Manuel Gil de Salcedo's historical novel entitled *De pescador a soberano, o el Alzamiento general de un pueblo* (Madrid, 1859), is dedicated to The People. The rising in question is that of Masaniello in seventeenth-century Naples, and Gil de Salcedo may well have taken some of his material from the Duque de Rivas' earlier study of the insurrection. Both Rivas and Gil de Salcedo see plenty to justify the revolt but also point out the suffering it involved. Gil de Salcedo tells the people in his dedicatory preface that he will be happy «si logro con [estas elocuentes páginas] abrirte los ojos». Adolfo de Castro's *Serena* (Madrid, 1868) is an historical novel on the theme of religious tolerance, a vexed nineteenth-century question in Spain, but set in the days of the Roman Empire. It is interesting to note that Pereda, when he wrote to acknowledge the copy of *El audaz* which Galdós sent him described it as a «novela política» rather than a «novela histórica» (cf. Soledad Ortega, *Cartas a Galdós*, Madrid, 1964, 40).

[57] The brotherhood of man and the peaceful coexistence of nations is not an uncommon theme in the First series. In *Trafalgar* the subject is more particularly argued in Chapter 13 and it is implicit in the treatment of English and Spanish soldiers by the novelist. Both sides are equally humane and heroic. Plobertín's pathetic humanity in *Juan Martín el Empecinado* has similar overtones and so does the verdict on Gabriel's belief in the justice of a French invasion of Portugal as «juvenil ignorancia y equivocado patriotismo» (*OC*, I, 314). This underlying spirit of internationalism seems Krausist rather than Federalist in inspiration, and is perhaps similar to that expressed by Galdós's close friend José Alcalá Galiano in poems like *El titán* (steam uniting man thanks to travel) and *Mont-Cenis.* This last poem was published in the *Revista de España* in 1871 (Vol. XXII) and its vision of new peaceful links between nations instead of wars may well have appealed to the liberals who followed Albareda's line in that periodical: «La Verdad trazará nuestro camino / El amor nos hará justos y humanos, / La Paz completará nuestro destino, / La ciencia nos hará libres y hermanos» (op. cit., 409).

[58] Regalado García, 62.

to the *Revista de España,* registered his protests and appeals to try to ensure that the constitutional ground which the revolution of 1868 had won was not immediately lost as a result of extremist agitation and dissent within the main political parties. Galdós was far from opposed to changes in the social and political structure of Spain, but felt that his country needed above all stability. The revolution had removed the obstacles to political, philosophical and scientific as well as literary development in Spain. But an unstable government, now dictatorial now anarchical, inevitably held up the progress which liberals looked for. Above all the outbreaks of violence in Spain in the early 1870's shocked him and his colleagues as much as the *commune* in Paris. Galdós in 1872 appealed for «un antagonismo lógico y fecundo, en vez de esta guerra torpe y salvaje». [59] The faith of Galdós and other liberals in common sense and an instinct for good government, which they believed to exist particularly among city dwellers, was perhaps naive, and yet their constant criticism of those who contributed to the political instability of Spain cannot be said to reflect a lack of political purpose or justification.

A particularly interesting aspect of these political articles in the *Revista de España* is their use of techniques and assumptions which are common in the *Episodios.* Analogies with the past, for example, frequently occur. Albareda, when expressing dismay at the «recriminaciones personales» which had arisen after the assassination of Prim, notes that what had in fact re-emerged was «los incurables odios que desgarraron a los liberales en 1823, 1839, 1843 y 1856». [60] Galdós himself draws similar parallels when comparing the «clérigos belicosos y rudos» who supported Carlism in the Cortes of 1871 to «antiguos guerrilleros», who were accompanied by equally violent laymen «protegidos por el clericalismo y templados al rigor de la política militante y batalladora.» [61]

---

[59] *Revista de España,* Vol. XXV, 140. Galdós makes an identical appeal for constitutional government on a two-party basis in another *Crónica,* «en cuyo turno sosegado estriba que la política sea una fecunda lucha en vez de un pugilato de pasiones y de destinos» (id., Vol. XXIV, 614). The instability of the various political régimes between 1870 and 1875 is the constant preoccupation of writers of the Revista política interior in the *Revista de España.* It also finds literary expression in some of Núñez de Arce's poems in *Gritos de combate.*

[60] *Revista de España,* Vol. XXIII, 282.

[61] *Revista de España,* Vol. XXIV, 147. Elsewhere he speaks of «el rastro de odios y de resentimientos que ha dejado tras sí nuestra azarosa historia constitucional» (Id., Vol. XXIV, 610). He also, in another article for the same periodical, addresses the «consecuentes progresistas, que habéis sostenido *una*

León y Castillo, too, saw a significant similarity between the extremist excesses of 1872 and «los exaltados de 1820 al 23 que convirtieron la libertad en un liberalismo de bandería, [y] que aceptaron el poder como arma de venganza y de exterminio.» [62] Indeed, León y Castillo is quite explicit about the lessons which could be learned from the study of the past. «¡Cuánta enseñanza», he writes, «entraña la historia de aquel conturbado período [1820-1823], y a cuántas comparaciones, fundadas en la analogía de las circunstancias, no da lugar!» [63] The reviewer of the first volume of Gómez de Arteche's *Guerra de la Independencia (Revista de España,* Vol. V, p. 641), also pointed out that the Peninsular War period was of the greatest possible interest for «toda clase de estudios políticos, militares, sociales y administrativos». In his opinion the war did not merely exemplify heroic resistance to a foreign invader, it also saw «la inauguración de un nuevo sistema de gobierno... simultánea con la más radical de las revoluciones».

Equally evident in these articles is the interest in the relationship between character and psychology of individuals and their social behaviour, which I have suggested is an important concern of Galdós in the first series of *Episodios.* Certainly it is present in Galdós' own articles, as one of his *Crónicas* for 1872 shows. «Cuando los hombres se agrupan por resentimientos», he writes, «cuando antiguos rencores, o la fuerza de palabras consagradas, les sirve de enlace, las colectividades... sólo sirven para despertar en los hombres innobles ambiciones, para avivar la repugnante envidia, para producir inmorales elevaciones y desastrosas caídas, para someter lo más caro y lo más sagrado que hay en el mundo, que es la suerte de la nación, a la tremenda prueba de una constante y abominable intriga, único ejercicio de los espíritus turbados y cegados por la pasión.» [64] Given such a belief in the inter-relationship of psychology and politics, it is easy to see how the novel could become a natural form in which to depict

---

lucha de medio siglo por la libertad, primero en los campos de batalla, después en el Parlamento, después en la Prensa y siempre en la opinión pública con riesgo de vidas y haciendas». Later in the same article he writes of the country's divisions in the following historical terms: «Divididos desde hace medio siglo, y sin esperanza de que se reconcilien nunca los dos principios de la tradición y del liberalismo, a esta escisión fundamental se añaden muchas otras dentro de los que ven en las instituciones parlamentarias el único refugio contra la tiranía personal o demagógica» (Id., XXV, 291 and 297).

[62] *Revista de España,* XXIX, 547.
[63] Id., loc. cit.
[64] *Revista de España,* XXIV, 149.

social tension and political crisis. The analogies with the past then led naturally to the exploitation of the historical novel. When links with the past were no longer so obvious, or the political problems were too immediate to be treated in oblique terms Galdós could turn to the novel of contemporary society. But the essence of his novel-writing would remain, as it already was in the *Episodios,* «el engranaje de los caracteres... [que] es la clave del drama eterno que llamamos sociedad». [65]

University of Southampton.

---

[65]   *Obras inéditas,* Madrid, 1923, Vol. V, 141.

ARTHUR TERRY

'Lo prohibido':
Unreliable Narrator and Untruthful Narrative

Despite its very real merits, *Lo prohibido* (1885)[1] seems to have
made little headway with readers and critics of Galdós, and it still
remains one of the least studied of the novels about contemporary
society. In a sense, this is understandable: coming between *La de
Bringas* (1884) and *Fortunata y Jacinta* (1885-86), it has neither the
compact brilliance of the one nor the vast narrative sweep of the
other, and such compensating qualities as it possesses are perhaps less
immediately striking. For Robert Ricard, one of the few critics who
have written in detail about the novel, *Lo prohibido* clearly stands at
some distance from the more established works of this period: «[Il]
occupe dans la production de Galdós une place intermédiaire et, à la
manière de *Tristana,* par exemple, il fait un peu figure d'oeuvre mineure
et sans couleur».[2] This was not the view of Leopoldo Alas, who,
writing shortly after the publication of *Lo prohibido,* saw it as «un
episodio más de esta historia, la más difícil y hasta ahora la mejor de
cuantas lleva escritas el fecundo novelista», and went on: «Después
de *La desheredada,* es acaso *Lo prohibido* el libro más importante, por
la pureza, la verdad, la profundidad y la frescura de la composición,
entre todos los de esta época de Galdós.»[3] The discrepancy between
these judgements is not simply the difference between proximity and
hindsight; within the limits of its journalistic form, Alas' critique is

---

[1] Page and volume references are to the first edition of *Lo prohibido* (Madrid, 1885, 2 vols.); the second reference in each case is to the Aguilar edition
of the *Obras Completas,* ed. F. C. Sáinz de Robles (Madrid, 1964), vol. IV.

[2] *Un roman de Galdós: «Lo prohibido»*, in *Galdós et ses romans* (Paris,
1961), p. 75.

[3] *Galdós* (Madrid, 1912), pp. 139-40.

just and perceptive, though his praise of the novel has not on the whole been confirmed by later critics.

One reason for this has been the tendency to discuss *Lo prohibido* almost exclusively in the context of Naturalism, to see it, in fact, as Galdós' most «naturalistic» novel. Thus Sr. Casalduero summarizes the plot as follows: «La experiencia de que se informa al lector es la siguiente: dado los cuerpos A, B, C, cuyas propiedades llamaremos a', b', c', ver cómo reaccionan en cierto medio, que designaremos M, ante el cuerpo N, cuyas propiedades las conoceremos por n'. Los cuerpos A, B, C, son tres bellas hermanas casadas. N es su primo, mozo sin nada que hacer y con dinero. El medio: Madrid en 1880.»[4]

The important question, of course, is whether this corresponds to our experience of reading the novel. Before dismissing Casalduero's account as over-schematic, it is only fair to consider the ways in which *Lo prohibido* appears to echo the Naturalist formula. The obvious instance is Galdós' explanation of the neurotic tendencies which afflict the various members of the Bueno de Guzmán family. The physical symptoms of these tendencies (Eloísa's «pluma en la garganta» and María Juana's «pedazo de paño entre los dientes») are referred to impressionistically, rather than clinically, at various points in the narrative; José María's periodic moods of depresssion, though less dramatic, are given a more general resonance by the extravagant comments of Raimundo and Don Rafael: «el mal del siglo, el cual, forzando la actividad cerebral, creaba una diátesis neuropática constitutiva en toda la humanidad» (I, 12; IV, 1677). This last implication is not followed up in the rest of the novel, though later José María sees himself as representing other more general qualities. As for the phrases associated with Eloísa and María Juana, these tend to recur almost mechanically at moments of crisis without adding to the dramatic effect. Only once in the novel do they contribute to such an effect, and this is by implication, when José María refers to the obsessive nature of his passion for Camila as «[una] congestion espiritual» (II, 206; IV, 1833). Here, the sense of physical constriction experienced by the two sisters is associated metaphorically with the more complex mental condition of José María to suggest an important variation in the pattern of family neurosis. But this is exceptional: the physical symptoms of Eloísa and María Juana remain for the most part at the level of interest-

---

[4] *Vida y obra de Galdós* (Madrid, 1951), pp. 92-93.

ing data, without gathering any further weight in the course of the novel. [5]

The same may appear to be true of the heavily-emphasized contrast between José María's father and mother. They are both dead by the time the story begins, so that they are referred to entirely in terms of the narrator's heredity. In the course of the action it becomes clear that the oscillations in José María's behaviour reflect the clash between the two halves of his temperament, in which the father's sensuality and the puritanical nature of the mother are uneasily combined. This father-mother polarity is obviously connected with the twin themes of sex and money which figure so strikingly in José María's actions and motives. At something like a dozen points in the book, we are made aware that the balance has tipped in one direction or the other: «En mí renacía de súbito el hijo de mi madre, el inglés, que llevaba en el cerebro, desde la cuna, gérmenes de la cantidad» (I, 232; IV, 1744), or, conversely: «Mi dualismo estaba desequilibrado; mi madre dormía, y la sangre andaluza de mi padre era la que mangoneaba entonces en mí» (I, 209; IV, 1737).

If we remember Zola's insistence on the novelist as investigator, as someone who deliberately sets up an experiment under controlled conditions in order to deduce certain laws from the result, we may feel that Galdós is inviting us to judge the career of José María Bueno in Naturalist terms. If so, we may also feel that he overemphasizes the simple facts of José María's heredity: that these, like the neurotic symptoms of Eloísa and María Juana, are taken too much for granted, without any real attempt to work them into the dramatic structure of the novel. Yet here a doubt should arise: in the case of his cousins, José María is simply reporting something which he has been told, and which later he is able to observe for himself; in judging the workings of his own temperament, he is rationalizing his own behaviour after the event, excusing his conduct (something he tends to do even at moments of self-reproach) in terms of hereditary factors which he has convinced himself are inevitable, though in fact they are not necessarily

---

[5] In the early stages of the narrative, such data also have a unifying effect: the family neurosis, with its anticipations (dislike of dogs and birds, the imagined sexual incapacity of uncle Enrique, the kleptomania of uncle Serafín, etc.) gives cohesion, without enforcing a rigid framework on the story. Thus at certain points the family characteristics have structural importance, but are not a question of cause and effect and are not naturalistic.

so. This is in keeping with José María's view of himself as a passive character («yo soy pasivo» [II, 23; IV, 1777]), a judgement which is not entirely confirmed by the events of the novel, so that the frequency with which he returns to the father-mother situation becomes an index of his self-deception. This example shows how careful one must be in relating *Lo prohibido* to the context of Naturalism. Even if we suppose that Galdós began to write the novel after making a preliminary sketch something on the lines of Casalduero's summary, this in itself would not set him apart from many other novelists who would have rejected the Naturalist theory of fiction. What is lacking in the novel as it came to be written is any sense of «experimentation» in Zola's meaning of the word, of any notion that human actions are determined by «laws», whether of nature or society. The richness of *Lo prohibido* comes from the ways in which the suggestion of a basic scheme is overlaid and complicated in the interests of truthfulness, a fact which is brought out clearly by Galdós' use of first-person narrative.

Lo prohibido is cast in the form of an imaginary memoir: José María's account of his life in Madrid is given in three clearly-marked stages, the last of which reveals that he has already died. Thus, the entire action is refracted through the mind of a narrator who is himself a fictional character. The advantages of such a device are obvious: apart from the consistency achieved by seeing the action from a single viewpoint, there is also a gain in immediacy. A first-person narrative usually has the effect of decreasing the emotional distance between the reader and the narrator; by exploiting the reader's natural tendency to identify himself with the protagonist, the author is able to create a conflict between sympathy and detachment on the reader's part more easily than in a story told in the third person. At the same time, this apparent immediacy may be made to conceal a great amount of complexity. One common misconception is to suppose that the adoption of a first-person narrator implies a desire for objectivity on the part of the author. Casalduero, for example, seems to assume this when he writes that «*Lo prohibido* se debió al deseo de máxima objetivación de Galdós, de enfrentarse a solas con la materia y su mecanismo» (*op. cit.*, p. 93). It would be truer to say that a first-person narrative may be as objective or subjective as any other kind of fiction. The fact that the author gives up his right to comment directly on the action or the characters certainly need not mean that he is observing reality with greater detachment. Critics sometimes write as if a first-person narrator were not simply another character created by the author; whereas a character in a third-person narrative may be seen alternately from the outside and from the inside, the protagonist of a first-person narrative is really a character who is being presented entirely from the inside, though it follows from this that every other character may only be observed from the outside.

Complications occur in this scheme whenever the narrator is «unreliable», that is to say, when there are reasons to believe that a gap exists between his own values and those of the author. When this happens, it may often be difficult to judge where the author himself stands, though he may indicate his own position indirectly, for example by making the narrator criticize his own behaviour in retrospect. In *Lo prohibido,* José María is evidently an «unreliable» narrator: his shortcomings are made clear indirectly or directly from a very early stage in the book. Thus in the opening chapter, his uncle, in describing the neurotic tendencies which affect the various other members of his family, creates an atmosphere of expectancy in which we wait to see what form the hereditary weakness will take in the narrator. The effect of this is to make us question José María's valuation of his circumstances, to make us sense, for instance, a possible smugness in his interpretation of Don Rafael's affection for him: «De todo este panegírico saqué otra vez en limpio, leyendo en la intención y en el desconsuelo de mi tío, que éste habría deseado que sus tres hijas fuesen una sola, y que esta hija única suya hubiera sido mi mujer» (I, 22-23; IV, 1680). There is nothing crude about the way in which we are made aware of José María's shortcomings: our reaction to this kind of comment as we meet it for the first time can only be a tentative one, to be confirmed or discarded as the story advances. Eventually, as the nature of the society in which José María lives is made clear, we recognize the purely social criteria by which almost everything in these opening chapters has been judged. The characteristic note is struck, for example, in the account of his early feelings towards Eloísa when, after referring to her «talento superior», he goes on: «Eloísa hablaba con sencillez, sin pretensiones ni aun de buen sentido; pues el buen sentido, cuando quiere aguzarse mucho tiene pedanterías tan insufribles como las de la erudición; expresaba lo que sentía, claro, sincero y con gracia. Y lo que ella sentía parecíame trasunto fiel del sentimiento general; no chocaba ni por su originalidad ni por su vulgaridad. Observé que sus ideas religiosas venían a ser poco más o menos como las mías, tornadizas, convencionales y completamente adaptadas al temperamento tolerante, a este pacto provisional en que vivimos para poder vivir» (I, 81; IV, 1698). This kind of situation, in which we are invited to judge the narrator by the implications of what he says, is in fact more common than the direct comments which José María makes on his own behaviour. Though the first stage in the narrative is supposedly written after his affair with Eloísa has come to an end, he rarely takes advantage of his privilege of hindsight. However often we might expect him to say «If only I had known at the time», he does so only once, in the course of his description of Eloísa's dinner-parties, where it comes at the climax of an emotional outburst which marks a turning-point in his relations with her: «¡Comedia, o mejor, aristocrático sainete! Yo lo presenciaba aquellos días, y aún no me daba cuenta, por la embriaguez que narcotizaba mi espíritu, de lo absurdo, de lo peligroso, de lo infame que era» (I, 184; IV, 1729). The effect of this is to galvanize the whole of the long and painstaking description which it interrupts: once the account of Eloísa's circle is resumed, José María's impulsive reaction has heightened our sense of the fragility of the situation, so that the narrative appears to move quite naturally towards the climax of Carrillo's fatal illness. The directness of such a comment is justified by the need for a strong effect at a particular point in the story; if Galdós normally chooses more oblique ways of conveying José María's values, this is to some extent enforced on him by the nature of a plot which contains few spectacular climaxes. But the directness or otherwise of such effects is only of minor importance: what matters is that they should be convincing, and this is only possible if they arise naturally from the character of the narrator. There are no abstract rules for the use of a first-person narrator; such a protagonist is never convincing in himself; he can only be convincingly stupid, proud or unbalanced.

Once it has been shown that a particular narrator is unreliable, we must ask «to what extent?» If we apply this question to José María Bueno, we find that the answer is extremely complex: that it implies nothing less than the total effect of the novel. One guiding principle, however, stands out: if for the greater part of the novel José María is an unreliable narrator, by the time we reach the closing chapters he has become rather less so, though he still falls short of total reliability. One sign of this is a growing seriousness in his reflections on human behaviour: «Y a cada territorio que descubrimos en el planeta moral, parece que se ensancha el alma total del mundo, y por ende, la nuestra crece y...» (II, 171; IV, 1822), or, most striking of all: «...me ocurrió que la vida es un constante trabajo de asimilación en todos los órdenes; que en el moral vivimos, porque nos apropiamos constantemente ideas, sentimientos, modos de ser que se producen a nuestro lado, y que al paso de que las disgregaciones nuestras se nutren otros, nosotros nos nutrimos de los infinitos productos del vivir ajeno...» (II, 298; IV, 1861). Such reflections are immersed in the flow of the narrative in a way which avoids any suggestion that Galdós is guiding his character's pen; at the same time, if we are inclined to feel that the insights they contain are Galdós' own, this is simply a measure of the extent to which the gap between author and narrator has narrowed.[6] The increase in José María's self-awareness, however limited, is crucial to the meaning of the novel. In his groping attempts to understand his own experience, he is forced to consider his relationships with other people at a depth of which he is totally unaware when the action begins. The «unreliability» of the opening chapters is made to stand out more and more as the narrative develops: many of José María's original attitudes —for example, regarding the morality of the three sisters, the worth of their husbands and his own reputation within the family— are eventually shown to be false. And Galdós' skill is such that the reader is able to see further into this process than José María himself; because of this, *Lo prohibido* is not only a study of human relationships, but also, in a very real sense, of the whole concept of personality.

José María's most sustained piece of self-analysis occurs in Part II, chapter XVII. The passage is too long to quote in full, but the general drift of his thoughts is clear enough: «Aunque me duela confesarlo, no soy más que uno de tantos, un cualquiera... yo no soy *hérve;* yo, producto de mi edad y de mi raza, y hallándome en fatal armonía con el medio en que vivo, tengo en mí los componentes que corresponden al origen y al espacio... Carezco de base religiosa en mis sentimientos; filosofía, Dios la dé; por donde saco en consecuer.cia que mi ser moral se funda más en la arena de las circunstancias que en la roca de un sentir puro, superior y anterior a toda contingencia. No domino

---

[6] Professor S. H. Eoff comments on this last passage as if Galdós were speaking in his own person. Cf. *The novels of Pérez Galdós* (Saint Louis, 1954), p. 49.

yo las situaciones en que me ponen los sucesos y mi debilidad, no. Ellas me dominan a mí» (II, 22; IV, 1776). And the passage ends: «Yo no soy personaje *esencialmente activo*...; yo soy pasivo: las olas de la vida no se estrellan en mí, sacudiéndome sin arrancarme de mi base; yo no soy peña: yo floto, soy madera de naufragio que sobrenada en el mar de los acontecimientos. Las pasiones pueden más que yo. ¡Dios sabe que bien quisiera yo poder más que ellas y meterlas en un puño!» (II, 23; IV, 1777). As we have seen, José María's lack of will takes the form of a fatalistic acceptance of his heredity which comes out above all in his moral choices. These are usually made to appear as practical concessions rather than as genuine decisions, as in chapter VI, when he chooses to stay in Madrid and face the consequences of his feelings for Eloísa. Characteristically, he sees the situation in heroic terms: «Era una cobardía huir del peligro: se me presentaba la ocasión de vencer o morir. O yo tenía principios o no los tenía» (I, 105; IV, 1705). We know, of course, how weak these principles are; he has already admitted as much himself. However, in practice, José María's passive nature is modified by his vanity and sentimentality, and both these qualities count for a great deal in his approach to sexual relationships.

José María's vanity is most evident in his dealings with Eloísa: at times, he feels the need to draw attention to their relationship, knowing that it will arouse the admiration, if not the approval, of a society in which such things are common. His reactions to Camila are quite different: «La vanidad no tenía tanta parte en ella (i.e. mi pasión por Camila) como en la que me inspiró Eloísa. Ya me estaba yo recreando con la idea de que mi triunfo, si al fin lo lograba, permaneciese en dulce secreto, y que sólo ella y yo la paladeáramos, pues si en otra ocasión el escándalo me había sido grato, en ésta el misterio era mi ilusión» (II, 24-25; IV, 1777). At this stage, he is still hoping to seduce Camila; his vanity is only diminished («no tenía *tanta* parte en ella»). In the end, however, it is defeated and destroyed; as he approaches the final stage in his relationship with Camila, José María's frustration becomes increasingly humiliating: «Mi amor propio, herido también, se daba a los demonios» (II, 242; IV, 1843); «Mi amor propio, ultrajado y escupido, sugerióme venganzas soeces...» (II, 305; IV, 1863), until his final illness leaves him stripped of any possibility of self-esteem.

Whenever his vanity comes into play, José María reacts as a typical member of his *milieu;* even if we feel that his is a peculiarly masculine form of egoism, his attitudes are closely echoed, for example, by Eloísa and María Juana. Up to a point, the same is true of his sentimentality, though this has deeper roots in his individual experience, and at the same time is reflected in a greater number of ways by the other characters. Sentimentality, in general terms, is often a question of romantic attitudes which have become debased. It is significant how, for example, in several Galdós novels of this period, imagination is seen, not as the deepest origin of poetic insight, but as the source of uncontrolled fantasies. In *Lo prohibido,* its only associations are of this kind: in Raimundo, imagination appears as a solitary vice; in Eloísa, who at one point compares herself with Raimundo, it gives rise to a fantasy of riches. It is also the source of José María's fantasies about life with Camila, and when these threaten to overcome his reason, he refers to «(mi) furor imaginativo» (II, 256; IV, 1848). The roots of José María's sentimentality are not, however, to be found in any shared quality, but in his earliest sexual experience. The memory of the dead Kitty returns at certain moments in the story: he remembers her when he is introduced to Victoria Trujillo, the girl whom María Juana intends him to marry and, more significantly, in the first stages of his relationship with Eloísa: «Echaba la vista sobre Eloísa y veía en sus ojos el cariño apacible y confiado de Kitty. Era ella, la mismísima, reincarnada, como las diosas a quienes los antiguos suponían persiguiendo un fin humano entre los mortales; y asomada a la expresión de aquel semblante y de aquellos ojos, me decía: Aquí estoy otra vez: soy yo, tu pobrecita Kitty. Pero ahora tampoco me tendrás. Antes te lo vedó la muerte, ahora la ley» (I, 103; IV, 1705). There is a portion of José María's personality which has never outgrown this truncated idyll: his ill-fated engagement to Kitty belongs to his Anglo-Andalusian past; its essence is a combination of social convention and immature sexual feeling. In his mind, however, it forms a pattern which intrudes on his later experience and sometimes distorts it. In his comparison between Kitty and Eloísa, the earlier memory acts as a source of evasion in two ways: by preventing him from seeing Eloísa as a separate individual and by suggesting a fatalistic pattern in his life which it would be pointless to try to overcome. So the memory of Kitty confirms José María in one of his basic characteristics: the tendency to approach new experience through predetermined attitudes. Kitty is a dream of the past, but Eloísa, when he first meets her, is quickly transformed into a dream of the present: «Desde que la vi me gustó, y la tuve por mujer sin par, la que todos soñamos y no poseemos nunca, el bien que encontramos tarde y cuando ya no podemos cogerlo, en una vuelta inesperada del camino» (I, 27; IV, 1682). Here again, the note of fatalism is struck: though José María has no firm religious beliefs, he is conventionally superstitious, and his belief in providence makes him see his own life as a series of fixed patterns. The most obvious of these is the one indicated in the title of the book, and later we shall have to consider the implications of this; for the moment it is enough to say that José María's relations with Eloísa are coloured by a sentimental attachment to the past which makes it impossible for him to judge the moral consequences of his behaviour. Later, when his affair with Eloísa is over and he is about to begin the writing of his memoirs, he reflects: «el desatino con que me representaba todas las cosas, viéndolas distintas de como efectivamente eran» (II, 69; IV, 1791). But this moment of self-awareness is itself deceptive: if it forms a just comment on his relationship with Eloísa, it fails to protect him from further disillusionment at the hands of Camila.

The limitations of José María's vision are also shown in his awareness of other people and of his physical surroundings. In Lo prohibido, as in Galdós' other novels of contemporary society, there are no sharp boundaries between the real world and the fictional world; the merest mention of a historical event is enough to sustain our belief in the existence of the characters. Once this kind of confidence has been established between reader and narrator, José María is free to move between the wider setting of Madrid and the intensely localized surroundings of his private life. In this way, the narrative is made to follow a pattern of radiation and convergence as José María's field of vision widens or narrows.

The Madrid of Lo prohibido is felt rather than described: the form of the novel excludes the kind of sociological detail we find in Fortunata y Jacinta, and in its place we are given a sense of atmosphere which can be used to heighten particular moments in the story. There is nothing vague in this effect: by sheer economy, Galdós manages to suggest most of the essential features of Madrid society in the 1880's which are elaborated in the longer novel: the physical improvements which have taken place since 1868, the increasing flexibility of society and the peculiar kind of affluence which characterizes the Restoration period. Along with this goes a sense of the moral atmosphere of a society which endorses various forms of corruption. Significantly, this aspect of Madrid is presented through the various characters who surround the narrator; José María himself remains unaffected by other people's views on society until almost the end of the book, when his own disillusionment is made to coincide with that of Don Rafael. One characteristic reaction appears in the opening description of María Juana: «De sus conversaciones se desprendía un tufillo puritano, una filosófica reprobación de las farsas sociales, guerra sorda a los que suponen más de lo que son y gastan más de lo que tienen» (I, 26; IV, 1681). Later, a number of characters who cannot be accused of Puritanism —Fúcar, Torres, Sacamantecas— add their variations to this theme, until we reach the final outburst in which Don Rafael condemns the worthlessness of his own life: «Dirás que me faltó carácter y te responderé que ahí está el *quid*. Es el mal madrileño; esta indolencia, esta enervación que nos lleva a ser tolerantes con las infracciones de toda ley, así moral como económica, y a no ocuparnos de nada grave, con tal que no nos falte el teatrito o la tertulia para pasar el rato de noche, el carruajito para zarandearnos, la buena ropa para pintarla por ahí, los trapitos de novedad para que a nuestras mujeres y a nuestras hijas las llamen *elegantes* y *distinguidas,* y aquí paro de contar, porque no acabaría» (II, 315-16; IV, 1866). This judgement of a corrupt society has a direct bearing on the events of the novel, and in particular on the character of the narrator himself. But before we come to this, it is worth noticing the two points in the novel at which José María dwells on the physical setting of Madrid.

One of these occurs early in the book, the other immediately before his final collapse. The first time José María is recovering from a minor illness which has led to one of his periodic fits of depression. The scene in which he watches the life of the street from his study window is a good example of Galdós' skill in the selection of telling details. At the same time, it is a scene observed through the eyes of a fictional character. The sight of workmen at their lunch makes José María reflect: «Yo envidiaba su apetito, y habría dado quizá mi posición por poder comer con ellos, sentado al sol, aquel cocido de color de canario y aquel racimo de tintillo aragonés» (I, 78; IV, 1697). The passage ends with another reflection: «Un pobre hombre que pregonaba café hasta muy tarde con perezosa y oscura voz, me hacía pensar en la enorme diversidad de los destinos humanos» (I, 79; IV, 1698). The significant thing here is the most obvious: that José María is seeing life through a window, as a spectator, not as a participant. What he sees appeals to his senses; the best his mind can do is to produce a platitudinous comment on the diversity of fate. His mood of idle daydreaming appears harmless enough in the context, but when we remember it later in the book, it falls into place with a number of occasions on which José María's insulation from the life of the city is emphasized. One such occasion, in fact, seems deliberately to echo the earlier one: in chapter XII, José María and Eloísa plan to escape for the day to the Puente de Vallecas, «a retozar allí con las criadas y los artilleros» (I, 244; IV, 1747). This plan remains a fantasy; instead, they stay indoors, behind the «muralla chinesca» of José María's apartment which separates them from the world outside: «¡Con qué desprecio oíamos, desde mi gabinete, el rumor del tranvía, las voces de personas y el rodar de coches...! ¡Valiente cuidado nos daba que toda aquella gente viniera a rondarnos! Lo que hacía la sociedad con aquel ruido de pasos, voces y ruedas era arrullarnos en nuestro nido» (I, 245; IV, 1748). One form of the self-deception which exists in the relationship between José María and Eloísa is their inclination to see themselves in idyllic terms. It is entirely characteristic that they should imagine themselves as princes in disguise rubbing shoulders with the common people, just as on another occasion they indulge in the fantasy of a desert island. As far as they are concerned, the world outside only exists for such possibilities to be realized. Later, through the character of Juanito Santa Cruz in *Fortunata y Jacinta,* Galdós was to explore in much greater detail the sentimental middle-class view of «el pueblo»; in *Lo prohibido,* though the lower classes of society are only touched on in passing, the roots of such sentimentality are already suggested in the attitudes of José María and Eloísa.

The second description of Madrid is quite different. In Part II, chapter IX, just before José María hears of his financial ruin, he walks through the Retiro. Immediately before this, the superstitious side of his nature has persuaded him that his misfortunes in love will be compensated by financial success. As the description opens, the dramatic irony of the original situation is undermined for the reader by the anticipation of disaster: «Y por fin saliste de la serie tenebrosa del tiempo, día 2 de julio, el más horrible y ceñudo de los días nacidos, a pesar

73

de decorarte con toda la gala de la luz y cielo de Madrid» (II, 325; IV, 1869). In what follows, the holiday appearance of the city and the music of the barrel-organs contribute to José María's mood of optimism. Up to a point, José María is projecting his mood on to his surroundings; but the total effect of the scene comes also from the fact that this aspect of Madrid has been suppressed until just this point in the novel. For José María too, it is a moment of liberation: «el ir y venir de gente que no hace más que pasear, y otros mil perfiles característicos de un pueblo en que toda la semana es domingo, eran para mí la expresión externa del vivir al día y esa bendita ignorancia del mañana sin la cual no hay felicidad que sea verdadera» (II, 326; IV, 1869). One is tempted to compare this passage with others in which Galdós emphasizes the sanity of the ordinary life of Madrid which runs beneath the corruption of the higher levels of society. Yet this is not quite the effect which it has in its context, where it belongs to the drama of José María's final ruin. Perhaps it is nearer the truth to say that the sense of happiness rooted in apparent vulgarity which José María experiences in this scene echoes the similar quality which he has been compelled to recognize in the lives of Camila and Constantino. In both instances, José María is gradually made aware of a resilience which earlier he had ignored or despised, and the final irony of his situation is that the recognition has come too late to help him.

Somewhere between the presence of Madrid and the attractions of family life come the two driving forces of José María's existence, money and sex. Though his financial interests involve him in the general life of Madrid society and his sexual relationships take place within the family circle, there is a common area in which the two things meet and interact. As Robert Ricard has rightly said, «*Lo prohibido* est essentiellement le roman de l'argent» (*op. cit.*, p. 85); in no other Galdós novel are the details of private assets and speculations so meticulously recorded. Yet the important point is not so much the actual dramatization of wealth as the way in which so many of the characters are seen to base their entire sense of values on the pursuit of unearned income. Leopoldo Alas saw this aspect of the book very clearly: «José María representa el dinero que se gasta mal, que se desperdicia en locuras y tonterías, en sobornar a la virtud y levantar templos a la prostitución; el dinero de los ciegos, de los ignorantes, que aun en los momentos en que quieren trabajar, no encuentran más camino que el de la Bolsa; el dinero que se pierde por jugarse a espaldas de la misma ley, demasiado ancha y poco timorata; el dinero que va y viene en especulaciones artificiales, que nada tienen que ver con la natural circulación del capital en la vida de la riqueza» (*op. cit.*, pp. 143-44). Galdós suggests the connection between financial and sexual relations with great subtlety, by a steady accumulation of small details. One peculiarity of the language of *Lo prohibido* is the frequent use of economic metaphors in describing personal relationships. Eloísa's words to José María are «un veneno de palabras cariñosas, que después, *por maldita ley fiscal,* se había de convertir en zumbidos insoportables» (I, 240; IV, 1746); María Juana's feelings for José María are described as «moneda falsa» (II, 250; IV, 1846), or, in a more general way, Raimundo's feverish energy is seen as a squandering of his «capital vital» (I, 56; IV, 1691).

Here, Galdós is touching on an assumption which governs most serious nineteenth-century thinking on the subject of sex, the idea that sexual vitality and economic prosperity obey the same kind of laws. [7] Once the equation is made, the metaphors follow: sexual energy becomes a matter of spending or conserving; promiscuity may be compared to rash investments. By contrast, sexual fantasies envisage a world of plenty in which economic restrictions no longer apply. In *Lo prohibido,* Galdós is aware of both possibilities: José María's intermittent attempts to set his financial affairs in order are always accompanied by a falling-off in his sexual desire: «las benditas cifras ahogadas temporalmente por la pasión, se sublevaban, vencían y se posesionaban de mí con un bullicio, con un jaleo que me tenían por loco» (I, 233; IV, 1744). This is particularly evident in the later stages of his affair with Eloísa; as his love for Camila reaches the point of obsession, we see the reserve process, in which his refusal to face the facts of his financial situation eventually bring about his total ruin. It might be argued that any other kind of distraction would have served Galdós' purpose equally well, but apart from the fact that sexual liaisons are so evidently the principal source of distraction in the society he is describing, there is a peculiar fatalism in the advice which

---

[7] See the excellent discussion of Victorian attitudes to sex by Steven Marcus in *Partisan Review,* XXXI (1964); reprinted in *The Other Victorians* (London, 1966). In the basic metaphor, as Professor Marcus puts it, «the body is regarded as a productive system with only a limited amount of material at its disposal» (*The Other Victorians,* p. 22).

José María receives from the experienced financier Medina: «Es preciso que Vd. no se distraiga tanto con las faldas... Observe Vd. que todos los que al entrar por las puertas de la contratación no supieron desprenderse de los líos de mujeres, han salido con las manos en la cabeza. Hombre enamoriscado, cerebro inútil para trabajar» (II. 291; IV, 1859). As for the world of fantasy, Galdós achieves one of his most brilliant effects in the scene where José María reflects on Eloísa's vision of a state of pastoral innocence. This vision we know to be false; it comes too soon after José María's own fantasy of limitless wealth to be anything else. Yet in José María's mind, what began as a utopian evasion is destroyed by a moment of sexual jealousy, when he imagines an interloper who will play on Eloísa's lust for wealth: «Pero un día la señora Eva alcanza a ver a un ser extraño y desconocido que se aparece en aquel delicioso rincón del mundo donde sólo habitamos ella y yo. Esa tercera persona es el demonio... Es un viajero, un náufrago que acaba de arribar a aquellas playas, y para trastornar el seso a mi mujer, le muestra una sarta de cuentas de vidrio... Cae mi Eva en la tentación, se vende por las cuentas de vidrio y el demonio carga con ella» (I, 156; IV, 1721). The effect of the passage is complex: the biblical reference relates it, of course, to the central metaphor suggested in the title of the novel; more locally, the mention of «cuentas de vidrio» places the lovers in the position of noble savages exposed to the commercial greed of *conquistadores*. In the context, however, this is ironical, since José María's fear only arises because he knows that Eloísa is already corrupted. But as he later acknowledges, he is himself responsible for her corruption: «pensaba que aquella transformación de su carácter era obra mía, pues yo fui el descarrilador de su vida» (II, 11; IV, 1773). So the fantasy turns in a vicious circle: the devil who tempts Eloísa with his «cuentas de vidrio» is behaving as José María behaved at the beginning of his relationship with her. However unconscious he may be of his motives, it is clear that gifts form an important part of José María's approach to both Eloísa and Camila; gifts in this context, as in the fantasy, act as a substitute for sexual advances. With Eloísa, this succeeds; José María's first gifts to Camila, on the other hand, are only a poor reflection of those he makes to Eloísa: more than anything else, they serve to ease his conscience over his more extravagant treatment of Eloísa. Later, when his main aim is to seduce Camila, he places temptation in her way, notably during the expedition to Bayonne, but Camila refuses to be corrupted.

José María's opportunities for making gifts are, of course, increased by his ambiguous position within the family. If the ultimate aim of his gifts is sexual conquest, then at least his real motives can remain hidden from others —and at times from himself— as long as he is able to maintain his rôle as rich bachelor cousin. It is from the close domestic atmosphere of the Bueno de Guzmán family that José María's wider vision takes flight, only to return at crucial moments in the novel. In this, *Lo prohibido* resembles a great many other nineteenth-century novels: for Galdós, as for Balzac and Dickens, the home is not merely the centre of family life, it is also the place where people have serious illnesses and die, and the extraordinary power of the scenes describing the sufferings of Carrillo and Eloísa comes from their domestic settings. But the first thing we notice about the Bueno de Guzmán family is its atmosphere of permissiveness. This is suggested lightly, and almost humourously, in José María's first conversation with his uncle, Don Rafael: «Era un desconsuelo profundo, abrumador, el sentimiento de no verme casado con una de sus tres hijas; contrariedad irremediable, porque sus tres hijas ¡ay dolor! estaban ya casadas» (I, 10; IV, 1676). In itself, this suggests no more than an easy frankness, a frankness in which there is still a place for decorum, and this is confirmed by Don Rafael's description of his three daughters and their husbands. At the beginning of the novel, José María is in the position of an objective outsider who is none the less one of the family, a person to whom confidences may be made in safety. Yet, before long, his privileged position is strengthened by the opinions of Eloísa and her parents. Eloísa makes no secret of her admiration for him; Don Rafael and Doña Pilar continually reveal their lack of enthusiasm for Eloísa's husband, Carrillo. Once his affair with Eloísa has begun, José María is embarrassed by the thought of the family's reaction: «Con la familia me había hecho algo cohibido. Temía que el tío se enfadase, que mi tía Pilar me echase los tiempos por la situación poco decorosa en que había puesto a su hija. Pero ninguno se dio por entendido. O no lo sabían, o lo disimulaban.» His gifts to them are still gratefully received: «(mi generosidad era) en mí como una corruptela para comprar su tolerancia, o subvención otorgada a su silencio» (I, 142; IV, 1716). To the end of the book, in fact, it is never made clear whether Don Rafael knows of José María's relations with his daughters, and his final outburst to José María on the moral corruption of Madrid is delivered without a trace of personal reproach. [8]

Nevertheless, José María's rôle within the family is not simply that of a usurper. He is, as he admits, a gregarious person: he needs the proximity of his relations, though he wishes to enjoy the advantages of family life without its responsibilities. This is made clear early in the book: «Mi carácter fue siempre, salvo en las ocasiones de mal nervioso, refractario a la soledad. No me gustaba vivir en el interior de aquella república, sí en sus agradables cercanías» (I, 46; IV, 1688). Significantly, his first moment of intimacy with Eloísa arises directly from this atmosphere of domestic comfort. As Eloísa is nursing him after his first illness, he is struck by a sudden feeling that she is acting as if she were his wife. At the root of this feeling is a sense of «rightness» («Cada persona estaba en su sitio y yo en el mío» [I, 84; IV, 1699]). There is no suggestion that José María feels sexual desire; he is mainly aware of Eloísa's maternal warmth. The scene is revealing, since it shows a motive which appears in José María's relationship with all three of his cousins: his desire for security makes his imagination jump ahead continually to the vision of a settled married life. Though in the end he rejects the opportunity of marrying Eloísa, he continues to admire her maternal feelings towards her own son, even after she has ceased to have any sexual attraction for him. María Juana, unlike her sisters, never engages José María's feelings in this way; instead, she tends to parody the wife-mother relationship by seeing herself in the rôle of the older, more experienced woman who sacrifices herself in the cause of José María's sexual education. The motive appears quite clearly, however, in José María's relationship with Camila. Towards the end of the novel, when José María has had to admit defeat, he is willing to settle for the least suggestion of domestic security, though the irony of circumstances is that he is cheated even of this: «Deseaba con toda mi alma hacer las paces con ellos (Constantino y Camila), y arrimarme al fuego de su santo hogar, lo más digno de admiración que hasta entonces había visto yo en el mundo» (II, 333; IV, 1872).

---

[8] Don Rafael's behaviour throughout the book is very consistent: from the beginning, he lives in a world of fantasy, symbolized by his sensations of flying (I, 18-19; 1679); later, his chronic tendency to weep suggests that he expresses apparent feelings without actually experiencing them (II, 314; 1866). In the present passage, he voices a general condemnation of Madrid without being aware of the specific example he has in front of him.

This last remark points to what is perhaps the fundamental significance of family life in *Lo prohibido.* If traditionally the family is felt to possess a peculiar kind of sanctity, this is because it forms the earliest, most primitive type of society. Consequently, once society has become complex and possibly corrupt, there is a natural tendency to regard the family in idyllic terms, as a refuge from the loneliness and suffering of the world outside. This is a constantly recurring theme in nineteenth-century fiction, though there are as many bad families in the novels of this period as in those of any other. What is striking, however, is the persistence of the ideal, however cruelly betrayed, and the tension which often exists between the idyll and the reality. In *Lo prohibido,* José María has his own idyllic vision of family life, though this is limited by his egocentricity and the weakness of his moral principles. These eventually bring about his downfall, but the process by which they do so is not an inevitable one, since we could imagine a different novel in which the family influence was strong enough to restrain or correct this side of his character. However, as events turn out, the family has no such moral authority, so that the idyll which José María glimpses is undermined from the start. Instead of preserving the values which have been perverted in society at large, most of his relatives have submitted to social pressures, and the family itself has come to reflect the general corruption.

The only exceptions are Camila and Constantino, whose model family life is conducted in the teeth of society and in the absence of all conventional social virtue. The way in which we are made aware of their different scale of values after the misleading initial presentation is the main focus of interest in the second half of the novel. Both structurally and psychologically, this process serves to balance José María's earlier account of his relationship with Eloísa. The two parts of the story are held together by the single consciousness of the narrator, who sees them both in terms of the principle implied in the title of the novel. Galdós' use of abstract titles deserves a study to itself: generally speaking, he seems to be suggesting not so much the theme of a particular story as the area of moral interest within which the reader may expect to move. In *Lo prohibido,* the attraction which forbidden relationships exercise over José María is underscored at various points. Early in the novel, a certain fatalism overshadows his feelings for Eloísa when she reminds him of his dead fiancée. Shortly afterwards, he and Eloísa become lovers; but the very ease with which this comes about leads José María to argue that she may be unfaithful to him in turn. This mistrust is echoed by Eloísa, who at one point accuses him of spending too much time with Camila. The same feeling appears in the passage in which José María reflects on Eloísa's pastoral fantasy, and continues through the long description of Eloísa's dinner-parties, where the possibilities for temptation are multiplied by the social context. Eloísa does, in fact, remain faithful to José María, but their relationship is brought to a head by the illness and death of Carrillo. Looking at the situation objectively, we may feel that José María reacts as he does at this point because his love for Eloísa has grown stale. But he himself sees things less simply: «Lo que en vida de (Carrillo) me enorgullecía, ahora me hastiaba; lo que en vida de él era plenitud del amor propio, era ya recelos, suspicacia con vagos asomos de vergüenza. Si robarle fue mi vanidad y mi placer, heredarle era mi martirio. La idea de ser otro Carrillo me envenenaba la sangre» (I, 295; IV, 1763). Mistrust, that is to say, is still very much in his mind, coupled now with the idea that his love for Eloísa has been self-indulgent, that his self-esteem has been increased by his experience with her, but will be easily wounded if she becomes his wife. The attitude is a strange mixture of irrational fear and the desire to see a rational pattern in the events of his life; for a time, José María expects it to pass, but it does not, and eventually crystallizes in what proves to be his final judgement on the affair: «Era pasión de sentidos, pasión de vanidad, pasión de fantasía la que me había tenido cautivo por espacio de tres años largos; y alimentada por la ilegalidad, se debilitaba desde que la ilegalidad desaparecía. ¿Es tan perversa la naturaleza humana que no desea sino lo que le niegan y desdeña lo que le permiten poseer?» (I, 299; IV, 1764).

José María finds his self-deception much more difficult to maintain in his relationship with Camila, who at one point unconsciously parodies the very argument he has used for not marrying Eloísa: «¡Ay!, no te canses en seducirme... lo menos que piensas es que cuando tú quieres plantarles cuernecitos a otros, se te carga la cabeza de ellos sin que tú lo sepas, tontín...» (II, 34; IV, 1780). Almost to the end of the novel, José María has no illusions about his guilt in wishing to seduce Camila; his mind plays freely with the possibility of Constantino's death, and there are times when he seems prepared to bring this about himself. Characteristically, his melodramatic imagination persuades him that he is the biblical serpent who will corrupt Camila's innocence: «me pasé allí la tarde, encantado, embelesado, respirando a todo pulmón el delicado ambiente de aquel Paraíso terrestre y casero, en el cual yo quería hacer el papel de culebra» (II, 38; IV, 1781). There is no need to dwell on the various allusions to the Garden of Eden which are scattered through this part of the book, since they have been brought together by Sr. Gustavo Correa in his discussion of Galdós' use of religious symbolism. [9] The pattern which they form is simple enough, and is reinforced, though not altered, by the episode in which María Juana tries to find a wife for José María. By this stage in the novel, his reactions have become fixed: «no me agradan más que las cosas prohibidas, las que no debieran ser para mí» (II, 133; IV, 1810)... «Soy un desdichado que siempre llega tarde...» (II, 172; IV, 1822). However, to see the novel entirely in terms of the working-out of this very obvious symbolism, as Sr. Correa appears to do, is to oversimplify what in reality is a very complex structure. The main defect of this approach, as of the Naturalist interpretation, is that it fails to take into account the importance of the first-person narrative. Once we grant that the whole idea of «lo prohibido» and the religious symbolism which goes with it form part of José María's attempt to rationalize his behaviour —to rationalize it, rather than to understand it in any deeper sense— we find ourselves once again questioning his reading of experience, to the point of feeling that the real defects of José María's personality lie beyond the reach of his understanding. Professor Eoff goes further than most critics on this question when he writes that «José María's taste for *lo prohibido* is immoral in one important sense by reason of a lack of self-mastery, and hence a lack of wholeness» (*op. cit.*, pp. 37-38). If one tries to define the exact sense in which José María is incomplete, one sees something of the depths at which Galdós' moral imagination can work. For, surely, what is «prohibited» to José María goes beyond his literal situation *vis à vis* the women in his life? Can we not say, in fact, that the peculiar feature of his «lack of wholeness», to use Eoff's phrase, is that he is excluded by temperament from conceiving a mature sexual attitude towards women because he has difficulty in seeing them as unique individuals?

One of José María's most characteristic weaknesses is his tendency to generalize. Eloísa, when he first meets her, is not just a woman,

---

[9] *El simbolismo religioso en las novelas de Pérez Galdós* (Madrid, 1962), pp. 80-95.

she is «lo que todos soñamos y no poseemos nunca» (I, 27; IV, 1682); at various times she reminds him of the dead Kitty and even, at one point, of her sister Camila. Generalization here takes the form of a confusion of identities which blurs his sense of Eloísa as an individual. The roots of this failure in José María are both social and personal. The whole pressure of the society in which he lives is towards a standardization of personal relationships. Money, as it functions in such a society, is also a generalizing force; where everything has its price, aesthetic and moral values are inevitably at a discount: *objets d'art* are treated merely as signs of wealth, and Eloísa herself «tiene los espíritus muy metalizados» (I, 180; IV, 1728). At a more personal level, José María's «romanticism», as he terms it, is merely another set of conventional responses which casts a haze of self-indulgence over his awareness of other people. One aspect of his sentimentality, as I have already suggested, is his habit of dwelling on the maternal qualities of women. This is obvious in his early reactions to Eloísa and in his affection for Eloísa's son, Rafaelito. It is also significant that his feelings towards Camila are first aroused by her devotion to her sick child; at the other extreme, José María's own desire for a mother-figure is cruelly parodied in his more superficial relationship with María Juana.

All these things point to José María's sexual immaturity; there would be no need to stress this if it were not that certain positive values are made to stand out by contrast. *Lo prohibido,* like many other serious novels, is deeply concerned with the difference between sexual desire and genuine love. Sexual desire, like money, obeys a limited number of fixed patterns, and is destroyed or transformed when instinct is overruled by imagination. Love, on the other hand, depends for its existence on a sense of differentiation: desire knows what it wants, but love is continually surprising since it sees the other person as unique. As a description of desire fulfilled, there is no more brilliant passage in the novel than the scene in which Eloísa becomes José María's mistress: «Las cuatro serían cuando entré en la casa. No había nadie de la familia más que Eloísa. No tuve que llamar. La puerta estaba abierta, y un operario arreglaba la entrada del gas. Sentí martilleo en las habitaciones interiores, y, al pasar junto a una puerta, oí la conversación de unas mujeres que, sentadas en el suelo, estaban cosiendo alfombras. Parecióme que yo me introducía invisible, como el gas, pasando por escondidos, angostos y callados tubos. Avancé. Bien sabía yo a dónde iba. Tan seguro estaba de encontrarla como de la luz del día. Después de atravesar dos salones, vi a Eloísa de espaldas. Estaba repasando una colección de estampas puesta en voluminosa carpeta. Acerquéme a ella de puntillas; mas aún no estaba a dos pasos de su hermosa figura, cuando, sin volverse, dijo esto: «Sí, ya te siento; no creas que me asustas...» » (I, 136; IV, 1715). The lovers are meeting by assignment in Eloísa's new house; they both know in advance what is going to happen, and the absence of surprise is emphasized on both sides: «bien sabía yo a dónde iba...», «no creas que me asustas». Setting and feeling are perfectly matched: José María passes like a ghost through the outer rooms, and as he does so, his mind snatches at the detail which provides a metaphor for his own situation: «Parecióme que yo me introducía invisible, como el gas...». The sinister quality of the image invests the secrecy of the action with a kind of insidious anonymity; Eloísa, for her part, is inseparable from her surroundings: the book of prints she is holding and the labours of the workmen who are putting the finishing touches to the house all contribute to the atmosphere of material wealth which is to surround her through the rest of their affair.

Conversely, José María is never allowed to experience a genuine love relationship, though his dealings with Camila in the later part of the book compel him to abandon some of the preconceptions which blinded him to the nature of his feelings for Eloísa. The difference in his behaviour towards the two women poses a problem which Galdós solves with great skill. If the novel is to have any moral depth, the reader has to be made dramatically aware of the possibility of genuine love, though the story is told by a narrator who is himself barred from the experience. The creation of such an awareness depends largely on the successful handling of the relationship between José María and Camila, but the process is made doubly convincing by an earlier episode in the novel. If love depends on a sense of differentiation, there are times when our failure to understand another person's motives may also increase our awareness of his individuality. This may equally well happen between persons of the same sex, and when it does, the result may be to deepen our conception of the other's character. In *Lo prohibido,* the illness and eventual death of Pepe Carrillo increases the feeling of guilt which overshadows José María's affair with Eloísa. Though Carrillo is in some ways an ineffectual character (the contrast between his charitable schemes and his inadequacy in more personal affairs is stressed at various points), his rectitude compared with other members of his circle makes it possible to see him as the innocent victim of deceit. José María, at any rate, is made uneasy by what he takes to be Carrillo's superiority —«habría deseado que aquel hombre careciese de méritos» (I, 93; IV, 1702) — and this feeling comes to a head in chapter X («Carrillo valía más que yo»). Here, as he reflects on Carrillo's tireless activity in social causes, José María is forced to recognize something which he would prefer not to believe: «Fáltame contar lo más importante, lo más extraordinario y anómalo en el carácter de aquel hombre. Lo que voy a decir es una aberración moral, indefinible excepción de cuánto han instituido la Naturaleza y la Sociedad, pero tan cierto, tan evidente como es sol éste que nos alumbra. Carrillo me mostraba un afecto cordial...» (I, 163; IV, 1723). We already know the shallowness of the moral order to which José María appeals in his confusion; for the first time in the story, he has come up against someone whose motives he cannot understand. Carrillo remains a mystery to José María until his death removes all possibility of a solution, but, paradoxically, this enigmatic quality has the effect of heightening José María's awareness of Carrillo as a separate individual. This sense of fascination is brilliantly conveyed in the scene at Carrillo's deathbed. For a moment, José María's melodramatic imagination suggests that the mystery is about to be resolved; he actually hopes that Carrillo will die cursing him (this, at least, he could understand), but the final gesture of the dying man is unambiguous: «Le miré la cara, y en sus ojos vidriosos vi cuajada y congelada la misma expresión de amistad leal que me había mostrado siempre» (I, 284; IV, 1760). Carrillo's death leaves José María with a feeling of blank incomprehension — «Toda mi vida, ¡ay!, estará delante de mí, como pensativa esfinge, la imagen de Carrillo, sin que me sea dado descifrarla» (I, 290; IV, 1762) — and it is with a kind of superstitious horror that he feels that he is expected to step into Carrillo's shoes.

Though the emotional nature of the two situations is quite different, José María's feelings for Carrillo prepare us for his more complex relationship with Camila and Constantino. In both instances, he has the experience of dealing with human beings whose true nature cannot be grasped by his own conventional standards. Carrillo completely escapes his understanding, though for this very reason he remains indelibly stamped on José María's imagination. Camila, in the early part of the novel, has no particular attraction for him: he takes her at the valuation which the other members of his circle have given her, and

accepts without question that she is «barbarous» and completely lacking in social graces. Reading the account of her disastrous dinner-
party in chapter VII, we are probably inclined to agree with this valuation; it is mainly by contrast with the more sophisticated entertain-
ments in the house of Eloísa that a certain sanity begins to emerge
among the disorderly arrangements of the Miquis household. At this
stage in the novel, the contrast is stated more firmly in terms of Camila's contempt for money (particularly José María's) and her serious
and touching attempts at economy. José María's attitude towards her
first begins to change at the time of her child's illness, and before long
he has begun to regard her as an example, not of barbarousness, but of
primitive goodness. Her life with Constantino now appears «un fenómeno de inocencia pastoril» (I, 317; IV, 1770), and it is Camila's physical health which first arouses José María's sexual feelings. This emphasis on Camila's physical qualities, together with the original impression of Constantino as a mindless athlete, has led Robert Ricard to
speak of their marriage as a purely animal affair. [10] This is surely too
close to the conventional valuation which the later events of the story
undermine. Even if we discount their attempts at self-improvement,
which in Camila's case at least are serious and effective, the moral
rightness of their conduct is made clear at many points. José María
realizes this to his cost, and the discovery is a crucial stage in his self-
education. Even after he has admitted Camila's worth, he thinks of
her chiefly as a woman to be seduced and imagines that her innocence
will play into his hands. To this extent, he feels that nature is on his
side; later he is proved wrong, though he only abandons his hope of
corrupting Camila at a late stage in the novel. There is something
obsessive about José María's concern with Camila's health, as becomes
clear when he speculates on marriage with her as the one means of
curing his own neurosis: «Fijóseme entonces la idea de que todos los
males nerviosos, fueran o no provenientes de la diátesis de familia, se
me quitarían cuando me casara con ella» (II, 245; IV, 1844). Nature
in Camila, however, is more than mere physical health: her vitality
is confined to «los encantos lícitos de la vida», and the soundness of
her conscience is never in doubt. The scenes in which José María

---

[10] «Galdós ne dissimule pas la prépondérance de l'élément sensible dans
l'amour passionné qu'ils ressentent l'un pour l'autre. Ce qui les sauve, c'est
leur divine ignorance, leur merveilleuse et complète absence d'idées. Ils sont
tout instinct...» *Aspects de Galdós* (Paris, 1963), p. 19.

puts her resilience to the test contain some of Galdós' most delicate comedy, and it is clear that Camila touches a vein of humour in his character as no one else does. At the same time, we are made to feel the desperation which underlies such moments as José María consciously abandons his notions of social decorum.

José María's awareness of Constantino is of great importance in the final stages of the novel. For most of the time, he finds himself admiring Constantino's virtues while at the same time wishing he would die. This creates a curious effect on the reader which is surely part of Galdós' intention. For somehow, in the second half of the book, José María becomes a more reliable narrator, in the sense that we do not doubt that what he says of Constantino and Camila is true. Though he himself is torn by jealousy and wicked intentions, this does not affect the picture of the Miquis household as it emerges from his account. One of the ironies of José María's situation is that he has come to realize that the Miquis represent the ideal of family life which he has failed to find elsewhere, though his passion for Camila forces him to work towards its destruction. He is, of course, unsuccessful in this intention, as he is compelled to admit even before his final illness. Towards the end of the book, his sense of what the Miquis represent is strengthened by his growing sympathy for Constantino. There is still a certain ambivalence about this, in so far as he still continues to hope that Constantino will be removed from the scene, but there is a world of difference between his delight when Constantino seems on the point of challenging him to a duel and his earlier private fantasies about Constantino's death. The difference is one of openness: by this stage José María has come to recognize Constantino's capacity for friendship, so that the idea of a duel takes on something of a chivalrous aspect. Just as his awareness of Camila as an individual increases as he experiences her powers of resistance, so his respect for Constantino's personality grows as he comes to realize that there is a kind of friendship which goes deeper than conventional social relationships. This, as Augusto Miquis points out, belongs to the heroic side of Constantino's nature: «Es un bloque de honradez y nobleza, con nociones radicalísimas y cardinales del bien y del mal... Para él, lo que no es superior es ínfimo; moral bárbara si se quiere; pero yo, pregunto: ¿no es ésta la moral de los tiempos en que los hombres supieron hacer cosas grandes, que no se hacen ahora?» (II, 308; IV, 1846). This is why, when Constantino withdraws his friendship from José María, we feel the devastating force of his action, and it is partly José María's own awareness of this which drives him to the edge of despair. By this point in the novel, José María has become peculiarly dependent on Constantino and Camila, through his growing alienation from the rest of society. One measure of this is his complete failure to convince others of the innocence of his relations with Camila. This lack of comprehension serves to emphasize the extent to which José María's relationship with the Miquis has placed him beyond the reach of normal social valuations. Once he has been excluded from their company, there is nothing left for him but to hammer at their door. By this time, José María is willing to settle for very little, but shortly after this, the blow falls, and he is struck down by the illness from which he never recovers.

If we see the novel mainly as the working-out of a mythical pattern, we are likely to misread the ending. Sr. Correa does so, it seems to me, when he writes: «El daño causado en la opinión a los dos esposos rebotaba sobre él (José María) en forma violenta, llevándolo a su final destrucción. El héroe diabólico era rechazado del paraíso del amor legítimo y lanzado a los abismos de la desesperanza y de la impotencia física. Su diabolismo era, así, ejemplarmente castigado.» [11] But José María does not vanish in a puff of smoke, and his final relationship with Camila and Constantino is more subtle than this account suggests. The characteristic note occurs in the passage where he dreams that Camila has given birth to a second child. The dream becomes reality, and José María dies after sharing in the happiness of the woman who has shown him the possibility of genuine love. Camila and Constantino, far from being corrupted, maintain their resilience to the end. There is a moment shortly before José María's illness when their situation seems in danger: «Eran sin duda menos felices, porque eran menos inocentes; ambos sabían algo más de la malicia humana; sin ser pecadores, habían probado las amarguras de la sospecha, la manzana apetitosa e indigestible, y de buenas a primeras se habían avergonzado de la desnudez de su inocencia» (II, 310-11; IV, 1865). But Camila herself has the last word: «Nos ha dañado en nuestra opinión, pero bien caro lo paga —había dicho Camila con inocencia de niña de escuela—. No seamos más papistas que el Papa, ni más justicieros

[11] *Op. cit.*, pp. 87-88. Sr. Gullón's reading of the ending is much closer to my own. Cf. *Galdós, novelista moderno* (Madrid, 1960), pp. 191-92.

que la justicia de Dios. ¿No estamos bien tranquilos en nuestra conciencia? No sabemos tú y yo, como éste es día, que ni él pudo conquistarme, ni había tales carneros, ni Cristo que lo fundó?... Pues si hay algún necio que crea otra cosa, déjalo y con su pan se lo coma» (II, 369; IV, 1883). So José María is forgiven and he makes Camila and Constantino his heirs, certain at last that they will remember him with affection. The great strength of the ending comes partly from the resignation of José María, but also from the absence of any obvious climax in the affairs of Camila and Constantino. The pleasure they take in the birth of their son is partly offset by our knowledge that this has happened before, and that their earlier child has died. Thus the final effect of the novel is to bring the moral strength which has served them so well into a steady relationship with the difficulties of life in such a way that we feel —as Galdós must have felt— that any possible sequel to their story would be superfluous.

The ending of Lo prohibido is only one example of the skill with which Galdós controls the complex life of the the novel without drawing undue attention to his craftsmanship. As in the other major novels, the illusion of life is conveyed less by the simple logical structure of events than by a series of variations on certain themes and situations. Thus the financial preoccupations of José María's society are echoed by the theorizing of Raimundo, which, though at times it amounts to parody (José María refers to him as «el bufón de mi opulencia»), nevertheless retains a core of seriousness which is acknowledged by other characters. Similarly, María Juana is made to reflect and distort certain aspects of both the sex and money themes. I have already discussed the way in which she parodies the romantic love situation by her attempts to reform José María. Compared with Eloísa, María Juana starts nearer to the money end of the scale; she identifies herself very closely with her husband's financial interests, to which the masculine side of her character is clearly attracted. Despite this, her moral values are eventually shown to be just as weak as Eloísa's, and are complicated by her claims to be a «superior woman». All this, of course, is seen through the eyes of José María, and plays an important part in shaping his final attitude towards Camila.

The points discussed by no means exhaust the number of occasions on which Galdós deepens a particular relationship by multiplying it into a number of different yet comparable images. Galdós's analogical imagination, to adopt a phrase which Professor Marcus uses of Dickens, [12] is so much a part of his vision of life in the novels of contemporary society that it goes beyond any mere technical devices. Nothing could be further, in fact, from the self-conscious techniques of Naturalism, or for that matter from any narrowly-conceived version of realism. What makes *Lo prohibido* a masterpiece is not the observation of society or the dissection of character, but the steady revelation of values which are in constant danger of being falsified by the narrator himself. This narrator, unreliable and unprincipled as he is, is the essential instrument in Galdós' imaginative achievement. «No one is more in error», Proust has written, «than the social novelists who analyse mercilessly from the outside the action of a snob or supposed snob, but never place themselves in his position at the moment when a whole social springtime is bursting into blossom in his imagination». This is a lesson which Galdós seems to have known instinctively by the time he came to write *Lo prohibido*. In following the course of events which is unfolded in the narrative of José María Bueno de Guzmán, we are made to realize, with the undogmatic sympathy which is the mark of a great novelist, the slow and irregular rhythm which comes closer than any preconceived structure to the sensation of life itself.

The Queen's University,
Belfast.

---

[12]   *Dickens: from Pickwick to Dombey* (London, 1965), p. 40.

GEOFFREY RIBBANS

Contemporary History in the Structure and Characterization of «Fortunata y Jacinta» *

It is nothing unusual for Galdós's *novelas contemporáneas* to be
clearly and deliberately pin-pointed in time and to refer to a period
of up to fifteen years before the date of composition. Thus the action
of *La desheredada* takes place between 1872 and 1875, the events of
La de Bringas immediately precede the expulsion of Isabella II in
September 1868 and *Lo prohibido* begins, with a retrospective gaze
backwards, in 1880. Similarly, the action of *Fortunata y Jacinta* is
firmly assigned to the period 1869 to 1876, with most of the incidents
described occurring between February 1873 and April 1876. The novel
is also remarkably precise in the dating of fictional occurrences. In
some cases actual dates to the very day are given: for instance, the
marriage of Don Baldomero and Doña Bárbara took place on 3 May
1835; in others simply the month is supplied: September 1845, the
birth of Juanito; May 1871, his marriage to Jacinta.

The process of making use of dates and political events in the
structure and characterization of the novel in fact goes far beyond
the simple fixing of the action within historical circumstance. Professor Sherman Eoff seems to me profoundly mistaken when he writes:
«Galdós takes note of political events relating to the Revolution of
1868, the interim between monarchies, the Restoration, and various
affairs of public interest; but neither political history nor political
theory concerns him seriously in his contemporary novels. Politics
sometimes forms the topic of conversation —usually among minor

---

* References are given to two editions of *Fortunata y Jacinta:* the first
edition, 4 vols. 1887, and *Obras completas*, V, ed. F. C. Sáinz de Robles, 3rd.
ed. Aguilar, 1961. The text followed is the Aguilar edition, with accentuation
modernised.

characters— but nowhere, after the semisocial novel *El audaz,* does it become a major force in the treatment of personality.» [1] I hope to prove, on the contrary, that political references play a considerable and deliberate part in the characterization of *Fortunata y Jacinta,* within the structure of which they have a clear and coherent purpose. First let us examine two characters who, introduced within the first three chapters of the first part, have the important function of bringing us into contact with aspects of the political history of the nineteenth century.

The first is doña Isabel Cordero Arnaiz, Jacinta's mother, who is as prolific as her daughter is barren. Her seventeen children, of whom nine survived, marked, we are told, the «fechas célebres» of the reign of her namesake, Isabella II:

> —Mi primer hijo —decía— nació cuando vino la tropa carlista hasta las tapias de Madrid. Mi Jacinta nació cuando se casó la reina [10 oct. 1846], con pocos días de diferencia. Mi Isabelita vino al mundo el día mismo en que el cura Merino le pegó la puñalada a su majestad, y tuve a Rupertito el día de San Juan del cincuenta y ocho, el mismo día que se inauguró la traída de aguas (I, 67; 31).

Finally, just as the engagement of Juan and Jacinta had been arranged, she died, pursued even at her death by «fechas célebres», for it was the same day as don Juan Prim died, 30 December 1870. [2] Such a coincidence as this serves not merely to fix firmly the date of the couple's engagement, but to link the story of Juanito's marriage with

---

[1] *The Novels of Pérez Galdós. The Concept of Life as Dynamic Process* (Washington, 1954), 102. In his account of the nineteenth-century novel in the *Historia general de las literaturas hispánicas,* ed. G. Díaz Plaja, vol. V (Barcelona, 1958), Mariano Baquero Goyanes remarks acutely in passing that «en *Fortunata* la historia nacional coincide con la particular. Así, en el capítulo II de la segunda parte *(sic) La Restauración vencedora,* este suceso histórico coincide con el cansancio de Juanito por Fortunata y su vuelta a Jacinta» *(op. cit.,* 109).

[2] Walter T. Pattison mentions in passing in *El naturalismo español* (Madrid, 1965), 127, this association of Isabel Cordero with historical events and notes that «la acción de la novela sucede sobre un fondo temporal y espacial que corresponde al *milieu* y al *moment* de la famosa fórmula de Taine» (127-28). There is an antecedent within the novel, for Doña Asunción Trujillo, Bárbara's mother, died in 1841 on the day that General León, who rose against Espartero, was shot. Similar too are the references to the Franco-Prussian War in Aurora's denunciations of Moreno Isla to Fortunata: «Yo fui Metz, que cayó demasiado pronto; y ella [Jacinta] es Bellfort, que se defiende; pero al fin cae también» (IV, 102; 444).

the vicissitudes of Spain's disturbed political life under Amadeo and the First Republic. Prim's assassination was historically an event of the greatest importance, for it was Prim, the determined and persistent leader of the Progressive party, who had been the principal instigator of the expulsion of Isabella II and the Bourbon dynasty in 1868. To replace it, Prim scoured Europe in search of a suitable constitutional monarch and eventually lighted upon Prince Amadeo of Savoy. The new king arrived in Spain just as Prim was killed by unknown hands, and the death of his sponsor ruined his chances of success. As far as the novel is concerned, the name of Prim, and in particular his vehement assertions that the Bourbons would never return,[3] recur repeatedly and significantly throughout.

The second character who serves to link the narration with recent Spanish history is Plácido Estupiñá, who is described in great detail in Chapter III of the first part. Estupiñá has a very considerable structural rôle in the novel; it is through him that Juanito comes to meet Fortunata; and at the end of the novel he acts as the go-between between the dying Fortunata and Jacinta when the former hands over the baby to the latter. But he also has another importance as a man «que fundaba su vanidad en *haber visto toda la historia de España* en el presente siglo» (I, 78; 34). Galdós fixes his date of birth on the same day —19 July 1803— as Ramón Mesonero Romanos, and thus links the chronicler of Madrid to whom he himself owed so much for the commercial details of this early part of the novel with the character who, more than Isabel Cordero, brings the external events of nineteenth-century history before the reader's eyes:

> Una sola frase suya probará su inmenso saber en esa historia viva que se aprende con los ojos:
> —Vi a José Primero como le estoy viendo a usted ahora.
> Y parecía que se relamía de gusto cuando le preguntaban:

---

[3] Part of a famous speech to Congress of 20 February 1869. Carlos Cambronero, *Las cortes de la revolución* (Madrid, n. d.), 3, quoted by A. Regalado García, *Benito Pérez Galdós y la novela histórica española, 1868-1912* (Madrid, 1966), 443, reports the incident as follows: «Se aventuró [Prim] a decir que la dinastía de los Borbones quedaba hecha trizas y que había desaparecido para siempre de España, y aunque es indiscreto aplicar el adverbio *siempre* tratándose de acontecimientos políticos, siempre inseguros y mudables, en aquel caso especial tenía la convicción de que los Borbones no volverían *jamás, jamás, jamás:* frase que produjo un efecto sorprendente, que se recordó cientos de veces y que hasta dio nombre a la sesión en que fue pronunciada, pues se la designó en aquella época por la 'sesión de los jamases'».

—¿Vio usted al duque de Angulema, a lord Wellington?...
—Pues ya lo creo —su contestación era siempre la misma—: como le estoy viendo a usted.

Hasta llegaba a incomodarse cuando se le interrogaba en tono dubitativo.

—¡Que si vi entrar a María Cristina!... Hombre, si eso es de ayer...

Para completar su erudición ocular, hablaba del *aspecto que presentaba Madrid* el 1 de septiembre de 1840 como si fuera cosa de la semana pasada. Había visto morir a Canterac; ajusticiar a Merino «nada menos que sobre el propio patíbulo», por ser él hermano de la Paz y Caridad; había visto matar a Chico..., precisamente ver no, pero oyó los tiritos hallándose en la calle de las Velas; había visto a Fernando VII el 7 de de julio cuando salió al balcón a decir a los milicianos que *sacudieran* a los de la Guardia; había visto a Rodil y al sargento García arengando desde otro balcón, el año 36; había visto a O'Donnell y Espartero abrazándose; a Espartero, solo, saludando al pueblo; a O'Donnell, solo, todo esto en un balcón; y por fin, en un balcón había visto, también, en fecha cercana, a otro personaje diciendo a gritos que se habían acabado los reyes. La historia que Estupiñá sabía estaba escrita en los balcones (I, 78-79; 34-35).

Employing here a device inherited from the *Episodios, nacionales,* Galdós offers us, in addition to an authentic and amusing characterization, a synopsis, on the purely superficial political plane, of the chaotic nineteenth century from the Napoleonic occupation onwards, with its revolutions, its flamboyant generals and futile *pronunciamientos* — all amounting to little more than speeches from a balcony: a rapid sketch of the immediate past, essential for a novel set in the 1870s. Far more significant, of course, in the real life of the country were the commercial developments, bringing in their train deep social and political changes, so painstakingly chronicled for the Santa Cruz and Arnaiz families in Chapter II of the first book.

Isabel Cordero and Estupiñá are, moreover, merely signposts indicating past historical events; they are not involved in them, and do not mirror them in any way. Of much greater importance is the political parallel consistently traced with one of the four principal characters, Juan Santa Cruz, with whom so much of the First Part is concerned. This is not the occasion to give a full character-sketch of Santa Cruz, but it is essential to note that he is quite clearly a representative of the second generation of the new Madrilenian bourgeoisie, deliberately and firmly attached to his period and to his class. [4] An only child spoilt by his doting mother, he lives in idleness on the inherited wealth accumulated by the work of his father and grandfather whose success-story epitomizes the rise of the commercial middle class to affluence and power. Juanito is treated in almost royal terms as heir-apparent (el *Delfín*), and his father delights in pointing out the contrast between his son's style of life and that of his own youth. It is a case not only of *nouveaux riches,* but of a new aristocracy.

In the initial presentation of Juanito through the eyes of the narrator in the first chapter, it is noteworthy that a political event is straightaway involved. In the company of various fellow-students he takes part in the disturbances of «la noche de San Daniel» (10 April 1865), [5] when there were strong student demonstrations over the expulsion of Castelar from his chair as a result of his criticisms of the Queen. Galdós gives the names of two or three (Juanito among them) of those taking part in the demonstration:

> Hasta el formalito Zalamero se descompuso en aquella ruidosa ocasión, dando pitidos y chillando como un salvaje, con lo cual se ganó bofetadas de un guardia veterano, sin más consecuencias. Pero Villalonga y Santa Cruz lo pasaron peor, porque el primero recibió un sablazo en el hombro que le tuvo derrengado por espacio de dos meses largos, y el segundo fue cogido junto a la esquina del teatro Real, y llevado a la Prevención... A la sombra me lo tuvieron veintitantas horas, y aún durara más su cautiverio si de él no le sacara, el día 11, su papá, sujeto respetabilísimo y muy bien relacionado (I, 6-7; 13).

---

[4] See Carlos Blanco Aguinaga, «On 'the birth of Fortunata'», *AG,* III (1968), 15: «Juanito... is, first of all, a characteristically non-productive product of one of the families of the then growing Spanish bourgeoisie; *la nobleza del dinero*». See also V. Llorens, «Galdós y la burguesía», *AG,* III (1968), 51-59.

[5] Raymond Carr, *Spain, 1808-1939* (Oxford, 1966), 296, describes it as the «first effective student agitation in Spain». Galdós himself witnessed the riot as a student recently arrived in Madrid: «Presencié, confundido con la turba estudiantil, el escandaloso motín de la noche de San Daniel... y en la Puerta del Sol me alcanzaron algunos linternazos de la Guardia Veterana», *Memorias de un desmemoriado, OC,* VI, 4th ed. 1961, 1655. The episode is also described in the *episodio nacional Prim,* chapters XII-XIV, *OC,* III, 6th ed. 1963, 565-70. In his article, «La palabra hablada en *Fortunata y Jacinta*», *NRFH,* XV (1961), 542-60, Professor Stephen Gilman comments on Galdós's use of the word *rasgo,* the term used by Castelar to characterize the queen's interested generosity in offering crown lands for sale at a quarter of their cost. It was the article «El rasgo» which caused his dismissal and sparked off the student riots of the *noche de San Daniel.*

We are told that Santa Cruz, like Villalonga, fares badly, but in fact, thanks to the impeccable respectability of his father, he comes off lightly in contrast with Villalonga, in what was quite a serious episode, notable, as Galdós witnessed, for the brutality of the police. From the first pages of the novel —and significantly enough, in a political incident— Juanito Santa Cruz is sheltered by his family circumstances. In the remainder of this first chapter, we see Juanito change abruptly from an unruly student to something approaching a bookworm, but then just as abruptly he abandons his reading: constancy is clearly not to be one of his characteristics. At the same time, Galdós studiously avoids any explicit criticism, adopting an apparent tone of understanding, tolerance and sympathy. Galdós describes him as follows at the age of 24:

> Era el hijo de don Baldomero muy bien parecido y además muy simpático, de estos hombres que se recomiendan con su figura antes de cautivar con su trato, de estos que en una hora de conversación ganan más amigos que otros repartiendo favores positivos. Por lo bien que decía las cosas y la gracia de sus juicios, aparentaba saber más de lo que sabía, y en su boca las paradojas eran más bonitas que las verdades. Vestía con elegancia y tenía tan buena educación, que se le perdonaba fácilmente el hablar demasiado. Su instrucción y su ingenio agudísimo le hacían descollar sobre todos los demás mozos de la partida, y aunque a primera vista tenía cierta semejanza con Joaquinito Pez, tratándolos se echaban de ver entre ambos profundas diferencias, pues el chico de Pez, por su ligereza de carácter y la garrullería de su entendimiento, era un verdadero botarate (I, 11; 14-15).

By this series of oblique contrasts and qualifications, Galdós accentuates the superficiality of his creation. He is «muy simpático», but his appearance is superior to his way of dealing with people; he impresses by his fluency without really doing anything for anyone; his knowledge appears greater than it is; he excels in slick paradoxes; he talks too much. Finally, the comparison with the notorious Joaquinito Pez, deftly modified in Juanito's favour, so that he is represented as *not quite* «un verdadero botarate», labels him as a typical *señorito,* a characterization which is reiterated by the use of the diminutive Juanito. Santa Cruz, explains Galdós, is one of those destined to be known by a diminutive all his life. Carrying with it the implication of grace, luck, urbanity, frivolity, it links Juanito, not only explicitly with Juan Valera (whose presence in this company is presumably not intended to be a compliment) but with the tribe of *señoritos* of the Pez type who people Galdós's novels, the progeny of the administrative or commercial bourgeoisie of Madrid.

Finally, the narrator's last observation in the chapter, about life experienced at first hand instead of through books, presents Juanito's complete abandonment of study in its most favourable light possible, but the comparison between eating a chop and hearing a description of the digestive process anticipates the self-indulgent caprice with which he later enjoys witnessing José Ido's ravenous consumption of a chop and its disastrous consequences.

The second section of Chapter I deals with doña Bárbara's cloying and anxious efforts to restrain her son's amorous proclivities. In describing Juanito's pursuits, Galdós once more employs the technique of assuming an air of indulgent relativism, underplaying the moral implications of what is described:

> En honor de la verdad, debo decir que los desvaríos de Juanito no eran ninguna cosa del otro jueves. En esto, como en todo lo malo, hemos progresado de tal modo, que las barrabasadas de aquel niño bonito hace quince años nos parecerían hoy timideces y aun actos de ejemplaridad relativa (I, 16; 16).

Similarly, his complete lack of occupation is emphasised, not explicitly as it is later (Chapter VIII, ii: «Por lo dicho se habrá comprendido que el *Delfín* era un hombre enteramente desocupado», I, 245; 85), but in the account of how, to the great concern of his mother, he comes to make his first trip to Paris:

> Presentóse en aquellos días al simpático joven la coyuntura de hacer su primer viaje a París, adonde iban Villalonga y Federico Ruiz, comisionados por el Gobierno, el uno a comprar máquinas de agricultura, el otro a adquirir aparatos de Astronomía (I, 16; 16).

The casually dropped details of the business which took Villalonga and Federico Ruiz to Paris throw into relief the fact that Juanito is even more idle than his fellows.

The first significant contemporary reference occurs considerably later, after the leisurely account of the Santa Cruz and Arnaiz families, the indirect indications of Juanito's affair with Fortunata and the marriage and honeymoon of Juanito and Jacinta. The couple have returned home and settled down in the house of Juanito's parents. In the middle of a family discussion, the household learns of the abdication of King Amadeo in February 1873. The men discuss the disastrous fall in stocks and shares, the imminence of the proclamation of the Republic and the possible disturbances it may entail; don Baldomero laments that Prim is no longer alive. The following chapter, VIII, returns to the domestic life of the young Santa Cruz couple. Jacinta is concerned, not with political questions, but with her increasing suspicions of her supposedly model husband:

> ¿qué le importaba a ella que hubiese República o Monarquía, ni que don Amadeo se fuese o se quedase? Más le importaba la conducta de aquel ingrato que a su lado dormía tan tranquilo (I, 239; 83).

The two themes, however, are presented by Galdós in parallel terms, and this chapter contains the first explicit statement about Juanito's moral characteristics:

> En el fondo de la naturaleza humana hay también, como en la superficie social, una sucesión de modas, períodos en que es de rigor cambiar de apetitos. Juan tenía temporadas. En épocas periódicas y casi fijas se hastiaba de sus correrías, y entonces su mujer, tan mona y cariñosa, le ilusionaba como si fuera la mujer de otro. Así lo muy antiguo y conocido se convierte en nuevo (I, 243; 84).

Juanito is supremely representative of the society to which he belongs: he obeys an impulse for change for the sake of change, an alternation of fashion, just as politically the country alternates capriciously between authority and revolution.

From this point onwards Galdós begins to become more categorical and less elusive about a figure he has until now skilfully built up by dint of contrast and insinuation: he now comments directly on his self-centredness, his desire to have it both ways, his calculated cultivation of sensual pleasure: «de la cantidad con que cualquier mani-roto se proporciona un placer, Juanito Santa Cruz sacaba siempre dos» (I, 246; 85). In the next section, no. ii of Chapter VIII, his father regrets Juanito's lack of firm political beliefs. Don Baldomero, we are told on several occasions, is a somewhat timid *progresista* who has retained in 1871 the same convictions he had in 1845. His somewhat unusual name is the same as that of the first *progresista* general Espartero —«su tocayo Espartero», he is called on p. 25. Espartero was seriously considered as candidate for the vacant throne on the expulsion of Isabella II in 1868; the use of quasi-regal numbers to distinguish Juanito's father from the founder of the family business (Baldomero I, Baldomero II) adds to this clear reminiscence of Espartero's recent candidature. Moreover, in the firmness of his political opinions, D. Baldomero is in marked contrast with his son.

Juan era la inconsecuencia misma. En los tiempos de Prim manifestóse entusiasta por la candidatura del duque de Montpensier:

—Es el hombre que conviene, desengañaos; un hombre que lleva al dedillo las cuentas de su casa, un modelo de padres de familia.

Vino don Amadeo, y el *Delfín* se hizo tan republicano que daba miedo oirle:

—La Monarquía es imposible; hay que convencerse de ello. Dicen que el país no está preparado para la República; pues que lo preparen. Es como si se pretendiera que un hombre supiera nadar sin decidirse a entrar en el agua. No hay más remedio que pasar algún mal trago... La desgracia enseña..., y si no, vean esa Francia, esa prosperidad, esa inteligencia, ese patriotismo..., esa manera de pagar los cinco mil millones...

Pues, señor, vino el 11 de febrero, y al principio le pareció a Juan que todo iba a qué quieres boca:

—Es admirable. La Europa está atónita. Digan lo que quieran, el pueblo español tiene un gran sentido.

Pero a los dos meses, las ideas pesimistas habían ganado ya por completo su ánimo:

—Esto es una pillería, esto es una vergüenza. Cada país tiene el Gobierno que merece, y aquí no puede gobernar más que un hombre que esté siempre con una estaca en la mano.

Por graduaciones lentas, Juanito llegó a defender con calor la idea alfonsina.

—Por Dios, hijo —decía don Baldomero con inocencia—, si eso no puede ser.

Y sacaba a relucir los *jamases* de Prim... (I, 247-48; 85-86).

The Duke of Montpensier as candidate for the throne vacated by his sister-in-law Isabella, King Amadeo, the Republic, the restoration of the Bourbon dynasty in the figure of don Alfonso, against which the posthumous force of Prim's peremptory refusal to countenance a Bourbon return is to be no more effective than any of the other absolute refusals of politicians —all these possible solutions, tried or untried, show the parallel fickleness of both Spain's political life and of Juanito.

The women in the family, significantly, support don Alfonso, especially Jacinta who, in marked contrast with her later attitude, bases herself simply on the fact that the Bourbon claimant is still a child.

The chaotic vicissitudes of the First Republic find in actual fact little echo in the novel. Only on one occasion, in December 1873, when Juanito is laid low with a severe cold, is there some talk of the constant fall of the values of stocks and shares, of the cantonalist disturbances and the need for ruthless measures, and the names of Castelar and Salmerón crop up: this corresponds to the last weeks of the presidency of Castelar, who had succeeded Salmerón on 7 September with the intention of taking a much tougher line with the Murcian insurgents. [6] At the same time, we learn that Juanito has returned to his periodic hankering for the rule of law:

> En los días precursores del catarro, hallábase mi hombre en una de aquellas etapas o mareas de su inconstante naturaleza, las cuales, alejándole de las aventuras, le aproximaban a su mujer. Las personas más hechas a la vida ilegal sienten en ocasiones vivo anhelo de ponerse bajo la ley por poco tiempo. La ley los tienta como puede tentar el capricho (I, 256; 88).

Like Juanito's rapprochements with his wife, Spain's desire for strong authoritarian government has roots no stronger than those of caprice. For the moment this is all: it is not until the last chapter of the first part, Chapter XI, that political parallels with Juanito become important again, though the events utilised are separated in time by only a few days from those just described. In between, the mistaken revelations of José Ido about *El Pitusín* give a new twist to the story which is occupied for some two hundred pages of the original edition with Jacinta's project of adopting her husband's supposed son.

---

[6] See Carr, *op. cit.*, 327-37, and C. A. M. Hennessy, *The Federal Republic in Spain 1868-74* (Oxford, 1962).

In the last chapter, *Final que viene a ser principio,* Juanito has become formal, judicious and cold in his behaviour to Jacinta, a sure sign for her that he has taken a mistress. Politically, it is the moment of the unceremonious and decisive denouement of the chaotic experiment of the First Republic. On the morning of 3 January 1874, when Castelar, the last hope of the more conservative forces, is outvoted, General Pavía sent his troops into the parliament building and cleared the Assembly by opening fire in the central passage of the Chamber. [7] Galdós introduces the subject as follows:

> Vinieron días marcados en la historia patria por sucesos resonantes, y aquella familia feliz discutía estos sucesos como los discutíamos todos. ¡El tres de enero de 1874!... ¡El golpe de Estado de Pavía! No se hablaba de otra cosa, ni había nada mejor de qué hablar. Era grato al temperamento español un cambio teatral de instituciones, y volcar una situación como se vuelca un puchero electoral. Había estado admirablemente hecho, según don Baldomero, y el ejército había salvado *una vez más* a la desgraciada nación española (I, 459; 151).

Galdós also provides us with an eyewitness account of the events in the Assembly —Jacinto Villalonga, Juanito's friend and accomplice in his affair with Fortunata, the *señorito* who had done what don Baldomero wanted for his son— who had gone into politics. Villalonga does not appear to tell his story until *el día de Reyes,* 6 January. When he enters, Jacinta, who knows him as the confidant and suspects him to be the corrupter of her husband, listens to as much of the conversation as she can. She is right in her suspicions: when she is out of the room, Villalonga tells Juanito that he has met Fortunata; as soon as she appears, he changes quickly to describing the dramatic events in the assembly. The episode is well built up: on the first occasion the two men hear Jacinta's steps outside and have time to change their subject; later they come very near to being caught out. In the first instance there was only time for Villalonga to proclaim that he had seen Fortunata and that she had improved out of all description. In Jacinta's presence he gives a fairly detailed account of the scenes in the Chamber, but as soon as she is called away he resumes the story: Fortunata has become elegant without losing her

---

[7] Galdós describes the scene in the Cortes in the *episodio nacional De Cartago a Sagunto,* Chapter IX, *OC,* III, 6th ed. 1963, 1204-08.

popular charms, and he quotes Juanito's views, so often repeated by other characters, that «el pueblo es la cantera. De él salen las grandes ideas y las grandes bellezas» (I, 464; 152). Fortunata has learnt everything pertaining to dress and outward appearance —she even wears a hat now— without learning to read or speak correctly.

> Las que tienen genio, aprenden en un abrir y cerrar de ojos. La raza española es tremenda, chico, para la asimilación de todo lo que pertenece a la forma. Pero si habías de verla tú. Yo, te lo confieso, estaba pasmado, absorto, embebe...
> ¡Ay Dios mío!, entró Jacinta, y Villalonga tuvo que dar un quiebro violentísimo...
> —Te digo que estaba embebecido. El discurso de Salmerón fue admirable..., pero de lo más admirable... (I, 465; 153).

At the next opportunity Juanito tries to find out who the man was who was with her, but they are again interrupted, this time by Bárbara as well as Jacinta. Villalonga now gives quite a long description of the actual scene in the chamber when the fatal vote took place, and is conscious enough of the importance of the events he is describing to continue for a moment even after the ladies have left:

> —¿Y Salmerón, qué hizo?
> —Yo puse toda mi atención en Castelar, y le vi llevarse la mano a los ojos y decir: «¡Qué ignominia!» En la mesa se armó un barullo espantoso..., gritos, protestas. Desde el reloj vi una masa de gente, todos en pie... No distinguía al presidente. Los quintos, inmóviles... De repente, ¡pum!, sonó un tiro en el pasillo...
> —Y empezó la desbandada... Pero dime otra cosa, chico. No puedo apartar de mi pensamiento... ¿Decías que llevaba sombrero?
> —¿Quién?... ¡Ah! ¿Aquélla? Sí, sombrero, y de muchísimo gusto —dijo el compinche con tanto énfasis como si continuara narrando el suceso histórico—, y vestido azul elegantísimo y abrigo de terciopelo...
> —¿Tú estás de guasa? Abrigo de terciopelo.
> —Vaya... y con pieles: un abrigo soberbio. La caía tan bien..., que...
> Entró Jacinta sin anunciarse ni con ruido de pasos ni de ninguna otra manera. Villalonga giró sobre el último concepto como una veleta impulsada por fuerte racha de viento.
> —El abrigo que yo llevaba..., mi gabán de pieles..., quiero decir, que en aquella marimorena me arrancaron una solapa..., la piel de una solapa, quiero decir...

8

—Cuando se metió usted debajo del banco.
—Yo no me metí debajo de ningún banco, tocaya. Lo que hice fue ponerme a salvo como los demás, por lo que pudiera tronar (I, 469-70; 154).

Finally, Villalonga is able to explain where Fortunata now lives, and when interrupted passes a final comment on the downfall of the Republic:

> Os diré el último detalle para que os asombréis. Los cañones que puso Pavía en las bocacalles estaban descargados. Y ya veis lo que pasó dentro. Dos tiros al aire, y lo mismo que se desbandan los pájaros posados en un árbol cuando dais debajo de él dos palmadas, así se desbandó la Asamblea de la República (I, 471; 154).

And Galdós himself comments at the end of the sub-chapter:

> Estas referencias o noticias sueltas eran en aquella triste historia como las uvas desgranadas que quedan en el fondo del cesto después de sacar los racimos. Eran las más maduras, y quizá por esto las más sabrosas (I, 472; 155).

The parallel established between Spain's political disturbances and Juanito Santa Cruz's promiscuity culminates in this lively and amusing episode in which the two themes alternate and interact. Polically, Spain is to experience an utterly chaotic and anarchical year before an established and outwardly legitimate form of government is restored. And as a result of Villalonga's revelations, Juanito kicks over the traces and sets out to find his former lover. Instead, he catches pneumonia. This is the end of the first book.

Juanito Santa Cruz, to whom such detailed attention is paid in the first part, disappears almost completely from the second part of the novel, the starting point of which is, not the prosperous world of the Santa Cruz and Arnaiz families, but the lower middle class world of Doña Lupe and the Rubín brothers. Nor are the events of the second part —Maxi's life and meeting with Fortunata, her confinement in Las Micaelas, their marriage and Fortunata's renewal of relations with Juanito— viewed in any way against the political background. In the third book, however, Juanito and his family circle come back into the foreground for a time; and, significantly, it is the moment of the next swing of the political pendulum, the decisive event of the period, the *Restauración*. In January 1875, following the *pronunciamiento* of General Martínez Campos in December 1874, the Bourbon dynasty is restored in the person of Alfonso XII, four years exactly after Prim's assassination and Amadeo's succession, nearly two years after the latter's abdication, one year after the *golpe de estado de Pavía*. But, while King Alfonso is triumphantly entering Madrid and the Santa Cruz family is, as usual, discussing the news, Jacinta, after four years of similar turmoil, has once more her own troubles, as she confided in the all-knowing narrator.

La noche a que Jacinta se refería, contando estas cosas, noche tristísima para ella por haber adquirido recientemente noticias fidedignas de la infidelidad de su marido, hubo en la casa gran regocijo. Aquel día había entrado en Madrid el rey Alfonso XII, y don Baldomero estaba con la Restauración como chiquillo con zapatos nuevos. Barbarita también reventaba de gozo, y decía:
—Pero ¡qué chico más salado y más simpático!
Jacinta tenía que entusiasmarse también, a pesar de aquella procesión que por dentro le andaba, y poner cara de Pascua a todos los que entraron felicitándose del suceso...
Jacinta se indignaba en su interior. Tenía un volcán en el pecho, y la alegría de los demás la mortificaba. Por su gusto se hubiera echado a llorar en medio de la reunión; mas érale forzoso contenerse y sonreír cuando su suegro la miraba. Retorciendo en su corazón la cuerda con que a sí propia se ahogaba, se decía: «Pero a este buen señor, ¿qué le va ni le viene con el rey?... ¡Qué les importará!... Yo estoy volada, y aquí mismo me pondría a dar chillidos, si no temiera escandalizar. ¡Esto es horrible!»
Don Alfonso érale antipático, porque su imagen estaba asociada a la horrible pena que la infeliz sufría (III, 58-60; 309).

As a result of her anguish, Jacinta's earlier sympathy for Alfonso has dissipated, for the new king and the alternations of power of which he is the latest example mirror her husband's inconstancy. As the chapter, which is called «La Restauración vencedora», proceeds, the latest turn in the Spanish political roundabout is brought closer to Juanito's private life. His father, don Baldomero, makes a statement which is called «muy sensata»:

—Yo no sé lo que sucederá dentro de veinte, dentro de cincuenta años. En la sociedad española no se puede nunca fiar tan largo. Lo único que sabemos es que nuestro país padece alternativas o fiebres intermitentes de revolución y de paz. En ciertos períodos todos deseamos que haya mucha autoridad. ¡Venga leña! Pero nos cansamos de ella, y todos queremos echar el pie fuera del plato. Vuelven los días de jarana y ya estamos suspirando otra vez porque se acorte la cuerda. Así somos, y así creo que seremos hasta que se afeiten las ranas (III, 62; 310).

The parallel with Juanito's alternations between freedom and legality, between Fortunata and Jacinta, is exact.

Juan himself is not as optimistic as the other men of his circle; he does not think that restorations ever prevail (his personal «restoration» to his wife certainly will not last) and he dislikes the military intervention. Finally, he adds sententiously:

> —Es la condición humana. Así viven y se educan las socie-
> dades —dijo el *Delfín*—. Lo que a mí no me gusta es que esto
> se haga por otra vía que la de la ley (III, 62; 310);

to which Jacinta, to herself, points the falsity:

> «¡Pillo, tunante! —pensaba Jacinta comiéndose las palabras,
> y con las palabras la hiel que se le quería salir—. ¿Qué sabes
> tú lo que es ley? ¡Farsante, demagogo, anarquista! Cómo se
> hace el purito... Quien no te conoce...» (III, 62-63; 310).

This is the moment of Jacinta's greatest exasperation with her husband, but as Juanito is now, as the words just quoted indicate, in one of his temporary phases of applauding law and order, authority and tranquillity, and he has a most persuasive tongue, he is quite easily able to placate once again his offended wife. Being tired of his mistress, he readily agrees to break absolutely with her. It is significant, incidentally, that he characterizes Fortunata, in unexpressed contrast with himself, as constant in her affections: «Otras mujeres, las de complexión viciosa, son en sus pasiones tan vehementes como inconstantes. Pronto olvidan al que adoraron y cambian de ilusión como de moda. Esta, no» (III, 79; 315). Once more, like Spain, he is ready to return to a settled way of life, not through conviction but through weariness:

> El *Delfín* había entrado, desde los últimos días del 74, en
> aquel período sedante que seguía infaliblemente a sus desva-
> ríos. En realidad, no era aquello virtud, sino cansancio del
> pecado; no era el sentimiento puro y regular del orden, sino

el hastío de la revolución. Verificábase en él lo que don Baldomero había dicho del país: que padecía fiebres alternativas
de libertad y de paz. A los dos meses de una de las más graves distracciones de su vida, su mujer empezaba a gustarle lo
mismito que si fuera la mujer de otro. La bondad de ella favo-
recía este movimiento centrípeto, que se había determinado
por quinta o sexta vez desde que estaban casados. Ya en otras
ocasiones pudo creer Jacinta que la vuelta a los deberes con-
yugales sería definitiva; pero se equivocó, porque el *Delfín,*
que tenía en el cuerpo el demonio malo de la variedad, cansá-
base de ser bueno y fiel, y tornaba a dejarse mover de la fuerza centrífuga (III, 66-67; 311-12).

Thus a domestic *Restauración,* parallel to the political one, takes
place and with it, as reflected in the title of the following chapter,
when the rupture with Fortunata ensues, «La revolución, vencida».
Galdós makes it quite clear that the change regarding Juanito is strict-
ly temporary, thus implying at the same time serious doubts about the
durability o fthe *Restauración* system.

He continues:

> Había que cambiar de forma de gobierno cada poco tiem-
> po, y cuando estaba en república, le parecía la monarquía tan
> seductora (III, 97; 321).

Galdós is speaking of Juanito in these unambiguously political terms.
The following sentences, as he goes to break with Fortunata, are:

> Al salir de su casa aquella tarde iba pensando en esto. Su mu-
> jer le estaba gustando más, mucho más que aquella situación
> revolucionaria que había implantado pisoteando los derechos
> de dos matrimonios (III, 97; 321).

Galdós has now entirely abandoned the technique of avoiding direct criticism he had employed so effectively in the first part: we see
Juanito Santa Cruz for what he is: capricious, selfish and irresponsible
—the embodiment, not only of his class but of the public life of his
time.

References to contemporary politics are by no means limited to
this parallelism, important though this is. Three other characters, in
three different ways, epitomize three distinct political attitudes, representing at the same time their respective social classes. One of them
we have already seen: Juanito's bosom friend Villalonga. As much

a *señorito* as Santa Cruz and his companion in his youthful excursions to the *Cuarto Estado,* Villalonga becomes a minister in the cynical stability of the *Restauración.* We quickly see him distributing patronage in a typically arbitrary and personal way: he listens to Feijoo's recommendations concerning Nicolás and Juan Pablo Rubín and the unfortunate Villaamil, gives the governorship of a province to Juan Pablo and is clearly engaged at various points in rigging elections.

If Villalonga represents the politician of the prosperous middle class who comes into his own with the *Restauración,* other social classes also have their political representatives. The proletarian figure is Fortunata's uncle, José Izquierdo, a revolutionary fulminator from the slums, nicknamed most inappropriately *Platón.* He is introduced to us early, during Jacinta's visit to the *Cuarto Estado* in search of Juanito's illegitimate son, and is an excellent example of Galdós's supreme linguistic power in capturing the illiterate, confused rhetoric of an absurd demagogue. Izquierdo voices his resentment at having been passed over by the politicians of the First Republic. («No colocarme a mí, a mí, que soy el endivido que más bregó por la Repóblica en esta judía tierra» (I, 324; 109),[8] but the part he attributes to himself in the heroic revolutionary struggles, especially in the Cartagena canton, is all wishful thinking. His terrifying denunciations of Republican leaders are the result of a chronic inferiority complex, as doña Guillermina points out when she confronts him. Izquierdo is by no means a worthy representative of the working-class revolutionary activity which was beginning to take shape at this time. In the structure of the novel, however, he serves to bring to our attention the unsuccessful figures of the Republic and the insurrectionary activity which preceded it, aspects of political life barely touched on in the world of the Santa Cruz family. Though personally a coward and a braggart, he may be said to represent the inarticulate fury of the underprivileged against the intellectual leaders of the left as well as the institutions of the oppressive state:

> ¿Estos de ahora?, es la que se dice: ni liberales, ni repobli-
> canos, ni na. Mirosté a ese Pi... un mequetrefe. ¿Y Castelar?
> Otro mequetrefe. ¿Y Salmerón? Otro mequetrefe. ¿Roque Bar-

---

[8] I have adopted the more phonetic spelling, reflecting Izquierdo's pronunciation (*endivido,* etc.) of the 1st ed. rather than the somewhat standardized form of *OC.*

cia? Mismamente. Luego, si es caso, vendrán a pedir que les ayudemos, pero ¿yo...? No me pienso menear; basta de *yeciones*. Si se junde la Repóblica, que se junda, y si se junde el judío pueblo, que se junda también... Dicen que les van a traer a Alifonso... ¡Pa chasco! Por mí, que lo traigan... Y yo digo que es menester acantonar a Madriz, pegarle fuego a las Cortes, al Palacio Real y a los judíos ministerios, al Monte de Piedad, al cuartel de la Guardia Cevil y al Depósito de las Aguas, y luego hacer un racimo de horca con Castelar, Pi, Figueras, Martos, Bicerra y los demás, por moderaos, por moderaos... (I, 326-29; 110-11).

Finally, in accord with the somewhat burlesque treatment Galdós gives the character, Izquierdo too finds his vocation, with the *Restauración,* as an artist's model. His empty fury is assuaged and, when we meet him again in Book IV (February 1876), contemporary politicians have been ousted as the subjects of his incoherent garrulity by an incongruous assortment of historical figures, safely embedded in the past, for whom he has sat as a model: Aeneas, Nebuchadnezzar, James the Conqueror, Hernán Cortés, etc.

Another essential, if ineffectual, aspect of nineteenth-century political life is introduced at the opening of the third book, in the first chapter «Costumbres turcas»: the interminable discussions of the cafés, of which Juan Pablo Rubín is the most assiduous representative. The world in which Juan Pablo moves is also clearly based on class; his *tertulia* consists largely of members of the lower administrative class, disgruntled office-seekers or *cesantes;* apart from Juan Pablo and Feijoo, the member described in most detail is Basilio Andrés de la Caña, who alternates between hack journalism and minor administrative jobs; and the shadow of the eternal *cesante* Villaamil leans long over the group. In addition, the incessant emigration from one café to another recalls the political alternations of the time, each with its new crop of *cesantes*.

In the first section of the first chapter we have a description of café life which clearly foreshadows the attitude of conciliation between divergent opinion, —in other words, of unprincipled temporizing— which characterized the *Restauración:*

Allí brillaba espléndidamente esa fraternidad española en cuyo seno se dan mano de amigo el carlista y el republicano, el progresista de cabeza dura y el moderado implacable. Antiguamente, los partidos separados en público, estábanlo también en las relaciones privadas; pero el progreso de las costumbres trajo primero cierta suavidad en las relaciones personales, y, por fin, la suavidad se trocó en blandura. Algunos creen que hemos pasado de un extremado mal a otro, sin detenernos en el medio conveniente, y ven en esta fraternidad una relajación de los caracteres. Esto de que todo el mundo sea amigo particular de todo el mundo es síntoma de que las ideas van siendo tan sólo un pretexto para conquistar o defender el pan. Existe una confabulación tácita (no tan escondida que no se encuentre a poco que se rasque en los políticos), por la cual se establece el turno en el dominio. En esto consiste que no hay aspiración, por extraviada que sea, que no se tenga por probable; en esto consiste la inseguridad, única cosa que es constante entre nosotros; la ayuda masónica que se prestan todos los partidos, desde el clerical al anarquista, lo mismo dándose una credencial vergonzante en tiempo de paces, que otorgándose perdones e indultos en las guerras y revoluciones. Hay algo de seguros mutuos contra el castigo, razón por la cual se miran los hechos de fuerza como la cosa más natural del mundo. La moral política es como una capa de tantos remiendos, que no se sabe ya cuál es el paño primitivo (III, 10-11; 294-95).

Thus principles disappear before the prospect of sampling a taste of the fruits of office, the tacit understanding of an alternation in power providing the incentive towards hidden alliances for mutual benefit and protection. Original political convictions are lost in the constant shifts of allegiance occasioned by self-interest. This position of compromise derives, as Feijoo remarks, from disillusion with formerly dogmatically held views:

—Yo —decía Feijoo— soy progresista desengañado, y usted [Juan Pablo Rubín], tradicionalista arrepentido. Tenemos algo en común: el creer que todo esto es una comedia y que sólo se trata de saber a quién le toca mamar y a quién no (III, 11-12; 295).

The detailed portrayal of Feijoo emerges quite naturally from the description of these heterogeneous café politicians united in one thing only: their personal hopes and aspirations. His practical philosophy, his relativist morality, his regard for forms typify the moral climate which leads to the *Restauración,* while at the same time his primary structural function in the novel is to bring about the second domestic restoration between Fortunata and Maxi — in the chapter entitled «Otra restauración».

The position of Juan Pablo Rubín himself is symptomatic of his class and circumstances. First of all, a commercial traveller, then a *funcionario* who quickly becomes a *cesante,* he goes over to the Carlists on the outbreak of the Second Carlist War, but soon quarrels with them and returns to Madrid. After his Carlist experience, he takes an aversion towards the clerical faction, but remains authoritarian, advocating a «gobierno de leña». At the end of 1874 he resumes his indiscriminate reading and produces, like his younger brother, a philosophy of sorts on the basis of a concept of Nature. Politically he continues to be resolutely opposed to the *solución alfonsina,* the preparations for which we see reflected in the pretentious tittle-tattle of the *tertulia* and in the mysterious visit described by La Caña to Cánovas's house. Even after Sagunto, when he is given, thanks to the intervention of Feijoo with Villalonga, a minor governmental post, his virulent complaints against the *Restauración* persist. For a moment, after he has been twice refused a loan by doña Lupe to pay his pressing debts, he becomes openly revolutionary and incendiary: «¿Y qué menos podía hacer el desgraciado Rubín que descargar contra el orden social y los poderes históricos la horrible angustia que llenaba su alma?» (IV, 268; 495). But theory recedes very rapidly when faced with opportunity; when Villalonga, now a minister of the Cánovas government, offers him, not just the post of secretary he was expecting, but the governorship of a third-class province, he at once casts off his reckless hostility to Don Alfonso and his adherence to principle, discards his mistress Refugio and assumes a proper gravity of manner. Having run the whole gamut of Spanish political attitudes from Carlism to incendiary nihilism, Juan Pablo Rubín is brought back into the fold by the all-embracing *Restauración.*

A further important point to observe is that Galdós treats the reconciliation of opposing interests in the *Restauración* as one of those happenings which seem to be predestined, just as it was inevitable that Fortunata, through sheer force of circumstances, [9] should accept Feijoo's protection and later, under his guidance, seek a reconciliation

---

[9] Section iii of Chapter V «Un curso de filosofía práctica» begins: «Como lo que debe suceder sucede, y no hay bromas con la realidad, las cosas vinieron y ocurrieron conforme a los deseos de don Evaristo González Feijoo» (III, 134; 332).

with her husband. Maxi, in turn, is bound in the end to accept Fortunata back, his initial refusal to countenance such a possibility being as vain as the *jamases* of Prim to the Bourbon restoration: [10]

[Maxi]   —Le aseguro a usted que eso... *Jamás, jamás, jamás.*
[Doña Lupe] —Ya te he dicho que no es prudente soltar *jamases* tan a boca llena sobre ningún punto que se refiera a las cosas humanas. Ya ves el bueno de don Juan Prim qué lucido ha quedado con sus *jamases* (III, 228; 361).

This second restoration, concludes Galdós, «fue de las cosas que pasan, sin que se pueda determinar cómo pasaron; hechos fatales en la historia de una familia como lo son sus similares en la historia de los pueblos; hechos que los sabios presienten, que los expertos vaticinan sin poder decir en qué se fundan, y que llegan a ser efectivos sin que se sepa cómo, pues aunque se les sienta venir, no se ve el disimulado mecanismo que los trae» (III, 233; 362). Galdós's form of historical determinism leads him to claim that some events have an inevitability which no human opposition or denial can overcome.

Galdós has woven political motifs most skilfully into his overall picture of the Madrid of the 1870s, seeing in them a necessary part of the social life of the time. First of all, he makes sure that his readers have a certain historical background by identifying Doña Isabel Cordero and Estupiñá with salient external events of the nineteenth century, while paying detailed attention to the rise of the commercial bourgeoisie. Second, he provides three characters of different classes —none of them at all admirable or high-principled— who all eventually find protection of one sort or another under the ample umbrella of the *Restauración*. Third and most important is the parallel drawn between the political turmoil of the period culminating in the return of the Bourbons and the character and private life of Juanito Santa Cruz. The historical envolvement, then, of the major novel of the *novelas contemporáneas* is far greater than has normally been recognised. Moreover, as Hans Hinterhäuser's excellent work on the *episodios na-*

---

[10] Compare Juanito's observation when, on abandoning her, he callously advises Fortunata to return to Maxi: «Solemos decir: 'Tal cosa no llega nunca'. Y, sin embargo, llega, y apenas nos sorprende por la suavidad con que ha venido» (III, 105; 323).

cionales clearly indicates, it is important not to neglect the *episodios* in any consideration of the *novelas contemporáneas*. In fact, I would suggest that the method adopted in *Fortunata y Jacinta* of integrating contemporary history as a consistent but incidental facet of the dominant fictional impulse largely overcomes the basic faults which Hinterhäuser has rightly discerned in the *episodios:* the irritating and delaying effect of the historical occurrences on the very limited novelistic action, and the over-insistent explanations Galdós feels obliged to offer of his procedure. [11]

What conclusions can we arrive at regarding Galdós's view of the *Restauración* from the parallel traced between Santa Cruz and politics? A novel is not a political treatise and we must be wary of deducing from an oblique and functional treatment of politics within *Fortunata y Jacinta* a dispassionate scientific view of the event. Indeed, taken as an explanation of the disturbed political scene of the time, the idea of a simple swing of the pendulum between authority and freedom seems shallow in the extreme; but it is making the wrong demands on a novelist to expect a view of contemporary society which is not somewhat unilinear and simplified if the fictional narrative is not to suffer, as it tends to suffer in the *episodios*. On the other hand, there appears to be a certain contradiction —more apparent than real— between Galdós the novelist and Galdós the quiescent supporter of the new dispensation. On the one hand, in the novel written in 1887, he portrays the *Restauración, pace* Professor Regalado, [12] in an essentially

---

[11]   Hans Hinteräuser, *Los «Episodios nacionales» de Benito Pérez Galdós,* (Madrid, 1963), 233-47, particularly: «En la mayoría de los casos, estas relaciones y ensamblamientos no suelen producir, en la obra de Galdós, un efecto demoledor sino, sencillamente, de cansancio; para expresarlo técnicamente, diríamos retardador» (241); and «la exagerada e incluso meticulosa insistencia con que el novelista explica y aclara su procedimiento» (245).   Hinterhäuser's discussion of the relation between «la gran historia» and «la pequeña» is particularly relevant to my theme, and he refers acutely, in passing, to *Fortunata y Jacinta* (237, 240).

[12]   A. Regalado García, *op. cit.,* 193: «Toda la obra novelística de Galdós está orientada en favor del *Statu quo* de la Restauración y contra los dos mayores peligros que lo amenazaban, la revolución política y el cambio de la estructura social propugnado por las aspiraciones del cuarto estado, encarnadas en la ideología de socialistas y anarquistas. La sucesión de sus novelas presentan al autor como creyente liberal en la ley del progreso, pero el examen detenido de sus ideas permite descubrir en el fondo del liberal vetas de conservador y de tradicionalista».   See also Raymond Carr's comments in *AG*, III (1968), 185-89.   For Galdós's political attitude to the *Restauración*, see Clara E. Lida, «Galdós y los *Episodios nacionales:* una historia del liberalismo español», *AG*, III (1968), 61-73.

negative light : a period of peace after agitation, virtue after vice, authority after revolution — one more fad of fashion of a man like Santa
Cruz, who symbolizes the ruling classes as a whole. On the other
hand, as *diputado* for Puerto Rico in Sagasta's interest, Galdós public-
ly supported the system during the same years. The explanation of
this anomaly lies, I suggest, in Galdós's general concept of history, be
this Hegelian or *krausista*. Since the *Restauración* is, for Galdós, an
inevitable occurrence, «de las cosas que pasan, sin que se pueda determinar cómo pasaron», a natural process, inherent in the earlier fruit-
less alternations of power, towards the reconciliation of divergent interests without eliminating the underlying differences, it forms part of
the very slow evolution towards improvement which he believes to be
predetermined.[13] Neither of the two domestic restorations in the novel is permanent, nor, Galdós seems to imply, does the *Restauración*'s
capacity to be all things to all men —to have something to offer Villalonga, Juan Pablo Rubín and Izquierdo— hold out any real solution to
Spain's problems; but it is a stage in the almost imperceptible advance,
so that Galdós sees no objection at this moment to playing his passive rôle within the system, as little more than an observer in Congress.

What, in fact, is really significant and original about the parallel so
carefully and thoroughly established is not the political outlook Galdós
reveals, but its integration within the structure of the novel. By this
parallel Galdós forges an intimate correlation between the individual
and the society in which he lives : Santa Cruz's fickleness, superficiality, glibness and egocentricity in his private life reflect attitudes which
derive from a specific historical situation and which pervade Spanish
politics : Spain's civic defects are mirrored in him. At the same time,
as they are common human defects, the analysis of both individual and
society is of universal application. The nation is made up of individuals, and individuals like Santa Cruz, from the class which dominates
politics, give rise to the political characteristics specifically of the Spain
of the 1870s and by extension of any other similar community. The
technique Galdós has adopted clearly has its dangers, for the historical details which were common knowledge in the country a mere ten
years or so after the event quickly pass into obscurity, but when the

---

[13]   See Hinterhäuser, *op. cit.*, 115-28: «la concepción dominante es, pues, la
de una evolución lentísima, aunque constante, hasta alcanzar la 'plenitud de
los tiempos'» (119).

fictional impulse is sufficiently strong and the characterization sufficiently firm, it seems to me that the novel can only gain by a close immersion in contemporary fact: Stendhal, Tolstoi, Dostoievsky, Proust, in their various ways, demonstrate this clearly.

Moreover, the process I have been describing is used discreetly, applying to one only of the four major characters. Even Juanito is not to be explained solely in political terms; though it is the most significant feature in his characterization, it does not determine his actions and reactions to incidents within the novel. The two female characters, Fortunata and Jacinta, have to some extent symbolic rôles, representing *pueblo* and inbred middle class respectively, but this does not drown their very individual response to situation; whereas the fourth main character, Maximiliano Rubín, though recognisably an authentic representative of the lower middle class, falls completely outside the scope of this particular socio-political parallelism. The very creation of Maxi —for me, one of Galdós's greatest achievements— shows how partial and relative the sort of political identification I have been describing is; it is one factor among many in the structure of a most complex novel. I would claim, however, that it constitutes a highly successful method of adding to the significance and depth of a key character and relating him firmly to the social and political environment of which he forms part.

University of Liverpool.

VERA COLIN

Tolstoy and «Angel Guerra»*

In an earlier article [1] I have shown how interest in the novels of Tolstoy became significant in Spain in the late 1880s. I have also listed the works of Tolstoy to be found in Galdós's personal library, one of which is *What I Believe,* in the French translation of Paris, 1885, where it appears under the title of *Ma Religion.* In this copy some of the pages have been turned down, as was Galdós's habit, and these pages deal, as noted in my previous article, with Tolstoy's interpretation of the Gospel according to St Matthew, V, verses 33-34 and 40, with Tolstoy's views on power and property, and with a summary of Tolstoy's creed. As will be demonstrated in the following brief summary of Tolstoy's work, the pages of *Ma Religion* which are turned down contain significant passages. The purpose of the present article is to suggest that these passages are crucial to an understanding of Galdós's novel, *Angel Guerra,* and, indeed, provide a key to the interpretation of that work.

* * *

What I Believe, written in 1884, formulated Tolstoy's belief in non-resistance to evil. We learn from the introduction that he had lost his faith at the age of fifteen, lived for 35 years without faith, and at fifty had come to believe in Christ's teaching.

From early childhood Tolstoy was deeply touched by the teaching

---

* Page and volume references are to the first edition of *Angel Guerra* (Madrid, 1891); these are immediately followed by a second reference to the Aguilar edition of the *Obras completas,* ed. F. C. Sáinz de Robles, Vol. V (2nd. ed., Madrid, 1950). Accentuation has been modernised.
[1] «A Note on Tolstoy and Galdós», *AG,* II (1967), 155-168.

of Christ concerning love, meekness, humility, renunciation and the
repayment of evil with good. He considered that the Greek Orthodox
Church treated these principles as peripheral to the teaching of Jesus
rather than as essential, and that it paid more attention to dogma than
to faith. He therefore broke with the ecclesiastical interpretation of
Christ's teaching and decided to rework the text of many passages of
the New Testament in order to retain the basic teaching which, in his
opinion, Christ gave to the world. Tolstoy believed that the key to
the Sermon on the Mount is contained in the words «Do not resist
evil», which for him means the refusal to resort to violence, since violence is an act opposed to love. He points out that from childhood he
had been taught to respect institutions which made use of force to se-
cure immunity from evil, to avenge national and personal insults and
to judge and punish. The Church taught that Christian teaching was
divine, but that its execution was impossible on account of human frail-
ty. Tolstoy himself felt that Christ's teaching was impractical until
the moment when he suddenly noticed the contradictions in which he
lived: he confessed Christ in words but denied him in fact; now he
understood that Christ's teaching would be fulfilled only when the commandment of non-resistance to evil should become law. It became
clear to him that the whole social structure of the so-called «Christian»
society was founded upon principles disapproved of by Christ. Pri-
sons, the Church, science and civilization were based on coercion and
violence. Christians acted on the principle of «an eye for an eye», dis-
carding the law of Christ and following that of Moses.

According to Tolstoy Christian teaching concerns not only personal
salvation but general questions of the state. Humanity on the whole,
and every individual personally, must make the choice between the
law of God and the law of man. Christ said: «Judge not, and ye shall
not be judged: condemn not, and ye shall not be condemned» (Luke,
VI, 37). Before he had arrived at his new understanding of Christ's
teaching, Tolstoy had believed that these words meant only a prohibition of gossip, but now he became convinced that Christ forbade all
human law-courts or institutions of judgment. The words «Judge
not, and ye shall not be judged» are, according to Tolstoy, the logical
result of the commandment «Resist no evil». Christ enjoins us to do
good in return for evil, to forgive all men and to love our enemies.
The courts do not forgive, but punish; they do no good, but evil.
Therefore Christ must have rejected courts. Christ also said: «Con-

demn not, and ye shall not be condemned». Tolstoy interprets these words as «Do not sentence» and «Forgive all». Tolstoy remarks that the apostles, Christ's disciples, the martyrs and Christianity up to the times of Constantine, interpreted Christ's words as he did.

Tolstoy says that neither patriotic and conservative Christians, nor aesthetic revolutionaries, will renounce the right forcibly to resist what they regard as evil. The so-called believers devote themselves to the building of churches, perfomance of sacraments, confessions of faith and so forth, but they refuse to live according to the law of non-resistance to evil which would free humanity from evil. They think that the law of non-resistance to evil is impractical and that all they can do is to strive towards an ideal which is attained by prayer and by faith in the sacraments, in the Redemption and in the resurrection of the dead. They also say that Christ's teaching is not in accord with human nature; Tolstoy's view is that violence is repulsive to human nature and that judges, soldiers and others who find themselves in similar positions would not use it if they were not forced to do so.

Christ's teaching concerning non-resistance to evil, as Tolstoy now understood it, appeared entirely new to him. He realized that Christ did not reject that which in the old law is eternal, but that he rejected the law of Moses. Tolstoy quotes John Chrysostom who, together with the Church, recognized the authority of God the Father, that is Moses, and rejected that of the Son. Where punishment for crime was concerned John Chrysostom and the Church both accepted the Mosaic law, «A tooth for a tooth». Tolstoy says that a man who believes in Christ disregards the law of Moses. After Tolstoy had understood Christ's law as Christ's, and not that of Moses, he was able to discover the essence of Christ's teaching in the following five commandments:

1) Matthew V, 21-26 (of which only verses 21 and 22 are quoted):

> Ye have heard that it was said by them of old time, Thou shalt not kill; and whosoever shall kill shall be in danger of the judgment;
> But I say unto you, That whosoever is angry with his brother without a cause shall be in danger of the judgment: and whosoever shall say to his brother, Raca, shall be in danger of the council: but whosoever shall say, Thou fool, shall be in danger of hell fire.

116

Tolstoy rejects the words «without a cause» as contrary to Christ's teaching, and he takes «Raca» and «fool» to mean worthless and senseless. He interprets verse 22 as «Be at peace with all men» and «Do not allow yourself to be angry or superior», and verses 23-26 as «Try to re-establish peace if it has been broken; the service of God is the annihilation of enmity».

2) Matthew V, 27-32 (of which only verses 31 and 32 are quoted):

> It hath been said, Whosoever shall put away his wife, let him give her a writing of divorcement;
> But I say unto you, That whosoever shall put away his wife, saving for the cause of fornication, causeth her to commit adultery: and whosoever shall marry her that is divorced committeth adultery.

Tolstoy was puzzled by the words «saving for the cause of fornication». He came to the conclusion that it is the law of Moses which permits a husband to divorce his wife, but that Christ meant that the putting away of the wife causes her to commit adultery. He interprets this commandment in the following way: «Do not regard the beauty of the flesh as an amusement; avoid this snare in advance (verses 28-30); let a man take one wife and a woman one husband and on no account abandon one another (verse 32)». For Tolstoy every union between man and woman is binding — whether blessed by the Church or not.

3) Matthew V, 33-37 (of which only verses 33 and 34 are quoted):

> Again, ye have heard that it hath been said by them of old time, Thou shalt not forswear thyself, but shalt perform unto the Lord thine oaths:
> But I say unto you, Swear not at all...

This commandment is understood by Tolstoy as referring not only to ordinary swearing, but to all kinds of oaths as sworn in courts of law, in military service and at marriages. Tolstoy considers that every oath extorted has an evil purpose. On page 92 of the French translation of *Ma Religion* in Galdós's library we find:

> ...Je compris que le commandement de Jésus concernant le serment est loin d'être insignifiant, facile à pratiquer et superficiel, comme cela m'avait semblé, tant que j'exceptais du serment défendu par Jésus le serment de fidélité à l'Etat.
> N'y a-t-il pas ici une défense de prêter serment, ce serment

9

indispensable à la division des hommes en groupes politiques et à la formation de la caste militaire? Le soldat est bien l'instrument de toutes les violences, et, en Russie, il prend le soubriquet de «prisséaga» (assermenté). Si j'avais causé avec le grenadier pour savoir comment il résolvait la contradiction entre l'Evangile et le règlement militaire, il m'aurait répondu qu'il avait prêté serment, c'est à dire qu'il avait juré sur l'Evangile. C'est la réponse que m'ont faite tous les militaires.

The idea is further extended by Tolstoy to include a refusal to take any part in courts of law, an attitude based on an interpretation of Luke VI, 31 and Matthew VII, 1. The following passage from page 31 of the French translation refers to this verse:

Jésus, dans sa prière, exhorte tous les hommes sans exception à pardonner, afin que leurs fautes leur soient également remises. Comment donc un homme qui, d'après sa religion, doit pardonner sans fin à tout le monde pourrait-il juger et condamner? Ainsi je vois, que selon la doctrine de Jésus, il ne saurait y avoir de juge chrétien qui condamne. Mais peut-être, d'après le rapport qui existe entre les mots: «Ne jugez point et vous ne serez pas jugés» et les paroles précédentes ou subséquentes, pourrait-on conclure que Jésus, en disant: «Ne jugez pas», ne pensait pas aux institutions judiciares? Cela n'est non plus le cas; au contraire, il est clair, d'après le rapport des phrases, qu'en disant: «Ne jugez point», Jésus parle précisement des institutions judiciaires. Selon Matthieu et Luc, avant de dire: «Ne jugez point» il dit: «de ne pas résister au mal».

4) Matthew V, 38-39:

Ye have heard that it hath been said, An eye for an eye, and a tooth for a tooth;
But I say unto you, That ye resist not evil; but whosoever shall smite thee on thy right cheek, turn to him the other also.

Tolstoy considers this commandment to be the key to the interpretation of the other four commandments. For him it means never to resist evil by force, never to use violence, to accept physical assault without retaliation, to give what is taken from you, and to labour if forced to work. Verse 40 continues:

And if any man will sue thee at the law, and take away thy coat, let him have thy cloke also.

This commandment is closely bound up with the fifth.

5) Matthew V, 43-48 (of which only verses 43 and 44 are quoted):

> Ye have heard that it hath been said, Thou shalt love thy
> neighbour, and hate thine enemy.
> But I say unto you, Love your enemies, bless them that curse
> you, do good to them that hate you, and pray for them which
> despitefully use you, and persecute you.

For Tolstoy, «neighbour» means fellow-countryman, and «enemies», national enemy. The law of Moses teaches us to love those of our own race and hate the foreigner. But Christ taught us to love everyone without distinction of nationality. Tolstoy points out that Christ did not explicitly forbid war because he never foresaw that Christians could take part in wars. The early Christians followed Christ's teaching.

Tolstoy acknowledges that those who are going to follow Christ's teaching will suffer, but he points out that they are going to suffer much more if they follow the teaching of the world. The accumulation of wealth, wars and the struggle for power have caused much more suffering than would arise from the practice of non-resistance to evil. On page 199 of the French translation we read:

> ...il suffit d'accepter franchement et simplement la doctrine
> de Jésus pour mettre au jour l'horrible mensonge dans
> lequel nous vivons tous et chacun en particulier. Une généra-
> tion après l'autre s'efforce de trouver la sécurité de son exis-
> tence dans la violence et de se garantir ainsi la proprieté. Nous
> croyons voir le bonheur de notre vie dans la puissance, la do-
> mination et l'abondance des biens. Nous sommes tellement
> habitués à cela, que la doctrine de Jésus, qui enseigne que le
> bonheur des hommes ne peut pas dépendre du pouvoir et de
> la fortune, et que le riche ne peut pas être heureux, nous
> semble d'exiger trop de sacrifices.

According to Tolstoy, the richer and more powerful a man is, the less happy he can be. Death is inevitable and no amount of possessions can save us from it. There is thus no sacrifice involved in following Christ's teaching; on the contrary, by following him we can become free to live for our own good and for that of others. On page 248 of the French translation, the last of the four pages turned down in the copy preserved in Galdós's library, we find the following passage:

> Jésus m'a dit: ton bien, c'est l'union avec tous les hommes;
> le mal, c'est la violation de l'unité du Fils et de l'homme.

Jésus m'a montré que l'unité du Fils et de l'homme, c'est à
dire l'amour des hommes entre eux, n'est pas seulement le but
auquel doivent tendre les hommes, un idéal placé devant eux,
mais que cette union, cet amour des hommes les uns pour les
autres est leur état normal et bienheureux, celui dans lequel
naissent les enfants, comme l'a dit Jésus, dans lequel vivent
toujours les hommes, jusqu'à ce que cet état soit troublé par
le mensonge, les chimères et les tentations.

The doctrines of Original Sin, of the Atonement, of the Trinity
and of the Resurrection were all without foundation for him. He
believed in a purely rational solution of the problems of life as preached
by Christ. Nevertheless his doctrine was a mystical doctrine of life
and of man. He strove after union with man and he rejected wealth,
rank and power because they tend to separate men. He saw the
purpose of life as the fulfilment of God's will. Tolstoy's doctrine
broke with both the Church and the world.

* * *

Angel Guerra's conversion from a revolutionary with anarchist
leanings to a man who died loving humanity was a gradual one. When
we first meet him, he has just taken part in an abortive rising during
which he has been involved in the death of a loyalist officer. This
act he endeavours to rationalise as a chance of war, but his conscience refuses to allow him to forget his part in the officer's death.
Disillusioned by his revolutionary activities, he returns home and there
quarrels with his mother, Doña Sales. She is bitterly opposed to her
son's way of life, and dies in the act of reprehending him. The death
of Angel's mother is quickly followed by that of his beloved daughter,
Ción. In his grief and loneliness Angel falls under the influence of
Leré, formerly his mother's trusted servant, whose sincere faith he
respects. It is with her that for the first time he seriously discusses
life from the religious point of view. And it is in this discussion
that we can see reflected Tolstoy's ideals.

Angel is counselled by Leré not to allow himself to become angry:

...Mi primer sermón... no va a lo externo, sino al alma. Lo
primero que le recomiendo a usted es que no se enfade nunca.
—Si yo no me enfado... Estoy hecho un cordero.
—Que no se incomode absolutamente por nada.

—¡Por nada!... Según lo que sea. Ya no me encolerizo, como antes, por cualquier contrariedad.

—Eso es poco... Hay que sofocar la ira en absoluto, y por todos los motivos.

—De modo que si voy por la calle, y me largan una bofetada, me quedaré muy complacido.

—Por ahora sería mucho pretender; pero allá se ha de ir. Pase que todavía no se resigne usted a que le den una guantada en la calle; pero mientras llega eso, hay que irse educando, y limpiar el alma de esa suciedad de la cólera (I, 292-293; *OC*, V, 1284-1285).

The second lesson which Angel must learn is the need to be charitable:

...Segundo sermón... Ahora lo que recomiendo es... que no sea usted avaro.

—¡Avaro yo! ¿Cuándo has visto en mí señales de sordidez?

—Es avaricia guardar lo que nos sobra después de haber satisfecho nuestras necesidades más apremiantes (I, 293; *OC*, V, 1285).

The third lesson is the prohibition of violence:

El tercer sermón fue breve. En pocas y resueltas palabras, *Leré* recomendaba a su amo que no se metiera en política, que dejase a los demás la misión de arreglar las cosas del Gobierno como quisiesen, que no llamase nunca enemigo al que pensara de otra manera que él, y afirmaba que en ningún caso se debe herir ni matar al prójimo, por la sola razón de llamarse blanco o llamarse azul. Llevado del íntimo placer que tales escarceos le producían, Angel la estrechaba con dialéctica ingeniosa; pero la toledana se encastillaba con terquedad en sus afirmaciones, y no había medio de sacarla de ellas. No admitía el uso de las armas ni para el ataque ni para la defensa.

—De modo —observó Guerra—, que según tú, no debe haber Guardia Civil.

—Yo no sé más sino que no se debe matar.

—Y la justicia humana tampoco, según tú, debe aplicar la pena de muerte.

—«No matar», digo.

—Entonces, también suprimirás los ejércitos, que son la salvaguardia de las naciones.

¿Y qué es eso de naciones? Si para que haya naciones es preciso matar, fuera naciones.

—Eso, y que no haya más que curas... Bonita situación.

Y cuando nos invada el francés, o el inglés nos quite una co-
lonia, saldrán los clérigos con el hisopo...

—¿Qué habla usted ahí del inglés y el francés? —dijo Leré,
moviendo vertiginosamente los ojos—. Yo digo que se deben
suprimir las armas, y que pecaron grandemente los que inventa-
ron los cañones, fusiles y demás herramientas de matar.

—Eso es, sí; fuera navajas, pistolas, y por fin suprimamos
los cuchillos y tenedores con que comemos, y en último caso,
hasta los bastones, que también son armas.

—Bah... quite usted. Yo digo *(con inspirado semblante)*
que la guerra es pecado; y ponerse dos hombres uno frente a
otro, con armas, pecado; y el salir todos en fila, pegando tiros,
pecado.

—Y la política, también pecado.

—También... Si no quiere usted entenderlo, ¿qué culpa tengo yo *(Mirándole con lástima.)* Es que somos demasiado sabios,
y lo primero que tendría usted que hacer es olvidar toda esa
faramalla, y quedarse ignorante mondo y lirondo... En fin, ya no
predico más. Basta de sermones perdidos (I, 296-297; *OC,* V,
1285-1286).

The similarity of these three sermons with the teaching of Tolstoy
in *Ma Religion* is self-evident. The insistence on charity, the rejection
of anger and violence, are all clear reflections of the Tolstoyan creed.
Leré advises Guerra not to take part in activities bound up with
the Government, because it is the State which imposes so-called justice,
including the death-penalty, and it is the State that wages wars,
maintains armies, makes armaments and is occupied in politics. Like
Tolstoy, Leré deduces from the New Testament commandment to
render good for evil, that resistance to an aggressive war should not be
permitted and that the punishment by death of criminals is indefen-
sible. It is interesting, too, to note that Leré, the ardent Catholic,
accepts the law of Jesus according to Tolstoy, whilst Guerra, at the
time of this discussion an agnostic, thinks on the lines of an eye for
an eye, the Mosaic law, which is the one accepted by the Church.

In the course of his conversion, guided in his spiritual life by
Leré, Guerra tries to live up to the ideals expounded by her, following
her commandments to the letter:

Era que fascinado por Leré, y sometido a una especie de obe-
diencia sugestiva, ponía en práctica casi maquinalmente alguna
de las máximas contenidas en los estrafalarios sermones de la
iluminada. Esta le había dicho: «socorre a los necesitados, sean

122

los que fueren», y él sentía inclinación instintiva hacia ellos, principiando por la caridad elemental de oirles y considerarles, concluyendo por socorrerles en cierta medida discreta (I, 299; *OC, V,* 1286).

Leré is indeed clearly shown to be the mainspring, not only of his gradual conversion, but also of his later attempt to found a religious order:

> La iniciativa o el germen de esta acción partía de su amiga, encarnándose luego en la mente de él y revistiéndose de la substancia de cosa práctica y real. Trocados los organismos, a Leré correspondía la obra paterna, y a Guerra la gestación pasiva y laboriosa. El proyecto de fundación sería Leré reproducida en la realidad... (II, 211; *OC, V,* 1369).

Angel Guerra, an ordinary mortal, a man of wrath, is thus seen trying to put into effect the doctrines of Leré (that is to say, some of the ideals expounded by Tolstoy in *Ma Religion):* the novel teaches us, as it teaches Guerra, that these ideas are, for the ordinary mortal, far too lofty and impractical. Galdós demonstrates to us that a human being, even if he strives to live up to the commandment of non-resistance to evil, cannot do so because of his human nature. Tolstoy's ideal is impossible of realisation in real life. A change of heart is not enough to alter human nature entirely and with it the whole structure of human society. Galdós does not deny the fact that individuals can grow spiritually, and Guerra is an example of such spiritual growth; but he does not see how non-resistance to evil could be consistently practised by ordinary mortals.

* * *

Tolstoy's influence is also apparent in the discussion between Angel Guerra and don Juan Casado concerning the rules of the religious society which Guerra is about to found and the ideas of Guerra's doctrine, which comes to be called *dominismo. Dominismo* is a mixture of a purely Spanish Utopia and Tolstoyan ideals. The Spanish elements can be listed as follows:

1. Guerra's decision to turn his back on the world and become a priest.
2. His readiness to put aside his scruples and to accept everything that the Church commands.

3. His readiness to die for his ideal.

4. His acceptance of social administration, art, culture and philanthropy in his future dream state.

5. His belief that «Christianisation» of the world will come about through the re-birth of the Catholic Church under a Spanish Pope.

Nevertheless, certain elements in *dominismo* are clearly of Tolstoyan origin:

1. Guerra's profound conviction that by putting his theory into practice, by practising charity as preached by Christ, the existing order of things could be altered peacefully.

Tolstoy believed that the Kingdom of Heaven could be established on earth if Christ's commandments (according to his interpretation) were followed. He says in *Ma Religion:*

> La doctrine de Jésus rétablit le règne de Dieu sur la terre. Il n'est pas vrai que la pratique de cette doctrine soit difficile, mais elle s'impose naturellement à tout homme qui a reconnu la vérité (p. 212 of the French translation).
> Je crois à la doctrine de Jésus, et voici ma religion: Je crois que seul l'accomplissement de la doctrine de Jésus donne le vrai bien à tous les hommes. Je crois que l'accomplissement de cette doctrine est possible, facile et joyeux (p. 247 of the French translation).

Guerra too is firmly convinced that his theory could be turned into practice. He says to Casado:

> La práctica, amigo mío, no puede menos de responder a toda buena teoría. No seamos timoratos; no pensemos mal de la realidad, juzgándola como la infalible desilusión de nuestras ideas, como el hálito vicioso y malsano que ha de convertirlas en humo. Cultivemos la idea sin desconfiar de la realidad, que vendrá ¿pues no ha de venir? a dar forma y vida al pensamiento, pues para eso existe. El mundo físico, ¿qué es más que un esclavo del mundo ideal y el ejecutor ciego de sus planes? (III, 296; *OC*, V, 1509).

Guerra, like Tolstoy, is of the opinion that neither philosophers nor politicians have been able to renovate society and benefit humanity. Only by applying Christ's teaching to actual life can the way to salvation be found. Here are Guerra's words relating to this theme:

124

La aplicación rigurosa de las leyes de caridad, que Cristo Nuestro Señor nos dio, aplicación que hasta el presente está a la mitad del camino entre las palabras y los hechos, traerá de fijo la reforma completa de la sociedad, esa renovación benéfica que en vano buscan la política y la filosofía (III, 310; *OC,* V, 1513).

The conviction that adherence to the three commandments: «Do not judge», «Do not defend yourself by violence» and «Do not make war» will in time revolutionise society, is shared both by Tolstoy and Guerra. Guerra, like Tolstoy, considers the existing Church as one which does not practise real Christianity. He says to Casado:

No, la Iglesia no practica la caridad más que en la parte que le conviene, para sostener su organización temporal. Yo me río de la organización temporal de la Iglesia, y mis *ciudades* son de una consistencia indestructible (III, 311; *OC,* V, 1514).

2. *The absence of armies and politicians in Guerra's new utopian state.*

In Guerra's society there will be no politicians, and no wars:

Yo no pronunciaré discursos, yo no echaré mi voto en una urna, yo no emplearé un arma, ni aun la más inofensiva. Mi misión es practicar las obras de misericordia estrictamente, a la letra. Dentro de algunos años, verán si hay muchedumbres o no hay muchedumbres al lado mío (III, 311; *OC,* V, 1513).

3. *Guerra's condemnation of existing state administrations, private property and family life: everything is to be dissolved in order to be built up again.*

Tolstoy writes:

L'Eglise chrétienne depuis Constantin n'a prescrit aucune activité à ses membres. Elle n'a même jamais exigé qu'on abstienne de n'importe quoi. L'Eglise chrétienne a reconnu et sanctionné le divorce, l'esclavage, les tribunaux, tous les pouvoirs existants, ainsi que les exécutions et les guerres; elle n'exigeait (et cela seulement dans les commencements) que le renoncement au mal à l'occasion du baptême; mais plus tard quand on a introduit le baptême des nouveau-nés, elle cessa d'exiger même cela...

Le pouvoir de l'Etat est basé sur la tradition, sur la science, sur le suffrage du peuple, sur la force brutale, sur tout ce que vous voudrez, mais non sur l'Eglise. Les guerres, les relations d'Etat à l'Etat, reposent sur le principe de nationalité, d'equilibre, sur tout ce que l'on voudra, mais non sur le principe de l'Eglise. Les institutions de l'Etat ignorent carrément l'Eglise. L'idée que l'Eglise peut servir de base à la justice, à la propriété, n'est que plaisante à notre époque. La science non seulement ne soutient pas la doctrine de l'Eglise, mais, sans le vouloir, est toujours hostile à l'Eglise dans son développement. L'art, qui ne servait jadis que l'Eglise, l'a complètement abandonnée (pp. 223, 225-226 of the French translation).

Guerra expresses this point of view in a different way, but the essence of his thought is the same : namely that the existing State is not a Christian State and that it ought to be abolished and rebuilt anew. He says to Casado:

Pues qué, ¿hay quién se atreva a declarar perfecto el estado social, ni aun en las naciones cristianas, ni siquiera en las que obedecen al sucesor de San Pedro? ¿No estamos viendo que todo ello es un edificio caduco y vacilante que amenaza caer y cubrir de ruinas la tierra? La propiedad y la familia, los poderes públicos, la administración, la Iglesia, la fuerza pública, todo, todo necesita ser deshecho y construido de nuevo (III, 310-311; OC, V, 1513).

Taking into account the points mentioned above, it is clear that there are definite Tolstoyan elements incorporated in Guerra's new doctrine, in itself a purely Spanish one, since the framework on which the world-government is going to rest is the Catholic Church headed by a Spanish Pope. But apart from this fact, the main characteristics of this new world-brotherhood are identical with Tolstoy's dream of a Kingdom of Heaven on earth, where there is no nationalism, no armies, no politicians, and where everything is achieved by the practice of charity.

* * *

In order that Guerra's *dominismo* could develop and gradually spread throughout the world, it had first to be put into practice on a small scale. For this reason, Guerra decided to found a brotherhood which would live according to the commandments of Christ. The emphasis laid on non-resistance to evil and the annulment of personality denotes the influence of Tolstoy, as does the point of view taken on contagious diseases and the resolve not to appeal to law-courts when dealing with criminals.

The following points represent the Tolstoyan elements in the rules laid down for Guerra's new foundation:

1. The decision not to appeal to law-courts.

Guerra plans to open the doors of his brotherhood to everyone needing help, including people sought by the police. According to Tolstoy's interpretation of St. Luke VI, verse 37 (his commandment 3) —(Do not take oath or judge»— Guerra is prepared not to hand over criminals to the police although he would not put up any resistance in the case of criminals arrested on his premises. Guerra remarks to Casado:

> Así como entran y salen los pecadores y los necesitados y los enfermos, la justicia tiene también la puerta franca. No se disputa al César lo que le pertenece. Aquí, ni negamos consuelo a quien lo ha menester, ni ocultamos al que no lo merece, ni vendemos a la justicia secretos de nadie. Nos entendemos con Cristo, y creemos trabajar por El organizando nuestros auxilios en la forma que va usted viendo (III, 167; OC, V, 1471).

Like Tolstoy, Guerra is of the opinion that the only judge of one's behaviour is one's own conscience and that the expiation of crimes has to be forthcoming from the sinner himself. When he encounters Arístides in hiding, Guerra tells him:

> No me importa a mí la justicia oficial. Sí me importa la moral, o sea la que el cristianismo llama penitencia (III, 279-280; OC, V, 1504);

and later when Arístides asks for asylum:

> ¿Estás loco? ¡Denunciarte! Mi opinión, ya te lo dije, es que debes imponerte tú mismo el sacrificio de entregarte a la justicia (III, 283; OC, V, 1505).

Guerra's words when he tries to induce Arístides to give himself up demonstrate another side of his relationship with justice: namely, that of non-resistance to evil. «Evil», which can refer to any kind of violence, may be applied here to the police, but, should they come, the doors of the brotherhood will be open to them.

2. *The refusal to use violence even in self-defence.*

In Tolstoy's interpretation of St. Matthew V, verses 38-39 —«Do not defend yourself by violence»— we find the most important rule which is going to be imposed in Guerra's proposed brotherhood. He says to Casado:

> Lo único que debo añadir es que en esta Casa de Dios se prohibe castigar al prójimo aun en defensa propia. El o la que recibe algún ultraje de palabra o de obra, se aguanta y espera más. Se ha dicho «no matarás», y hay que cumplirlo a la letra (III, 298; *OC,* V, 1510).

The same emphasis on non-resistance to evil is apparent when Guerra consents to admit Arístides to his asylum, telling him:

> ...no matar, no castigar, no defenderse..., sucumbir siempre ante la ingratitud y la violencia (III, 344; *OC,* V, 1523).

Guerra is fully aware that the practice of non-resistance to evil will claim its victims, but, like Tolstoy, he is convinced that after some people have been sacrificed to this doctrine, the law of non-resistance to evil will triumph. In his speech to Arístides he says the following:

> ...no alegar ningún derecho; hacer el bien a los demás y guardar el mal para sí; sucumbir siempre ante la ingratitud y la violencia. ¡Ya ves cuán sencillo! Tal sistema de conducta ha de producir, implantado bruscamente, algunas víctimas; pero la idea irá fructificando, y tras las víctimas vendrán los triunfadores. La perversidad concluirá por rendirse (III, 344; *OC,* V, 1523).

The problem of how non-resistance to evil would work out in practice was faced by Tolstoy in his fairy-tale *Ivan the Fool* (translated into

French in 1887 by E. Halpérine-Makinsky). In it Tostoy tells us a story about a small kingdom, where everyone worked happily on the land (including the King himself), where armies, police and law-courts were non-existent and where the use of money was unknown. When this kingdom was attacked by the neighbouring king, Tarakan, the people did not resist, but offered the soldiers all they had, inviting them to share their lives. The enemy soldiers refused to fight. The angered king then ordered his armies to destroy the villages, to burn the grain and the houses and to slaughter the cattle:

> But the fools still offered no resistance, and only wept. The old men wept, and the old women wept, and the young people wept. «Why do you harm us?» they said. «Why do you waste good things? If you need them why do you not take them for yourselves?» At last the soldiers could stand it no longer. They refused to go further and the army disbanded and fled. [2]

According to Tolstoy it was enough that the enemy should see the weeping people and hear their generous offer of all their goods for every hard-hearted soldier among them to become conscience-stricken and to stop committing atrocities. Tolstoy, when dreaming of his Kingdom of Heaven on earth, that is, in his didactic works especially, did not take into account that really wicked people do in fact exist.

We see this happening to Guerra too. Carried away by his determination to live up to the commandments of Christ, he presupposes that other people's hearts and souls are, like his, open to conversion. He receives Arístides like a brother, only to be attacked by him later.

3. The annulment of personality.

When Guerra tells Arístides that he should «anular la propia personalidad y no ver más que la del prójimo» (III, 344; *OC*, V, 1523), we can discern a direct Tolstoyan influence, because for Galdós spiritual development was always bound up with the expansion of the individual self. Guerra himself began his spiritual life by falling in love with Leré, a woman of flesh and blood, and gradually, by the utmost expansion of personal love, he succeeds in embracing in it love for all mankind. His dying words speak of:

---

[2] *The Works of Leo Tolstoy*, Tolstoy Centenary Edition, trans. Aylmer Maude (London, 1928-1937), XIII, 173, 174.

...el amor, si iniciado como sentimiento exclusivo y personal,
extendido luego a toda la humanidad, a todo ser menesteroso
y sin amparo (III, 371; *OC,* V, 1531).

It seems that Galdós never wavered from this conception of love:
it had to spring from individual, personal feelings for one or several
definite beings and expand until it embraced all mankind. Love, as
Galdós understood it, finally transcended the personal. Tolstoy
conceived it as selflessness: selflessness in the sense that in the place
of utmost expansion of oneself Tolstoy puts annihilation of one's
own individuality and its dissolution, or, better said, merging into
the human element that surrounds one. Tolstoy's ideal of such a
self-less person was Karataev, in *War and Peace.* Here is a description of his character:

> Karataev had no attachments, friendships or love, as Pierre
> understood them, but loved and lived affectionately with
> everything life brought him into contact with, particularly with
> man —not any man— but those with whom he happened to
> be. He loved his dog, the French and Pierre who was his
> neighbour, but Pierre felt that in spite of Karataev's affectionate
> tenderness for him (by which he gave Pierre's spiritual life
> its due) he would not have grieved for a moment at parting
> from him. [3]   And Pierre began to feel in the same way towards
> Karataev.

We can see from this extract that Karataev's love was not a strong
personal love, but a diffused impersonal one. It is Tolstoy's ideal love,
whereas Galdós's conception of love was the one preached by Christ:
«Love thy neighbour as thyself.» These words presuppose love for
oneself.   Christ spoke of the expansion of one's ego which leads to
an altruistic love for mankind, not an impersonal diffused love.

It may be argued at this point that Galdós was not influenced by
Tolstoy's inclination to depersonalization, but by the interest in oriental
religions which he shared with Tolstoy. The reason for supposing
that in this particular case Galdós was influenced by Tolstoy is the fact
that the new religious elements found in *Angel Guerra,* such as non-
resistance to evil and the interpretation of Christianity in connection
with the social order of things, stem from Tolstoy's *Ma Religion,* and

---

[3]   *The Works of Leo Tolstoy,* III, 204-205.

that therefore it would be natural to suppose that Galdós's decision
to include the idea of depersonalization in Guerra's rules for his
brotherhood, is also attributable to the influence of Tolstoy. Tolstoy
writes :

> The life of an individual, striving for his own welfare amid
> an infinite number of similar individuals destroying each other
> and destroying themselves, is an evil, an absurdity and true life
> cannot be such. [4]

These points represent an influence of Tolstoy on Galdós, because
the thoughts expressed by Guerra are not in harmony with those of the
Spanish writer. As has been pointed out by Casalduero, Galdós was
of the opinion that the enforcement of law was necessary for the
maintenance of order in a state, whilst Tolstoy was against the very
existence of law-courts :

> En *Prim,* Santiuste escribe la «Historia lógico-natural de los
> españoles de ambos mundos en el siglo XIX»... Lo lógico natural
> era que los españoles hubieran fusilado a Fernando VII y al
> Infante Don Carlos. Adviértase que no se trata de destronar
> (es el momento en que va a escribir el destronamiento de Isa-
> bel II), sino de fusilar, de atacar el mal en su raíz... En la zona
> de Libertad espiritual en que se encuentra, Galdós puede dis-
> tinguir y diferenciar la demagogia, el desorden, la anarquía, de
> la destrucción y el castigo. La destrucción, la muerte, pueden
> ser y son obra de la justicia y el amor ; obra de verdadero go-
> bierno, de verdadero orden. Galdós es capaz de separar lo
> falso de lo verdadero, y por eso puede ver que en el fondo
> hay Gobiernos de orden que son tan anárquicos, demagógicos
> y destructivos como los levantamientos sediciosos y los movi-
> mientos rebeldes, y en cambio que hay revoluciones que obe-
> decen a un espíritu de verdadero orden y gobierno. [5]

Galdós thought it imperative to destroy evil at its very root, whilst
Tolstoy preached non-resistance to evil under any circumstances. The
annulment of personality is also a Tolstoyan ideal, and quite contrary
to the spiritual development of Galdós's characters.

We come back to the thought that Galdós, in order to show us the

---

[4] *The Works of Leo Tolstoy,* XII, 20.
[5] Joaquín Casalduero, *Vida y obra de Galdós (1843-1920),* (Madrid, 1951),
193-195.

131

consequences of non-resistance to evil when practised in actual life, allows Guerra to act in part «à la Tolstoy». By doing so Galdós brings to one's notice how the application of non-resistance to evil and the conviction that in every human being there is a hidden «better nature» which invariably responds to loving treatment, leads to violence and death and makes victims of innocent people, while evil men are left free to continue their criminal activities.

The purely spiritual aspect of Guerra's tragedy is not in question; from a Christian point of view he attained the highest level of Christian perfection since he was able to forgive his assailants before he died:

> Me voy del mundo sin ningún rencor, ni aun contra los que me maltrataron (III, 369; *OC,* V, 1531).

The fact is that, unlike Tolstoy, Galdós had a clear vision of what might happen should non-resistance to evil become law. The incident of Guerra's death at the hands of people whom he had befriended confirms the opinion that Galdós was acquainted with Tolstoy's doctrine of non-resistance to evil and that he uses the character of Guerra to criticise Tolstoy's doctrine. Galdós wanted to prove for himself and to his readers that the commandment of non-resistance to evil as interpreted by Tolstoy, «Resist no evil at any time; never employ force, never do what is contrary to love; and if men offend you put up with the offence; employ no force against force», was impractical in life as it only led to greater evil.

* * *

Before dealing with the question of what part non-resistance to evil played in Guerra's tragic end, it is interesting to note a passage from Tolstoy's *The Kreutzer Sonata* which throws a strong light on why Galdós thought it impossible to create a Kingdom of Heaven on earth. The reason for Guerra's failure to live up to his ideal is foreshadowed in Posnyshev's speech when talking to Tolstoy on the train:

> Just think: if the aim of humanity is goodness, righteousness, love —call it what you will—, if it is what the prophets have said, that all mankind should be united together in love, that the spears should be beaten into pruning-hooks and so forth,

what is it that hinders attainment of this aim? The passions hinder it. Of all the passions the strongest, cruelest and most stubborn is the sex-passion, physical love; and therefore if the passions are destroyed, including the strongest of them —physical love— the prophesies will be fulfilled, mankind will be brought into unity, the aim of human existence will be attained, and there will be nothing further to live for. [6]

All through Guerra's spiritual development we see that every time he was faced with a situation involving sex-passion his good intentions to practise charity broke down. The first example of this was when he attacked Arístides for blaming him for Dulcenombre's illness and unhappiness:

> El temperamento bravo y altanero resurgía en él, llevándose por delante, como huracán impetuoso, las ideas nuevas, desbaratando y haciendo polvo la obra del sentimiento y de la razón en los últimos meses (II, 245-246; OC, V, 1379).

The second incident happens when Guerra finds Leré asleep. His passion is awakened. He relates what he felt in the following words:

> Todo el espiritualismo, toda la piedad, toda la ciencia religiosa de que me envanecía, salieron de mí de golpe... Era ya otro hombre, el viejo, el de marras, con mis instintos brutales, animal más o menos inteligente, ciego para todo lo divino (III, 118, OC, V, 1456).

And lastly when Arístides insinuates to Guerra that his love for Leré is not spiritual, but a human passion, his violence breaks out again:

> Angel, incapaz de reprimirse, corrió a él, le puso las manos en el pecho, le apretó contra el colchón, y rechinando los dientes, le dijo: «Cállate o te...» (III, 347; OC, V, 1524).

Although Tolstoy understood what sex-passion meant as a man and as an artist, he completely disregarded human nature in his religious philosophy. He was convinced that, once non-resistance to evil became law, humanity would be transformed. As K. S. Laurila puts it:

---

[6] *The Kreutzer Sonata and Other Stories* (Oxford, 1950), 141-142.

So ist für Tolstoy die absolute Enthaltung von jeder direkten und indirekten Gewaltsanwendung wie ein «Zauberstab» mit dem man die unglückliche Menschheit nur zu berühren hat, um sie flugs von allen Nöten zu befreien. [7]

In *Angel Guerra* Galdós presents us with a character who is capable of a great passion. This man he imbues with the determination to live according to the Gospels, as interpreted by Tolstoy. He puts him into situations where human passions come into conflict with the will to be meek and self-effacing. The outcome of this conflict is contrary to the one envisaged by Tolstoy. But it is not only the passion for love that wields such a terrific power even over those who, like Guerra, sincerely strive for perfection; it is also evil, when encountered face to face, that provokes, not meekness, but the will to resist. The impossibility of not resisting stark evil, even for those wishing to do so, is dramatically portrayed by Galdós in the scene where Arístides, Fausto and Poli come to rob Guerra:

> Hizo un esfuerzo de presión terrible sobre sí para sostenerse en el temperamento seráfico del *dominismo*. ¡Qué hermosura, qué majestad ofrecerse indefenso a las injurias y al saqueo de semejante canalla! ¡Qué mérito tan extraordinario dejarse pisotear; no proferir contra ellos ninguna expresión de protesta; no pedir auxilio ni hacer uso de su vigor muscular; proceder, en fin, ante los ultrajes, en perfecta imitación de la conducta del Divino Jesús! Pensándolo estaba Guerra, cuando vio a poca distancia de sí la cara de Arístides, flácida, compungida, macilenta, con expresión de traidora amistad en los ojos febriles, y lo mismo fue ver aquella máscara que sacudírsele interiormente todo el mecanismo nervioso, y explotar la ira con crujido formidable. La manotada fue terrible (III, 351-352; *OC*, V, 1525).

The salient point of this passage is the fact that on seeing Arístides's face Guerra suddenly realises that wicked men do exist. His belief in the «better nature» of men and his conviction that a change of heart could be brought about by practising charity, are shattered. He wishes now to oppose evil by force. But it is too late. Because he has followed the commandment, «Judge not, and ye shall not be judged: condemn not, and ye shall not be condemned», not in its

---

[7] K. S. Laurila, *Leo Tolstois politische Ansichten* (Helsingfors, 1923), 26.

original interpretation —applying it to one's fellow men in a personal sense— but in Tolstoy's interpretation which extended this commandment to all existing laws for the prevention of crime, Guerra has forfeited his life and the life of Jusepa. Instead of resisting evil, Guerra has, by his kind actions, fostered its growth. The tragic end of Angel Guerra proves what Galdós set out to prove, namely that the creation of a new society based on non-resistance to evil, as preached by Tolstoy, is inconceivable.

London.

Torquemada:
The Man and his Language*

«It can be said that all prose fiction is a variation on the theme of *Don Quixote*. Cervantes sets for the novel the problem of appearance and reality: the shifting and conflict of social classes becomes the field of the problem of knowledge... And the poverty of the Don suggests that the novel is born with the appearance of money as a social element —money the great solvent of the solid fabric of the old society, the great generator of illusion. Or, which is to say the same thing, the novel is born in response to snobbery...»[1]

Doubtless Galdós would have agreed with Trilling. His own statements on the novel —notably «Observaciones sobre la novela contemporánea en España» (1870)[2] and his Academy Discourse of 1897— make the point that the proper study for the novelist is the fluid society of his day, and in particular the most dynamic element in that society, the middle classes. His practice, of course, is precisely this, and time and again he exploits the theme of money «the great generator of illusion».

The *Torquemada* series, if not his greatest achievement, is the work most central to his concerns as a novelist, the most coherent expression, in almost pure linear form, of his vision of nineteenth-century man and society. Stated in the crudest terms, Torquemada is the cap-

---

* Page references are to the first editions of *Torquemada en la hoguera* (Madrid, 1889), *Torquemada en la cruz* (Madrid, 1893), *Torquemada en el purgatorio* (Madrid, 1894), and *Torquemada y San Pedro* (Madrid, 1895); these are immediately followed by a second reference to the Aguilar edition of the *Obras completas*, ed. F. C. Sáinz de Robles, vol. V (3rd. ed., Madrid, 1961).

[1] Lionel Trilling, *The Liberal Imagination* (London, 1951), 209.

[2] See G. Correa, «Pérez Galdós y su concepción de novelar», *BICC*, XIX (1964), 99-105.

italist class, his life the rise of that class and the transformation it effects in society. This somewhat obvious symbolism, together with the touches of caricature and the burlesque tone in which Galdós so frequently indulges, may lead the reader to underestimate the complexity and the humanity of this comic figure. For instance, M. Baquero Goyanes, echoing Angel del Río, considers that «El personaje... pierde la humanidad que tenía en *Torquemada en la hoguera* y se convierte un poco en caricaturesco *figurón*». [3]

Another factor which may contribute to this underestimation is the tendency among some critics to see the last three novels of the series as separate from the first. Casalduero puts this point of view in its most categorical form:

> Los tres volúmenes forman una novela completamente in-
> dependiente de *Torquemada en la hoguera*. El mismo Galdós
> debía considerarlo así, pues en *Torquemada en la cruz* hay una
> nota que dice: «Antecedentes: *Fortunata y Jacinta, Torque-
> mada en la hoguera*», y anuncia el volumen de *Torquemada
> y San Pedro* como el «*tercero* y último de la serie». Estos cua-
> tro volúmenes forman dos novelas distintas, las cuales sólo
> tienen de común los elementos puramente externos —nom-
> bres, gestos, algunos hechos, algunos personajes, entre los cua-
> les se encuentra el protagonista. [4]

The mere fact that over four years elapsed between the publication of *Torquemada en la hoguera* and that of *Torquemada en la cruz* would seem to lend force to this argument, but I believe that this kind of external evidence is less than conclusive. [5] Eoff, who has contributed more than most critics to our understanding of Galdós, insists that «the series must be considered as a single four-volume novel; for the whole comprises a single story consisting of progressive steps in the life of the leading character.» [6] It is not simply a matter of chronological sequence; the full richness and subtlety of the conception cannot be appreciated unless we see the four parts as an organic unity.

---

[3] *Historia general de las literaturas hispánicas,* ed. G. Díaz-Plaja, V (Barcelona, 1958), 111.

[4] J. Casalduero, *Vida y obra de Galdós* (Madrid, 1951), 138.

[5] Indeed, some external evidence may point in the other direction. One conclusion which could be drawn from R. J. Weber's article «Galdós's Preliminary Sketches for *Torquemada y San Pedro*», *BHS,* XLIV (1967), 16-27, is that Galdós began to plan this last novel of the series immediately after writing the first (though this does not seem to be Professor Weber's opinion).

[6] S. H. Eoff, *The Novels of Pérez Galdós* (Saint Louis, 1954), 105.

It is true that there are two distinct phases in the career of Torquemada, but the decisive shift occurs, naturally enough, at the moment when Galdós begins to write *Torquemada en la hoguera,* not later. The character has hitherto appeared briefly in *El doctor Centeno, La de Bringas, Lo prohibido, Fortunata y Jacinta* and *Realidad.* In these novels he is a fragment of the environment, one of the forces acting upon the major characters, identifiable by his physical appearance, certain gestures and tricks of speech, but having no life of his own. In *Fortunata y Jacinta* Galdós shows interest in him as a *costumbrista* type, alludes to his wife and daughter and describes his friendship with Doña Lupe, on whom he has exercised a powerful formative influence, but we do not see into the mind of the man.

No doubt at this stage the author realized the potentialities of this creation. It is in *Fortunata y Jacinta* that he remarks «por doquiera que el hombre vaya lleva consigo su novela» (I, 96; *OC,* V, 40). Of the scores of minor figures who make up the social context of this great work, he separates two — Villaamil and Torquemada — in order to follow them as they live out their respective novels. He seems to have referred to *Miau* as «las sobras de otra cosa».[7] There is a sense in which this is also true of *Torquemada en la hoguera,* but the reader is not allowed to feel this for long, for before he is half-way through this short work Galdós, with masterly speed and assurance, has established Torquemada as a three-dimensional figure, living his own novel in his own world.

The essential difference between the Torquemada we have seen in the earlier novels and the man we are now to see is made plain by Galdós in the opening paragraph where, as so often, he speaks quite explicitly about his purposes. We should not be misled by the half-comic rhetoric[8] into underestimating the seriousness and relevance of this exordium:

> Voy a contar cómo fue al quemadero el inhumano que tantas vidas infelices consumió en llamas; que a unos les traspasó los hígados con un hierro candente; a otros les puso en cazuela, bien mechados, y a los demás los achicharró por partes, a fuego lento, con rebuscada y metódica saña. Voy a contar

---

[7] See letter to Galdós from Alas, 13 July 1888, published by Soledad Ortega de Varela, *Cartas a Galdós* (Madrid, 1964), 248.

[8] For a possible interpretation of this, see P. L. Ullman, «The exordium of *Torquemada en la hoguera*», *MLN,* LXXX (1965), 258-60.

cómo vino el fiero sayón a ser víctima, cómo los odios que
provocó se le volvieron lástima, y las nubes de maldiciones
arrojaron sobre él lluvia de piedad; caso patético, caso muy
ejemplar, señores, digno de contarse para enseñanza de todos,
aviso de condenados y escarmiento de inquisidores (1; *OC,*
V, 906).

Perhaps the most important phrase here is «cómo vino el fiero sayón a
ser víctima». The notions of poetic justice and exemplariness are pertinent to this as to most of Galdós' novels, but more fundamental is
the simple fact that agent becomes patient. In order to render Torquemada credible as a human being and acceptable as protagonist, he
must be shown to suffer; it is no longer enough for him to act, much
less simply to act out the type-part in which he has hitherto been cast.
He is therefore plunged into a sudden crisis of suffering, an agony
such as he has never experienced or imagined. But not before we have
been told certain significant things about him.

First of all, he is not a pure miser, not one of

esos usureros que se pasan la vida multiplicando caudales
por el gustazo platónico de poseerlos, que viven sórdidamen-
te para no gastarlos y al morirse quisieran, o bien llevárselos
consigo a la tierra, o esconderlos donde alma viviente no los
pueda encontrar. No; don Francisco habría sido así en otra
época; pero no pudo eximirse de la influencia de esta segunda mitad del siglo XIX, que casi ha hecho una religión de las
materialidades decorosas de la existencia (9-10; *OC,* V, 908).

Galdós has not created another Harpagon, or even a Grandet, [9] but a
character who, for all his self-centredness, greed and hardness of heart,
shows a marked degree of sociability and susceptibility to outside pressures. The author tells us that Torquemada is what he is because he
lives in a particular society at a particular time:

Viviendo el *Peor* en una época que arranca de la desamorti-
zación, sufrió, sin comprenderlo, la metamorfosis que ha des-
naturalizado la usura metafísica, convirtiéndola en positivista
(10; *OC,* V, 908).

---

[9] J. J. Alfieri, «The Double Image of Avarice in Galdós' Novels», *Hispl*
(USA), XLVI (1963), 722-29, making the point that Torquemada enters the
main stream of nineteenth-century economic development, aptly quotes Marx
on the distinction between the miser and the capitalist.

In this historical situation and under the influence of his womenfolk, Torquemada has become more respectable, better dressed, *más persona,* and consequently an increasingly successful business man. The transformation is slow, meets with inner resistance and is incomplete: «y así como no varió nunca su manera de hablar, tampoco ciertas ideas y prácticas del oficio se modificaron» (14; *OC,* V, 909). Nevertheless, one can already discern in these expository pages the processes and the consequential tensions of what Eoff calls «socialization» (which is perhaps another way of saying humanization), and there is a strong suggestion that they are environmentally determined. This is one aspect of the continuity which exists between this first novel of the series and its sequels.

An important trait which is also emphasized at this early stage is Torquemada's respect for ideas, learning and eloquence. Not only does he stand in awe of the intellect of his child — «sentía ante él la ingénita cortedad de lo que es materia frente a lo que es espíritu» (16; *OC,* V, 910)— but he is also fascinated by the talk of Bailón, the only person with any pretensions to education with whom he regularly comes into contact. This fascination seems to be compounded of a real, if limited, interest in social and philosophical topics (their conversations range from *miasmas* to *el gran Conjunto*) and an as yet undiscriminating taste for words and admiration for one who can use them. The comic treatment of Bailón's windy rhetoric is the first hint of the preoccupation with style which is to run through the tetralogy.

But this character really comes to life only when disaster overtakes him. When Valentín falls ill, unsuspected dimensions of thought and feeling are revealed. The following passage will serve as an illustration:

Apretó el paso sin reparar en la cara burlona de su favorecido, y siguió dando, dando, hasta que le quedaron pocas piezas en el bolsillo. Corriendo hacia su casa, en retirada, miraba al cielo, cosa en él muy contraria a la costumbre, pues si alguna vez lo miró para enterarse del tiempo, jamás, hasta aquella noche, lo había contemplado. ¡Cuantísima estrella! Y qué claras y resplandecientes, cada una en su sitio, hermosas y graves, millones de millones de miradas que no aciertan a ver nuestra pequeñez. Lo que más suspendía el ánimo del tacaño era la idea de que todo aquel cielo estuviese indiferente a su gran dolor, o más bien ignorante de él. Por lo demás, como bonitas, ¡vaya si eran bonitas las estrellas! Las había chicas, medianas y grandes; algo así como pesetas, medios duros y duros. Al insigne prestamista le pasó por la cabeza lo siguiente: «Como se ponga bueno, me ha de ajustar esta cuenta: si acuñáramos todas las estrellas del cielo, ¿cuánto producirían al cinco por ciento de interés compuesto en los siglos que van desde que todo eso existe?» (56-57; *OC,* V, 921).

At this point of crisis, Torquemada seems on the one hand to show a new potentiality for spiritual growth, and on the other to confirm that he is as yet incapable of emerging from the role of hardened usurer in which he is cast — or, as Galdós almost appears to be saying, in which he has cast himself. He is under terrible stress: the agony of seeing his adored Valentín suffer is heightened by helpless rage at the crumbling of his vast ambitions for the brilliant child. He is driven to the lengths of questioning his own conduct in an attempt to find an explanation for his misfortune, and thence to acts of charity in the hope of propitiating a dimly-perceived but obviously irate Divinity. This activity is a parodic inversion of his usual role. He rushes out in search of beggars to whom to give alms «como si fuera en persecución de un deudor». They are on this occasion as elusive as debtors and almost as reluctant to receive as debtors to pay. Their amazement at Torquemada's new-found philanthropy is an understandable reaction; Torquemada has great difficulty in convincing himself that this is his true nature.

In the passage quoted, he is hastily divesting himself of his money («apretó el paso... siguió dando, dando»), without really seeing the recipients, who are no more than instruments for his giving, just as his debtors have been instruments for his acquiring. However, he cannot bring himself to part with all the money he is carrying (which, in any case, we have been told, «debían de ser calderilla»); he gives «hasta que le quedaron pocas piezas». [10] Wholehearted charity is quite alien to him, a fact which is underlined immediately after this incident by his giving away his cloak — but only his old one.

His suffering has even more far-reaching effects than the upsetting of his normal acquisitive function. As he makes his way home, he looks up at the sky. Not only does he look, he gazes. The symbolism is obvious. Hitherto, totally earth-bound, he has merely glanced

---

[10] This «vicio del descuento» is shared, however, by a character who is the very embodiment of Christian charity — Benina of *Misericordia* (66; *OC,* V, 1895).

at the sky to ascertain the weather. Now for the first time the heavens enter into his consciousness, adding a new dimension to his world. The pace of the narrative slackens; there is a moment of lirical contemplation: « ¡Cuantísima estrella! Y qué claras y resplandecientes, cada una en su sitio, hermosas y graves». At first, Torquemada's reaction is one of pure wonder; he is as a child seeing the stars for the first time; he admires their number, their brightness, their orderliness — qualities which appeal to us all, but especially to his methodical usurer's mentality. Then follows the inevitable human reaction to the vastness of the universe: the attempt to humanize the stars —«millones de millones de miradas» — and the realization of their blindness to the insignificant creature man —«que no aciertan a ver nuestra pequeñez». But, of course, it is not man's condition in general that concerns don Francisco; it is his own overwhelming grief, and the thought that the heavens are indifferent to it or unaware of it is wholly intolerable to him. Here, Galdós shifts back for a moment to the point of view of the author and, for the first time in this chapter, refers to Torquemada not by name but as «el tacaño», before introducing further reflections on the beauty of the stars as seen specifically by the usurer. Their brilliance, differences in size and order are translated into monetary terms: they become «pesetas, medios duros y duros». No greater tribute to the beauty of the heavenly bodies could come from Torquemada, but at the same time this constitutes a reduction of the universe to something manageable. It enables Torquemada momentarily to escape the anguished contemplation of his own littleness and suffering against a background of celestial indifference— an indifference which is the cosmic counterpart of the human misunderstanding of which he complains — and to effect a transition to an almost hopeful anticipation of the future: «Como se ponga bueno [Valentín] me ha de ajustar esta cuenta...» (The comedy amidst the pathos is reinforced by the ironical «insigne prestamista»). If only the child lives, his mathematical genius will enable him to cut the universe down to size for his father, by calculating what the stars are worth in hard cash.

Here, as elsewhere in this novel, Torquemada is presented as a creature who, in spite of his limited horizons, firmly ingrained habits and monumental self-centredness, is capable of being jolted out of his usual way of life by some major emotional upset. His new line of conduct, however, is severely conditioned by his old habits of thought. His philanthropy is conceived of as part of a business deal with the Deity by which he will be able to achieve certain ends in the here and now. His consciousness of the plight of others is subordinated to his overwhelming self-pity. His new awareness of the boundless universe beyond the streets of Madrid is bearable because even this is reducible, by a flight of fancy, to the language of the ledger.

Valentín dies, and his father, feeling himself defrauded by the Deity's not having adhered to the bargain he has tried to drive, returns to his old ways. But this is a deliberate choice, not an unconscious reversion to type; Torquemada can never again be merely *el tacaño*. He has been shown to be a human being. He suffers, and is changed by suffering. He adapts himself to circumstances, but as yet this adaptation is grudging, limited and subject to regression. The process of «socialization» is indeed to be a remarkable transformation, but the interest of these novels lies even more in the hesitancies and tensions involved, the restraints put upon it, and the ultimate ambiguity of the status, spiritual if not social, achieved by the protagonist.

To maintain that there is an essential continuity between *Torquemada en la hoguera* and the three later novels of the series is not, of course, to argue that there are no significant new departures in the latter. There are several. One of the most interesting is the attention Galdós now pays to the speech of Torquemada as an index of his personal and social development. In the first of the novels the author, as always, makes most efficient use of the spoken language to fix the character of his hero. Torquemada speaks a vigorous popular language marked by one or two personal idiosyncrasies of vocabulary, notably expletives,[11] and varying in tone, within fairly narrow limits, according to circumstances. That he is not totally uninfluenced by the language he hears is already apparent from the way in which he echoes the philosophical verbiage of Bailón and even, in a grotesquely distorted form, phrases of a devotional nature: «El demonio está contigo, y maldita tú eres entre todas las brujas...» (103; *OC,* V, 933). On the other hand, he is often brutally straightforward in his speech, and occasionally movingly so:

> Me ve cómo estoy, ¡puñales!, muerto de pena, y me viene a hablar de la condenada leche... Hábleme de cómo se consigue que Dios nos haga caso cuando pedimos lo que necesitamos,

---

[11] Discussed by V. A. Chamberlin, «The *muletilla:* an important facet of Galdós' characterization technique», *HR,* XXIX (1961), 296-309.

> hábleme de lo que... no sé cómo explicarlo... de lo que signi-
> fica ser bueno y ser malo... porque, o yo soy un zote o ésta
> es de las cosas que tienen más busilis... (65-66; *OC*, V, 923).

When he attempts to grapple with spiritual matters, his language betrays the deficiencies of his thought and feeling. Two aspects of this
failure are particularly striking. One is the comic confusion in his
handling of such abstractions as «la Humanidad», a confusion which
does not merely show up Torquemada's inadequacies, but also reflects,
in caricature, the fundamental vacuity of the model he is imitating.
The other is the tendency to translate difficult and unpalatable ideas
into the readily understandable terms of business dealing. Thus, the
God-man relationship becomes a creditor-debtor relationship, and, as
we have already seen, the stars become coins.

Both these features point in the direction of the subsequent novels
of the series, but in *Torquemada en la hoguera,* because of its structure and its brevity, there is no room for any appreciable development
in the speech habits of its hero. This is to come, in response to new
stimuli, with the more leisurely narratives spanning the whole of the
rest of his life.

Doubtless an awareness of the comic potentialities of incongruous
language is something that goes back to the beginnings of literature.
In the Spanish novel, from the *Lazarillo* onward, these potentialities
have been much exploited. Isla, indeed, derives a whole novel from
one specialized aspect of this theme. Innumerable minor characters
have been identified and fixed in the mind of the reader by the attri-
bution of oddities of speech. Cervantes himself does not despise this
technique, but in the creation of Sancho Panza he goes far beyond it;
the felicitous ineptitudes and inevitable proverbs with which Sancho's
speech is strewn do not disguise the fact that his language, like his
whole personality, undergoes a process of change and enlargement. It
is not, however, a steady movement in one direction: the «quixotifi-
cation» of his character is incomplete and insecure, [12] but Cervantes
seems to be even more hesitant about the sporadic ennoblement of
his language. As Riley points out, [13] the notion of literary decorum
is called into question when Sancho Panza, conscious of his potential

---

[12] Cf. Dámaso Alonso, «Sancho-Quijote; Sancho-Sancho», *Del siglo de oro
a este siglo de siglas* (Madrid, 1962), 9-19.
[13] E. C. Riley, *Cervantes's Theory of the Novel* (Oxford, 1962), 137.

role as governor and full of high ambitions for the marriage of his daughter, talks to his wife in a style of such unwonted dignity and correctness (*Don Quixote,* II, v) that not only does Teresa complain («después que os hicisteis miembro de caballero andante habláis de tan rodeada manera que no hay quien os entienda»), but the author himself repeatedly intervenes to cast doubt on the authenticity of the whole passage. This metamorphosis of Sancho —ephemeral though it be— involves more than a mere infringement of canons of literary taste. The literary concept of decorum is a fragment of the wider concept of a static social order. Sancho's new language reflects his ambitions to rise out of his class, ambitions which threaten to disrupt such a social order. Perhaps Cervantes felt constrained to laugh them away; he certainly found it easy to do so. Later in the century, *O Fidalgo aprendiz* and *Le Bourgeois gentilhomme* were still grotesque figures of fun, but by the nineteenth century literature, even in Spain, had come to terms with such unseemly upstarts. Society had long since —if not always— done so.

This is not to suggest that nineteenth-century Spanish novelists did not have at hand a rich source of comedy in such characters. It is easy to find examples who share with Torquemada a pretentiousness of speech allied to social ambitions, [14] but there is no need to postulate a model for him outside Galdós' own work, which offers a number of parallels and partial antecedents for Torquemada's linguistic evolution. The novelist frequently makes use of newly-acquired speech habits as an index of the aspirations of his characters. It may be Celepín's rudimentary attempts to refine his language by a profuse and indiscriminate application of the prefix *des-* (*El doctor Centeno,* I, iv), the enhancing of Manuel Peña's oratorical powers by Manso's efforts to educate him in a somewhat different sense (*El amigo Manso,* IV, VII), Fortunata's unsuccessful striving to correct her pronunciation as part of an equally unsuccessful programme of reform and respectability (*Fortunata y Jacinta,* II, ii), the talk and the epistolary style of Tristana —extravagant, incoherent, stuffed with Italian phrases— as a wonderful new world of love and art and literature seems to be opening up before her (*Tristana,* XV, ff.), or José María's facile acquisition of the

---

[14] E.g. Pepe Ronzal of *La Regenta* and Pereda's Don Gonzalo González de la Gonzalera.

clichés of parliamentary oratory as political ambitions take hold of him (*El amigo Manso,* XV).

José María, indeed, has more than this in common with Torquemada. Galdós, through Manso, points to him as a representative figure of the age:

> José reproducía en su desenvolvimiento personal la serie de fenómenos generales que caracterizan a estas oligarquías eclécticas, producto de un estado de crisis intelectual y política que eslabona el mundo destruido con el que se está elaborando. Es curioso estudiar la filosofía de la historia en el individuo, en el corpúsculo, en la célula. Como las ciencias naturales, aquélla exige también el uso del microscopio.
> Indudablemente, estas democracias blasonadas... esta sociedad que despedaza la aristocracia antigua y crea otra nueva con hombres que han pasado su juventud detrás de un mostrador... todo... reclama y quizás anuncia un paso o transformación, que será quizás la más grande que ha visto la historia. Mi hermano, que había fregado platos, liado cigarrillos, azotado negros, vendido sombreros y zapatos, racionado tropas y traficado en estiércoles, iba a entrar en esa escondida falange de próceres, que son la imagen del poder histórico inamovible y como su garantía de permanencia y solidez (95-96; *OC,* IV, 1203).

Here, changing speech is the outward sign of just such a social transformation as Torquemada undergoes, whilst this transformation of the individual is seen as exemplifying the shifting class-structure of nineteenth-century Spain. Galdós is already adumbrating some of the principal themes of the *Torquemada* series, but neither in *El amigo Manso* nor elsewhere does he subject the parallel evolution and interaction of language, personality and social role to such a sustained scrutiny.

There has been some study of specific aspects of the language of the tetralogy. Chamberlin has made pertinent observations on Torquemada's use of the *muletilla* in an article already alluded to, [15] showing how it varies according to the hero's states of mind and the stages in his career; far from being haphazard and meaningless, the form taken by the *muletilla* is part of the imagery whereby the innermost concerns of the character are made apparent (e.g. «¡Cristo!» is associ-

---

[15] See above, note 11.

ated with his hopes for the reincarnation of his son). A recent examination of Galdós' use of colloquialisms [16] has shown that their frequency diminishes over the four novels of this series :

> La cantidad de expresiones por novela es la siguiente : *Torquemada en la hoguera* (4,9 por página), *Torquemada en la cruz* (3,2 por página), *Torquemada en el purgatorio* (2,3 por página), *Torquemada y San Pedro* (2,3 por página). Cuando Galdós quiere mostrar el ascenso de clase social de un personaje, disminuye el número de expresiones familiares como en el caso de Torquemada y de Fortunata, con el propósito de producir un efecto más marcado de mejoramiento social del individuo. [17]

There seems to be some justification for the conclusion drawn here from the data, although it would be easy to attach too much importance to these raw statistics, as indeed to any purely quantitative assessment. One must agree with Gilman in his insistence on careful consideration of the context in which a particular type of language occurs. [18]

Yet Gilman himself fails to pay proper regard to his own dictum. Whilst rightly pointing out that «Fortunata existe en un estado de constante metamorfosis lingüística», [19] he ignores the possibility that this may also be true of Torquemada, whose language he treats as if it were all of a piece :

> Pero el más notable de los numerosos estilos de la falsificación (de lo que Fielding llamaría *affectation*) es tal vez el de Torquemada. Su lenguaje es una obra maestra de caricatura verbal. Podemos oír la melosidad, el subir y bajar de la voz, la dureza de corazón que hay en el fondo, la radical traición del sentido interior por la forma externa. Si en algún lugar «el estilo es la mentira», es justamente aquí. [A footnote refers to Torquemada's «increíble discurso» as an example of «esta obra maestra de la caricatura oral»]. [20]

---

[16] Graciela Andrade Alfieri and J. J. Alfieri, «El lenguaje familiar de Pérez Galdós», *Hispanófila*, VIII (1964-65), No. 1, 27-73.

[17] *Art. cit.*, 31-32. Of the score of novels scrutinized, *Torquemada en la hoguera* has the highest density of colloquialisms. From a very low frequency in *La Fontana de Oro* there is a fairly steady increase up to *Torquemada en la hoguera* and a fairly steady decline after it. It could therefore conceivably be argued that the later novels of the series merely follow the overall pattern of Galdós' stylistic development and that the frequency of these expressions is not necessarily a function of Torquemada's shifting social status.

[18] S. Gilman, «La palabra hablada y *Fortunata y Jacinta*», *NRFH*, XV (1961), 542-60.

[19] *Art. cit.*, 551.

[20] *Art. cit.*, 550.

There is some truth in this, or there would be if it were a question of a static character with a fixed mode of utterance. But Torquemada is no Uriah Heep; his language is not merely a mask donned deliberately to hide the reality beneath. At times, it is true, that is part of its function, but, as often as not, it reveals more than it hides, because it is an extension of his developing personality, an externalization (as Chamberlin has shown in the case of the *muletilla*) of the inner reality. [21]

If «El estilo es la mentira» is the comment that immediately springs to mind when one thinks about Galdós' language, there is another — this time a remark by Galdós himself, not one of his characters — that is worth recalling. In a conversation with Luis Bello, he is reported as saying «Para mí el estilo empieza en el plan». [22] This is peculiarly appropriate to the *Torquemada* series, of which the author might almost have said «El plan empieza en el estilo», so intimately related are *estilo* and *plan*. For the novels, looked at from one point of view, are about style —Torquemada's style— and whether style is the man, or may become the man.

A glance at some of the important points in the evolution of the hero in the last three of the novels may help us to see more clearly the nature of this relationship between the man and his manner. In the second chapter of *Torquemada en la cruz* he is confronted with Cruz del Aguila, impressed by her aristocratic elegance, and overwhelmed by the contrast between her graciousness and his own oafish tactlessness. His fear of ridicule, his awareness of his own talents and a new-found — and doubtless rationalizing — consciousness of the role the well-to-do should play in society now impel him into a deliberate quest for self-improvement:

> «Pero ello es que no tengo política, no la tengo; en viéndome delante de una persona principal, ya estoy hecho un zángano y no sé qué decir, ni qué hacer con las manos... Pues hay que

---

[21] Gilman and Chamberlin refer to Joaquín Gimeno Casalduero, «El tópico en la obra de Galdós», *Boletín informativo del Seminario de Derecho Político de la Universidad de Salamanca* (enero-abril 1956), 35-52, which I have not seen. Judging from the brief quotations given (e.g. «El tópico aparece como una cortina de humo que oculta una realidad...», p. 46), Gimeno seems to lend support to Gilman's argument that Torquemada's acquired speech characteristics are a disguise.

[22] Luis Bello, «Aniversario de Galdós: Diálogo antiguo», *El Sol*, 4 Jan. 1928; quoted by Ángel del Río, «Aspectos del pensamiento de Galdós» in *Estudios galdosianos* (Zaragoza, 1953), 13.

aprenderlo, ¡ñales!, que cosas más difíciles se aprenden cuando sobran buena voluntad y entendederas... Animo, Francisco, que a nuevas posiciones, nuevos modos, y el rico no es bien que haga malos papeles. ¡Bueno andaría el mundo, si los hombres de peso, los hombres afincados, los hombres de riñón cubierto, fueran cuento de risa!... ¡Eso, no, no, no!» (23-24; *OC,* V, 942).

He perceives that language is crucial to this undertaking and reflects on the shortcomings of even the best of his past associates in this respect:

«Doña Lupe, me acuerdo bien, decía *ibierno, áccido, Jacometrenzo,* palabras que, según me ha advertido Bailón, no se dicen así... No vaya a creer que la ofendo por eso... Cualquiera equivoca el discurso cuando no ha tenido principios. Yo estuve diciendo *diferiencia* hasta el año ochenta y cinco... Pero para eso está el fijarse, el poner oído a cómo hablan los que saben hablar...» (26; *OC,* V, 943).

In his second conversation with Cruz he is overjoyed when he is able to use a «palabra bonita» — *higiénico* — at an appropriate moment, but thrown into confusion by his error, which he recognizes instantly, in using *óptico* instead of *oculista.* This linguistic awareness is associated with a degree of sensitivity in other respects that emphasizes his human vulnerability, already disclosed in *Torquemada en la hoguera.* He is charmed by Fidela, moved by the first sight of the blind Rafael. He cannot bring himself to get down to business, out of «miedo, verdadero temor de faltar al respeto a la infeliz cuanto hidalga familia» (50; *OC,* V, 950). That night, his conscience, in the form of his adored Valentín (whose cult has ousted all other notions of religion), rebukes him — «fuiste un grandísimo puerco» — and commands him to return the interest. He assents:

«Lo haremos; es menester hacerlo... ¡Devolución..., caballerosidad..., rasgo! Pero ¿cómo se compone uno para el rasgo? ¿Qué se dice? ¿De qué manera y con qué retóricas hay que arrancarse? Diréles, ¡ñales!, que fue una equivocación..., que me distraje..., ¡ea!, que me daba vergüenza de ser rumboso..., la verdad, la verdad por delante..., que no acertaba con el vocablo... por ser la primera vez que...» (64; *OC,* V, 954).

In this reply and in his writhings as he gropes for words to explain his action to Cruz we see how the man's speech derives directly from

149

his innermost nature, how a linguistic deficiency is at bottom a moral deficiency.

The encounter with the Aguila family has aroused in him an unsuspected social ambition, but it has shown him how vast is the gulf to be bridged. By a happy coincidence, it also introduces him to a person uniquely equipped to be his guide, whose bearing, dress and speech fill him with admiration, almost with awe:

> Todo, Señor, todo en don José Ruiz Donoso delataba al caballero de estos tiempos, tal y como debían ser los caballeros, como Torquemada deseaba serlo, desde que esta idea de la caballería se le metió entre ceja y ceja.
> El estilo, o lo que don Francisco llamaba *la explicadera*, le cautivaba aún más que la ropa... (73-74; *OC*, V, 956).

Torquemada eagerly takes Donoso as his model, but the latter's influence is not confined to externals; he becomes Torquemada's mentor in domestic and business affairs, acts as intermediary in matters of delicacy, and is a symbolic catalytic agent in the whole social process. There is a profoundly true irony in this figure of monumental respectability who with his conventional rhetoric preaches a doctrine of decorum that constitutes a ready-made apologia for Torquemada's future social climbing and a justification of the revolutionary shifts of power and prestige taking place in Spanish society.

> «La riqueza impone deberes, señor mío: ser pudiente, y no figurar como tal en el cuadro social, es yerro grave. El rico está obligado a vivir armónicamente con sus posibles, gastándolos con la prudencia debida, y presentándose ante el mundo con esplendor decoroso. La posición, amigo mío, es cosa muy esencial. La sociedad designa los puestos a quienes deben ocuparlos...» (81; *OC*, V, 958-59).

Torquemada's reaction is one of avid and reverential acceptance:

> Lo que le había dicho sobre los deberes del rico y la ley de las posiciones sociales era cosa que se debía oír de rodillas, algo como el sermón de la Montaña, la nueva ley que debía transformar el mundo. El mundo en aquel caso era él, y Donoso el Mesías que había venido a volverlo todo patas arriba, y a fundar nueva sociedad sobre las ruinas de la vieja (86; *OC*, V, 960).

But even more than the doctrine, it is the platitudinous language in which it is enshrined that enchants Torquemada. He has learned new words, words which will help him to find his place in the polite society of which it is his duty to become a member.

> Ya sabía decir *ad hoc* (pronunciaba *azoc*), *partiendo del principio, admitiendo la hipótesis, en la generalidad de los casos;* y, por último, gran conquista era aquello de llamar a todas las cosas el *elemento tal,* el *elemento cual.* Creía él que no había más elementos que el agua y el fuego, y ahora salíamos con que es muy bello decir los *elementos conservadores,* el *elemento militar, eclesiástico,* etc. (87; *OC,* V, 960).

Socially orientated and adequately motivated, as the jargon might have it, Torquemada learns fast. He dresses better, sheds the grosser habits, speaks with greater discretion, so that marriage with one of the Aguila sisters becomes feasible. It is here that Donoso's diplomatic skill is brought into play. One evening, Torquemada, anxious to know which of the sisters he is supposed to be on the point of marrying, can contain himself no longer and erupts in a flood of language — violent, vulgar, sprinkled with his peculiar oaths — belonging to his unreformed past.

> —Y, sobre todo, y esto es lo que más me revienta..., dígame, dígamelo pronto...; ¿con cuál de las dos me caso?... El demonio me lleve, si lo entiendo... ¡Puñales, y la Biblia en pasta!
> —Moderación, mi querido don Francisco. Y parta del principio de que yo no intervengo si...
> —Yo no parto de más más principio ni de más postre, ¡cuerno! si no del saber ahora mismo...
> —¿Con cuál...?
> —Sí, con *cuála!* Sépalo yo con cien mil gruesas de demonios y con la Biblia en pasta...

Donoso assures him that he himself does not yet know, and offers to resign his function as intermediary, unless Torquemada entrusts him with full powers. Torquemada's fury subsides :

> ...Yo creía..., vamos..., parecía natural *(calmándose)* que lo primero fuera saber cuál es la rama en que a uno le cuelgan...; De modo que...
> —Nada puedo decir aún sobre ese particular, cuya importancia soy el primero en reconocer.
> —Apañado estoy... Ya debe comprender que tengo razón...

hasta cierto punto, y que otro cualquiera, *en igualdad de cir-cunstancias...*

Al ver que se ponía otra vez la máscara de finura, Donoso le tuvo por vencido, y le encadenó más, diciéndole:

—Repito, que si mis gestiones no le acomodan, ahí va mi dimisión de ministro plenipotenciario...

—Oh, no, no... (132-133; *OC,* V, 973).

There is a fine contrast here between the speech of Donoso, who maintains —though not without a touch of humour— his pompous, cliché-ridden style throughout, and that of Torquemada which shows a remarkable gradation according to his shifting mood. Torquemada opens with a spontaneous outburst, comparable in style to the angrier moments of *Torquemada en la hoguera,* all refinement forgotten. Then he explicitly rejects Donoso's language, which has been the object of his fervent admiration; he mocks the phrase *partiendo del principio,* so eagerly seized upon when he first met Donoso, and ostentatiously prefers the vulgarism *cuála* to the correct form *cuál.* As he grows calmer, his speech loses its violent expletives but retains its popular flavour with the inelegant, if graphic, reference to the bride-to-be as «la rama en que a uno le cuelgan». Finally, as he descends to the level of moderate, reasonable argument, he once again has recourse to Donoso's phraseology and is tamed by Donoso.

Galdós describes this phraseology as «la máscara de la finura». The image seems apt to the extent that it refers to something consciously acquired which has covered, but not eliminated, the old habits and which may on occasion be shed. But it is not the whole truth. Torquemada learns a new language as part of his striving after a new way of life, a new personality. This can only grow; it cannot be super-imposed. The mask tends to become the face, or the face tends to conform to the mask. The transformation will never be complete, but once under way it cannot be wholly reversed. This incident is an early example of the frequent fluctuations in Torquemada's style of speech which occur throughout the whole period of his social ascent, and are the outward manifestations of a deep-seated duality which is never resolved. Already, the fact that his reversion to vulgar speech is not wholly an involuntary relapse but contains an element of deliberate choice suggests that his new persona is establishing itself as something against which he feels the need to react on occasion. It is beginning to take over.

Once the marriage is assured, the learning goes on apace. He greedily seizes upon each new fine phrase he hears, learns it and experiences childlike satisfaction in demonstrating that he knows how to use it. There is a dreadful lapse when on his wedding day he consumes too much champagne —purely in order not to waste it— and indulges in unconscious drunken mockery of his new language :

«porque yo *abrigo la convicción* de que no debemos *desabrigar* el bolsillo, ¡cuidado! y *parto del principio* de que *haiga* principio sólo los jueves y domingos; porque si, como dice el amigo Donoso, las leyes administrativas han venido a *llenar un vacío,* yo he venido a llenar el vacío de los estómagos de ustedes...» (272-273; *OC,* V, 1013).

However, when he is sober again, his submissiveness to Cruz's as yet temperate demands is accompanied by

un recrudecimiento de palabras finas, toda la adquisición de los últimos días empleada vertiginosamente, cual si temiera que los términos y frases que no tenían un uso inmediato, se le habían de escapar de la memoria... Cierto que la casa no tenía aspecto de casa de señores; faltaban en ella *no pocos elementos;* pero su hermana política, *dechado* de inteligencia y de buen gusto, etc., había venido a *llenar un vacío...* Todo *proyecto que ella abrigase* se lo debía manifestar a él, y se discutiría *ampliamente,* aunque él *previamente,* lo aceptaba... *en principio* (286-287; *OC,* V, 1017).

The novel ends on a hopeful note. Torquemada's first great social conquest —his marriage into the aristocracy (significantly, perhaps, on the «víspera o antevíspera... de la festividad de Santiago, patrón de las Españas»)— is successfully achieved, bringing with it the prospect of companionship of a charming wife, the birth of a son to take the place of Valentín, and even a possible reconciliation with Rafael, who has been utterly hostile to the match. All this is summed up with satisfaction by Don Francisco's latest «frase bonita» : «Toda la familia reunida..., ¡el bello ideal!»

The *tópico,* however worn or false it may appear to the sophisticated, is, at this moment, something new, true and splendid to Torquemada. It is integral to his new way of life. The first chapter of *Torquemada en el purgatorio* makes this point by setting forth a chronology of the stages of the family's re-entry into Madrid society, paralleled by a chronology of phrases newly acquired by Torquemada. By now, scarcely a sentence uttered by him, even in familiar conversation, is without its *tópico*.

A price has to be paid for this enormously accelerated climb up the social ladder. The transition from the old ways to the new is not a smooth one, and Torquemada's old self suffers savage wounds inflicted by Cruz in her ruthless battle against his miserliness. She is resolved not merely to enter polite society again, but to dominate it. Torquemada is now the instrument of her revenge, as previously he had been the instrument of the family's salvation from poverty. She drives him to ever more lavish expenditure. He makes a show of resistance, but knows himself to be defeated from the outset. His language during these disputes remains on the level of the «frase bonita». After one such battle with his sister-in-law

> se quedó allí ejerciendo, con grave detrimento de las alfombras, el derecho del pataleo, y desahogando su coraje con erupción de terminachos.
> —¡Maldita por jamás amén sea tu alma de *ñales!*... Re-Cristo, a este paso, pronto me dejarán en cueros vivos. ¡Biblia, para qué me habré yo dejado traer a este *elemento,* y por qué no rompería yo el ronzal cuando vi que tiraban para traerme!... (105; *OC*, V, 1046).

It is only after Cruz's departure that he reverts to his native tongue, and even in this moment of private rebellion such words as *elemento* show that he can now no longer free himself completely from the formulae of «polite» language.

His intellectual horizons are widened, after a fashion, by his conversations with the young pedant Zárate, who takes the place occupied by Bailón at an earlier stage and from whom he picks up a farrago of scraps of knowledge. He acquires «dicciones muy chuscas, como la *tela de Penélope,* enterándose del por qué tal cosa se decía; *la espada de Damocles* y *las kalendas griegas*». Moreover, he reads the whole of the Quixote,

> y se apropió infinidad de ejemplos y dichos, como *las monteras de Sancho, peor es meneallo, la razón de la sinrazón,* y otros que el indino aplicaba muy bien, con castellana socarronería, en la conversación (174; *OC*, V, 1065).

Galdós is not identifying his hero with Sancho Panza, but he is at least inviting the reader to consider what Torquemada would call the «puntos de contacto». The Cervantine association tends to reinforce the impression of his growing humanity at a moment when his relationship with the Aguilas, even with Rafael, seems to be mellowing. For Torquemada himself, however, literature has nothing to do with life, but is simply a source of useful phrases. Hamlet can be dismissed once it is realized that he is fictitious: «en sabiendo que ese *Jamle* es todo invención de poetas, no me interesa nada» (191; *OC*, V, 1070). [23] All that remains with Torquemada is one more «frase bonita», the inevitable tag «aquello de *ser o no ser*».

Thus equipped, he is ready for the severest test to which his new language and his new public persona are to be put —his speech delivered at the great banquet held in his honour. [24] Here the first impression is one of inner vacuity concealed by surface complexity and confusion. The event is presented simultaneously on four different levels: Torquemada's public words, his private thoughts, the reactions of the audience and the author's comments are interwoven, with the aid of parentheses and footnotes, to achieve a remarkably dramatic effect. The reader follows Torquemada as he alternately flounders and darts through the verbiage he generates; the interest, and indeed the suspense, derive from the struggle with the words as separate, refractory entities. We feel that the completion of each sentence is in itself a triumph; we are content not to look for the sense of the whole. Yet the discourse is, in essence, a simple, coherent statement of Torquemada's *credo,* a fairly crude but by no means falsified version of the commonplaces of bourgeois capitalist doctrine. The bulk of it could be summed up in his own words:

---

[23] Whilst this is in keeping with Torquemada's oft-expressed contempt for poets, it could also be seen as a sign of his eagerness to suppress all suggestion of his wife's infidelity. In this case, it would not be a question of obtuseness, of his blindness to literature being paralleled by a blindness to life, but rather of his perspicacity and wisdom in trusting Fidela without question.

[24] It is a matter for speculation whether this scene derives in any way from Galdós' own experience of a banquet (Oviedo, June 1894?) at about the time when he was working on the later stages of *Torquemada en el purgatorio* (see *Cartas a Galdós,* 266). It is just such a detachable incident as might have had this fortuitous point of origin. Nevertheless, it comes as an absolutely fitting culmination to Torquemada's public career. It seems right and inevitable that his greatest triumph should be a triumph of oratory.

¿Queréis que *os defina mi actitud* moral y religiosa? Pues sabed que mis dogmas son el trabajo, la honradez *(murmullos de aprobación)*, el amor al prójimo, y las buenas costumbres (301; *OC*, V, 1101).

He proclaims himself as the uneducated self-made man who by dint of hard work and thrift has shaped his own destiny. He dismisses the idea of luck as «pamplinas, tontería, *dilemas, antinomias, maquiavelismos*». Every man is responsible for his own fate. The cult of action must take the place of the cult of personality. Industriousness must be matched by sober living. «El amor al prójimo» is interpreted in characteristically parsimonious fashion; there can be no charity for the idle and vicious. The capitalist's self-interest is identified with the interests of the community. There is a nod in the direction of the Almighty and the *venerandas creencias,* followed by a moment of tender contemplation of the blessings of family life, but the object of his greatest enthusiasm is the material progress achieved by science and industry. As one of the pillars of society, Torquemada naturally expresses his respect for authority, but he does not disguise his amused contempt for political parties or his alarm at the mounting public expenditure that results from the proliferation of bureaucracy. Such benefits to mankind as the occasion for this banquet —the building of a railway— are the fruits of private enterprise, not of governmental initiative.

There can be no doubt that these ideas, such as they are, really belong to Torquemada, just as they really belong to his age. They are the common ground which he shares with his audience. In the anxious moments before he delivers his speech, he is quite clear about its substance, but uneasy about its form:

«¡Re-Cristo! —pensó, dándose ánimos—; que no me falten las palabritas que tengo bien estudiadas; que no me equivoque en el término, diciendo peras por manzanas, y saldremos bien. De las ideas responde Francisco Torquemada, y lo que debo pedir a Dios es que no se me atraviese el vocablo.» (281; *OC,* V, 1905).

The speech is a success; the audience bursts into rapturous applause, delighted and surprised at his unexpected near-mastery of the cliché, his quaint imagery (the locomotive is «la ordinaria del mundo entero»), his nimble justification of his errors (Damocles is happily transformed into Aristotle) and the occasional felicitous misapplication of a «palabra bonita» *(holocausto* for the banquet). The speaker is so overwhelmed by the reception that he suspects for a moment that he is being mocked :

> Pero no, no se burlaban, porque en efecto, había hablado *con sentido;* él lo conocía y se lo declaraba a sí mismo, *eliminando* la modestia. No se consolaría nunca de que no le hubiera oído el gran Donoso. (307; *OC,* V, 1103).

Yet his awareness of having spoken «*con sentido*» seems to be contradicted later when he and Rafael are talking frankly to each other for the first and last time. Torquemada modestly disclaims all oratorical art and social graces: «Fuera de los negocios, Rafaelito, *convengamos* en que soy un animal.» Rafael points out that he «sabe asimilarse a las formas sociales; se va identificando con la nueva posición» and asks him what he really thinks of his speech and its reception.

> Levantóse Torquemada, y llegándose pausadamente al ciego, le puso la mano en el hombro, y con voz grave, como quien revela un delicadísimo secreto, le dijo :
> —Rafaelito de mi alma, vas a oír la verdad, lo mismísimo que siento y pienso. Mi discurso no fue más que una *serie no interrumpida* de vaciedades, cuatro frases que recogí de los periódicos, alguna que otra expresioncilla que se me pegó en el Senado y otras tantas migajas del buen decir de nuestro amigo Donoso. Con todo ello hice una ensalada... Vamos, si aquello no tenía pies ni cabeza..., y lo fui soltando conforme se me iba ocurriendo. ¡Vaya con el efecto que causaba! Yo tengo para mí que aplaudían al hombre de dinero, no al *hablista* (326; *OC,* V, 1108).

Here Torquemada not only recognizes the objective truth of the matter, but goes beyond it as he humbles himself in an effort to win the esteem of his brother-in-law, who exercises a considerable power of suggestion over him and before whom he now finds it impossible to maintain his new role. Yet even in this moment of apparent plain speaking he cannot completely shed his «refined» language. Galdós italicizes *serie no interrumpida* to draw attention to this fact and to the element of insincerity in this confession. Torquemada has allowed himself to be persuaded into a momentary denial of the enormous satisfaction he derived from his oratorical success. He does not really want to believe, nor is it really true, that it was merely his money that drew the applause. At the banquet, as never before, he attained something approaching identification with distinguished society. This is not an achievement lightly to be cast away, yet he echoes what he supposes to be Rafael's opinion because Rafael's friendship matters more to him. Reconciliation with his brother-in-law will mean that his bitterest enemy has been won over and family unity —his *bello ideal*— consolidated. That same evening, however, Rafael commits suicide. Public prosperity is matched by private calamity.

This is the pattern for *Torquemada y San Pedro,* the last novel of the series. Once again suffering brings Torquemada face to face with the religious issues on which he turned his back after the death of his first son. Already in his banquet speech he has acknowledged that religion has its place:

> Y no creáis que doy de lado, *por decirlo así,* al dogma sagrado de nuestros mayores. No; yo sé dar *al César lo que es del César* y al Altísimo... también lo suyo. Porque a buen católico no me gana nadie... (301; *OC,* V, 1101).

In return, church dignitaries have joined the stream of flatterers calling to congratulate him on the speech. Such transparent humbug sets the seal on his respectability, but has little to do with the spiritual realities. Religion begins to seem relevant to Torquemada in his decline, when his family disintegrates and he is left with an imbecile child and a domineering sister-in-law. He is assailed by Padre Gamborena who is bent upon wresting his soul from Mammon. Once he attempts to meet Torquemada on his own ground, to speak his language, this priest, an amalgam of fervent piety and worldly wisdom, is unable to prevent the financier from approaching the matter of salvation as if he were negotiating a business deal, albeit a specially hard-driven one:

> Pero usted me ha de garantizar que, una vez en su poder mi conciencia toda, se me han de abrir las puertas de la Gloria eterna...
>
> —¿Conque nada menos que garantía? —dijo el clérigo, montando en cólera—. ¿Soy acaso algún corredor, o agente de Bolsa? Yo no necesito garantizar las verdades eternas. Las predico. El pecador que no las crea, carece de base para la enmienda. El negociante que dude de la seguridad de ese Banco en que deposite sus capitales, ya se las entenderá luego con

el demonio... no admito bromas en este terreno, y para que
nos entendamos olvide usted las mañas, los hábitos y hasta
el lenguaje de los negocios (165; OC, V, 1157).

With Torquemada's persistence in these habits and this language we
become aware of the parallel with *Torquemada en la hoguera*. Numer-
ous details link the last novel with the first and suggest that in essence
little has changed, e. g.: the identification of Gamborena with the
beggar to whom the usurer gave his cloak, and of both with St. Peter,
the re-emergence of Rufina, the references to his first wife, and the
revival of the coin image (this time applied to the doorway to heaven
rather than to the stars) as revealing Torquemada's spiritual horizons
(294; OC, V, 1194).

The most obvious instance of reversion, however, is Torquemada's
last appearance in society, when he returns to his old haunts in an
attempt to escape from his ducal palace, which seems to him a prison,
from his sister-in-law, and from the imagined danger of poisoning. He
experiences a momentary sense of release and well-being, as if he were
back in his true element, when he enjoys the hospitality of his old
crony, Matías Vallejo, and his associates. But he no longer belongs
to this society, and he is aware of it:

Por cierto que al comprender la necesidad de pagar verbal-
mente sus agasajos, pensó también, con seguro juicio, que en
tal lugar y ante tales personas debía sostener la dignidad de su
posición y de su nombre, empleando el lenguaje fino que no sin
trabajo aprendiera en la vida política y aristocrática.
—Señores —les dijo, rebuscando en su magín las ideas no-
bles y los conceptos escogidos—, yo agradezco mucho esas
manifestaciones, y tengo una verdadera satisfacción en sen-
tarme en medio de vosotros y en compartir estos manjares
suculentos y *gastronómicos*... Yo no oculto mi origen. Pueblo
fui, y pueblo seré siempre... Para que la nación prospere es
menester que entre las clases no haya antagonismos y que fra-
ternicen *tirios y troyanos*... (207-208; OC, V, 1169).

Reference is made to Cruz's many acts of charity, and in spite of his
enmity towards her, Torquemada feels that he must uphold «no sólo
su dignidad, sino la de toda la familia». His new-found class-con-
sciousness is reinforced by family solidarity and his language reflects
both:

—Gracias, señores, gracias. Yo también bebo a la salud de aquella *noble dama*... —dijo don Francisco, pensando que sus agravios particulares contra ella no debían manifestarse ante una sociedad extraña— ¡Ah! ¡Nos queremos tanto ella y yo...! Le dejo hacer su santa voluntad, porque tiene un talento y una... Cuantas reformas se *implantan* en mi casa-palacio, ella las dispone. Y si alguna disidencia o *discrepancia* surge entre nosotros, yo transijo, y sacrifico mi voluntad *en aras* de la familia. No hay otra mujer que *raye a mayor altura* para gobernar a una servidumbre numerosa. La mía es como los ejércitos de Jerges. ¿Sabéis vostros quién era ese Jerges? Un rey de la Persia, país que está allí por Filipinas... de aquí no me movería, si no me llamaran a otra parte los mil asuntos que tengo que *ventilar*. Esto es un *oasis*... ¿Sabéis lo que es un *oasis?* (209-210; *OC,* V, 1170).

Had Torquemada's «lenguaje fino» been no more than a mask, here, if anywhere, he would have laid it aside, for he is making a gesture of rebellion against his aristocratic environment. But he finds it impossible to shed his new role or the language which accompanies it. His protestations that he is still *pueblo* arise from a consciousness that this is no longer wholly true. He cannot now share the attitudes and interests of those he is talking to; he feels impelled to impress them by his elegant vocabulary, to half-conceal the truth about his family life from them with the aid of his store of clichés, to make a show of learning before them, and even to enlighten them with scraps of his new knowledge.

On the social plane, then, Torquemada has by now undergone a partial but irreversible metamorphosis whose principal outward manifestation is linguistic. On the spiritual plane, which, of course, is not wholly separable from the social, the situation is still unclear. Some critics have maintained that there is no real change in the man:

C'est pure apparence. La transformation est restée tout extérieure et superficielle: elle est sociale et mondaine, rien de plus. Le fond du caractère n'a pas changé, l'âme ne s'est ni affinée ni ennoblie: jusqu'au bout, jusque sur son lit d'agonie, Torquemada demeurera «el tacaño». [25]

Even more categorically:

Torquemada... personaje que encarna la *antítesis* de la criatura religiosa... el avaro a ultranza que no pierde en ningún mo-

---

[25] R. Ricard, *Aspects de Galdós* (Paris, 1963), 75-76.

mento los rasgos de su conformación individual. La vida lo coloca en circunstancias de ascensión social y espiritual, pero él es incapaz de un cambio a fondo y radical. Su naturaleza bastarda y animal no podrá nunca compenetrarse con esquemas de orden superior... Su pasión irreductible define la esencia última de su personalidad y lo sitúa al margen de toda posible transformación moral y religiosa. [26]

If this were true, there would be little interest in the latter part of the novel. Torquemada has taken the measure of polite society, which has accepted him. That this has not required a fundamental regeneration of the man is a criticism of the social order rather than of Torquemada. But it has at least opened up the possibility of further development in him. The question of his spiritual health is kept open by Galdós; we have good grounds for fearing the outcome, but his salvation still seems a possibility until the end.

According to the vicissitudes of his illness, his moods swing between joyful acceptance and fierce impious rejection of the hope of salvation offered by Gamborena. At one instant he is contrite, placing his trust in God and even showing affection for Cruz:

> —No, hija, no duermo —dijo el pobre señor con voz tan desmayada que parecía salir de lo profundo, y sin abrir los ojos—. Es que medito, es que pido a Dios que me lleve a su seno, y me perdone mis pecados. El Señor es muy bueno, ¿verdad?
> —¡Tan bueno, que...!
> La emoción que la noble dama sentía, ahogó su voz. Abrió al fin Torquemada sus ojuelos, y ella y él se contemplaron mudos un instante, confirmando en aquel cambio de miradas su respectivo convencimiento acerca de la bondad infinita (255; *OC,* V, 1183).

In this moment of humility and pathos he speaks a language of the simplest piety.

At another time, when he thinks that he is on the way to recovery, he ebulliently proclaims his faith:

> —¡Que viva Cristo y su Santa Madre! ¡Y yo, miserable de mí, que desconfiaba de la infinita misericordia! Pero ahora no desconfío; que bien clara la veo. Y no me vuelvo atrás, ¡cuidado!

---

[26] G. Correa, *El simbolismo religioso en las novelas de Pérez Galdós* (Madrid, 1962), 135-36.

de nada de lo que concedí y determiné. El Señor me ha ilumi-
nado, y ahora he de seguir una *línea de conducta diametral-
mente opuesta...* (268; *OC*, V, 1186).

Here, the interjection «¡cuidado!» and the pomposities of «concedí y
determiné» and *«línea de conducta...»* mark the return to a more
customary style; his confidence is re-established and calls for a language
befitting the man of affairs.

The improvement in his condition is short-lived; in great pain,
feeling himself to have been deceived, he violently repudiates the
consolation offered by Gamborena:

> — ¿Y qué me dice usted de esto, señor fraile, señor ministro
> del altar o de la *biblia en pasta?*... Esto es un engaño, una
> verdadera estafa, sí, señor... no me callo, no... Me da la gana
> de decirlo: yo soy muy claro... ¡Ay, ay! El alma se me quiere
> arrancar... ¡bribona! Ya sé lo que tú quieres, largarte volando,
> y dejarme aquí hecho un montón de basura. Pues te fastidias,
> que no te suelto... ¡No faltaba más sino que usted, señora
> alma, voluntariosa, hi de tal, pendanga, se fuera de picos pardos
> por esos mundos!... No, no... fastidiarse. Yo mando en mi
> santísimo yo, y todas esas arrogancias de usted, me las paso
> por las narices, so tía... (279-280; *OC*, V, 1190).

The tragic-grotesque effect is heightened by the interplay of a gross,
vulgar language with a still-nimble fancy, as Torquemada struggles to
retain his hold on life. A little later there is a reversion to low cun-
ning and sordid sub-human greed (aptly centred on his defective child)
as he turns his back on the charitable dispositions of his newly-made
will and on the more civilized aspects of the society which has assim-
ilated him:

> —No hay nada de lo tratado, y tiempo de sobra tenemos
> para revocarlo. Todo lo que la ley permita, y algo más que yo
> agencie con mis combinaciones, para Valentín, ese pedazo de
> ángel bárbaro y en estado de salvajismo, bruto, pero sin ma-
> licia. ¡Y que no quiere poco a su padre el borriquito de Dios!
> Ayer me decía: *pa pa ca ja la pa,* que quiere decir: «verás
> qué bien te lo guardo todo». ...el hombrecito mío ha de ser
> todo lo que se quiera, menos pródigo, pues de eso sí que no
> tiene trazas. Será cazador, y no comerá más que legumbres. Ni
> tendrá afición al teatro, ni a la poesía, que es por donde se
> pierden los hombres, y esconderá el dinero en una olla para

que no lo vea ni Dios... ¡Oh, qué hijo tengo, y qué gusto trabajar todavía unos cuantos años, muchos años, para llenarle
bien su hucha! (283-284; *OC,* V, 1191).

His suffering is less acute, hence the violence and coarseness have
gone from his speech, which is now a plain colloquial discourse without
a trace of the «frases bonitas». But Galdós calls this «desatinada pala-
brería» and makes it clear that this is not Torquemada's true self
speaking. Which, indeed, of these varied moods represents the «true»
Torquemada? He still eludes us.

What is clear is that he himself is lost. His personality has gained
in breadth and complexity as he has advanced in society and achieved
an unassailable public position, but he is only beginning to perceive
the possibility of a spiritual dimension to life. In this sphere he has
none of the acumen and capacity for learning and adaptation which
have brought worldly success and some degree of domestic happiness.
He has learned the language of high finance and senate politics, but
he does not understand the language of Gamborena:

> —¿No me salvaré? —preguntó de súbito don Francisco,
> abriendo mucho los ojos.
> —¿Qué entiende usted por salvarse?
> —Vivir. (291; *OC,* V, 1193).

In a situation reminiscent of *Torquemada en la hoguera* he attempts
to apply the language of worldly affairs to his dealings with God. It
is true that it is now *big* business and politics that supply his
vocabulary [27] («no quiero en manera alguna romper mis buenas relaciones con el Señor Dios» [269; *OC,* V, 1187]), not the transactions of
the petty usurer, and that he puts forward very plausible arguments
for seeing his grandiose loan conversion scheme as the carrying-out
of God's will for Spain, but he is still trying to do a deal with God
on his own terms. It is uncertain whether he is ever cured of this
spiritual blindness.

It is no accident that the fate of Torquemada in the next world
should seem to depend on the resolution of a linguistic ambiguity: the
meaning of the word *conversión.*

University of Liverpool.

---

[27] Even to the extent of applying the term *economía* to his own digestive
apparatus: «*Héme aquí* con ganas de comer, y sin poder meter en mi cuerpo
ni un buche de agua, porque lo mismo es tragarlo, que toda la *economía* se
me subleva, y se arma dentro de mí la de Dios es Cristo.» (279; *OC,* V, 1190).

Charity in «Misericordia» *

It is a critical truism to state that if the earliest novels of Galdós can be seen as novels of opposition —the head-long clashes of *La Fontana de Oro,* of *Doña Perfecta,* of *Gloria* and of *La familia de León Roch*— the later works are characterised by the synthesis of opposing views —the coming-together of Fortunata and Jacinta, the vision of Nazarín, the union of Pepet and Victoria. The clash of faiths in *Gloria* is replaced by the all-embracing nature of a figure such as Almudena. But to opposition and synthesis as key structural devices in the novels of Galdós must be added also diversity: the prismatic technique which Galdós employs to suggest the different facets of the problems with which he deals in his novels. As early as *Gloria,* the black-and-white presentation of Catholic Christianity of *Doña Perfecta* is replaced by a set of varying shades of grey. And this method persists throughout the *novelas contemporáneas.* The purpose of this essay is to study the presentation of the theme of charity in the last novel of this series, *Misericordia,* in terms of such gradations and shadings.

* * *

Galdós's most biting criticism is reserved in this novel for don Carlos Moreno Trujillo, a caricatured figure of the slippery businessman who hopes to bribe his way into heaven, and who is convinced that the balancing of the ledger is the crucial responsibility of the individual

---

* Page references are to the first edition of *Misericordia* (Madrid, 1897); these are immediately followed by a second reference to the Aguilar edition of the *Obras completas,* ed. F. C. Sáinz de Robles, vol. V (2nd. ed., Madrid, 1950).

in this life. The details of Trujillo's home life serve to give direction to the ironic comment. His books are all account books «todo muy limpio y ordenadito». In the centre wall of his study is a portrait of his dead wife, doña Pura, «en marco que parecía de oro puro», and next to it hang a «multitud de coronas de trapo con figuradas rosas, violetas y narcisos, y luengas cintas negras con letras de oro.» These are the wreaths —made not from real, living flowers, but from imitations— which accompanied the body of Doña Pura to the cemetery, but which don Carlos has chosen to keep at home, «porque no se estropeasen en la intemperie del camposanto». His fire is never lit, the bronze clock does not go, the calendar is a day behind, and don Carlos shuffles about wearing «la capa de *andar por casa,* bastante más vieja que la que usaba para salir». He has to wear his cape indoors because of the lack of heating, for he professes to believe that heating in the home is «la causa de tanta mortandad» (99-100; *OC,* V, 1904-5). When we see him at home, he has called Benina to him to explain to her that the cause of her mistress's downfall is an inability to balance her private budget: «Sin buen arreglo, no hay riqueza que no venga a parar en la mendicidad... Y el que no hace números, está perdido» (101-102; *OC,* V, 1905). He shows Benina his books in which everything is entered; 5 céntimos for a box of matches, and even the alms he gives. «Si Francisca hubiera hecho balance, no estaría como está» (103; *OC,* V, 1906).

The idea of the Recording Angel, duly entering all the acts of the individual as credit or debit, with the final examination before the awful Judge who will determine whether the account is in balance —when the examinee will be permitted to pass through the gates of Heaven— or whether all credit is exhausted and the account is in the red —in which event Hell will serve as the debtor's prison— is one which evidently appeals to Trujillo. But, be it noted, he approaches this great examination in the same spirit as he approached his dubious business deals on earth:

> Cree que repartiendo limosnas de ochavo, y proporcionándose por poco precio las oraciones de los humildes, podrá engañar al de arriba y estafar la gloria eterna, o colarse en el cielo de contrabando, haciéndose pasar por lo que no es, como introducía el hilo de Escocia declarándolo percal de a real y medio la vara, con marchamos falsos, facturas falsas, certificados de origen falsos también... (95; *OC,* V, 1903).

So says doña Paca. And whilst we must make allowances for her bitterness towards him, it is evident that he has not only insulted her —in her eyes— when she was left a widow, sending her a measly six *duros* «y unos pingajos de Purita, guantes sucios, faldas rotas, y un traje de sociedad, antiquísimo, de cuando se casó la Reina» (93; *OC,* V, 1903), but that in fact he turned his sister-in-law's affliction into pecuniary profit for himself and his wife. Don Carlos and doña Purita had always sponged on doña Francisca and her husband in the latter's life-time, dropping into coffee or sharing a theatre-box at the other's expense, but when doña Paca was left a widow, «se aprovechaban de mis apuros para hacer su negocio», says Paca.

> En vez de ayudarme, tiraban de la cuerda para extrangularme más pronto. Me veían devorada por la usura, y no eran para ofrecerme un préstamo en buenas condiciones. Ellos pudieron salvarme y me dejaron perecer. Y cuando me veía yo obligada a vender mis muebles, ellos me compraban, por un pedazo de pan, la sillería dorada de la sala y los cortinones de seda. (96; *OC,* V, 1903-1904).

Trujillo, then, showed himself to be the reverse of charitable on this occasion, and now he does little more than lecture doña Francisca, by way of Benina, on domestic economy, and gives her an account book and a pencil. Yet he still hopes to sneak into heaven, buying prayers at a discount, so to speak. He is a regular church-goer, respected by the beggars who crowd the doorway of the church of San Sebastián, for he regularly doles out the daily ration of coppers —all duly entered daily, weekly and annually in his ledger— not without «un sermoncillo gangoso, exhortándoles a la paciencia y humildad» (13; *OC,* V, 1879). And —a final touch of irony— as he prepares to scatter his bread upon the waters, he takes the coins one by one, «sobándolas un poquito antes de entregarlas, para que no se le escurriesen dos pegadas» (12; *OC,* V, 1879).

Juliana, doña Paca's daughter-in-law, becomes progressively harder as the novel unfolds. At first doña Paca looks down on her as *ordinaria,* «tan ordinaria, que no empareja ni emparejará nunca conmigo. Sus regalos me ofenden, pero se los agradezco por la buena voluntad» (91-92; *OC,* V, 1902). At this point Juliana appears to be genuinely charitable, offering gifts to Doña Paca with a certain delicacy: Benina reports that:

> La Juliana me dijo que probaremos algo de la *matanza* que le
> ha de mandar su tío el día del santo, y además dos cortes de
> botinas, de las echadas a perder en la zapatería para donde
> ella pespunta (91; *OC*, V. 1902).

But when the unexpected happens and doña Paca comes into money,
Juliana, the epitome of hard-faced common-sense, descends upon her.
«Doña Paca, ...no sea usted tan débil de natural, y déjese guiar por mí,
que no ha de engañarla» (346; *OC*, V, 1977). It is true that in the
financial sense Juliana does not deceive doña Paca, but it is clear that
she will make her life a misery. The flowers which Obdulia has bought
are cast out, as is Francisco Ponte, and preparations are made for a
move to a smaller flat. Paca acquiesces: «Era el eterno predominio de
la voluntad sobre el capricho, y de la razón sobre la insensatez» (347;
OC, V, 1977). Now this is all very well in its way. Doña Paca was
foolish and extravagant, and, without the use of common-sense, would
quickly have found herself once more in financial straits. But common-
sense alone is not enough. When Juliana counsels doña Paca to rid
herself of Benina, because her servant is too old to be of much service,
we lose sympathy with her:

> No piense usted más en la Niña, Doña Paca, ni cuente con
> ella aunque la encontremos, que ya lo voy dudando. Es muy
> buena, pero ya está caduca, mayormente, y no le sirve a usted
> para nada (347-348; *OC*, V, 1977).

And at once we observe that Juliana's advice is by no means disinter-
ested; she wishes to recommend her cousin Hilaria for the post.
Doña Paca at first rebels —«Pero es muy buena la Niña» (348; *OC*, V,
1977) she argues— but her adversary is much the stronger. «¡Ay, si
cuanto dices es la pura razón!» (350; *OC*, V, 1978). But is logic
alone enough? Clearly there is no charity here.

Doña Paca shows herself alive to the lack of charity in the treatment
meted out to her by Trujillo and his wife on the death of her husband:
«No sólo desconocieron siempre la verdadera caridad, sino que ni
por el forro conocían la delicadeza» (97; *OC*, V, 1904). This is true,
but it does not mean that doña Paca herself is necessarily either
delicate or charitable. Her attitude to Juliana is, as we have seen,
extremely disdainful at the outset of the novel, and her final submis-
sion to her daughter-in-law can be viewed as an example of the working

of poetic justice. When Ponte falls ill, doña Paca shows her generous side, although not without some attention to the financial aspects of the matter. As the apparently lifeless body is taken into the house, Benina assures her mistress.

> que aquél no era cadáver, como de su aspecto lastimoso podría colegirse, sino enfermo gravísimo, el propio don Frasquito Ponte Delgado, natural de Algeciras, a quien había encontrado en la calle; y sin meterse en más explicaciones del inaudito suceso, acudió a confortar el atribulado espíritu de doña Paca con la fausta noticia de que llevaba en su bolso nueve duros y pico, suma bastante para atender al compromiso más urgente, y poder respirar durante algunos días.
> —¡Ah, qué peso me quitas de encima de mi alma! —exclamó la señora elevando las manos—. El Señor le bendiga. Ya estamos en situación de hacer una obra de caridad, recogiendo a este desgraciado... ¿Ves? Dios en un solo punto y ocasión nos ampara y nos dice que amparemos. El favor y la obligación vienen aparejados (204-205; *OC,* V, 1935).

This is by no means a calculated generosity, and her subsequent actions underline her lack of common-sense, when she orders her servant to buy for Frasquito «dos botellas de Jerez, pavo en galantina, huevo hilado, y cabeza de jabalí» (236; *OC,* V, 1944). [1] Doña Paca is not herself giving anything up in order to allow this to be done; it is a generous gesture, but one which is at the same time ridiculous, given the financial situation in which the characters find themselves.

Paca's attitude to Frasquito Ponte is clearly contrasted with her attitude to Almudena, when Benina wishes to give shelter also to the blind Arab beggar. She is motivated here by social snobbery, but it is also significant that the change in her becomes evident after she has heard about the inheritance. Once the priest, don Romualdo, has told her the good news, her worries about the absent Nina are forgotten:

> ¡Cuál sería su emoción, cuáles su sorpresa y júbilo, que se borró de su mente la imagen de Benina, como si la ausencia y pérdida de ésta fuese suceso ocurrido muchos años antes! (305; *OC,* V, 1964).

---

[1] Compare the way in which Doña Pura, in *Miau,* foolishly spends the money begged from Carolina Lantigua.

Eventually she hears news of Benina: that she is to be found begging, and in the company of Almudena. She is plunged into doubt. What shall she do? She has just inherited money; her dear Nina, companion of her misery, is a beggar:

> —Bueno —exclamó al fin con súbito arranque. Pues viva Nina y viva con su moro, y con toda la morería de Argel, y véala yo, y vuelva a casa, aunque se traiga al africano metido en la cesta (316; OC, V, 1968).

The impulse again is a generous one, and the reaction is sound. Without Nina, her joy in her new wealth is diminished:

> Doña Paca, la verdad sea dicha, sentía que se le aguaba la felicidad por no poder hacer partícipe de ella a su compañera y sostén en tantos años de penuria. ¡Ah! Si Nina entrara en aquel momento, ¡qué gusto tendría su ama en darle la gran sorpresa, mostrándose primero muy afligida por la falta de cuartos, y enseñándole después el puñado de billetes! ¡Qué cara pondría! ¡Cómo se le alargarían los dientes! ¡Y qué cosas haría con aquel montón de metálico! (322; OC, V, 1969-70).

But the stress here is on the wealth, on the cash. Doña Paca, under the influence of the wealth, goes so far as to admit that Trujillo is right in his insistence on the sacredness of the balance-sheet. Paca still feels the loss of Benina — «no se consolaba doña Paca de la ausencia de Nina» (341; OC, V, 1975) — but she is by now firmly in the grip of Juliana. When Nina at last reappears, doña Paca welcomes her in a half-hearted fashion:

> Yo de buena gana te recibiría otra vez aquí, ...pero no cabemos en casa, y estaremos aquí muy incómodas... Mañana estaremos de mudanza, y se te hará un hueco en la nueva casa (363; OC, V, 1982).

This is putting off the evil hour, and when she hears that Benina will not abandon Almudena, she will not hear of her returning to the flat. Benina points out that

> A casa le traía, sí, señora, como traje a Frasquito Ponte, por caridad... Si hubo misericordia con el otro, ¿por qué no ha de haberla con éste? ¿O es que la caridad es una para el caballero de levita, y otra para el pobre desnudo? (365; OC, V, 1982).

This is indeed true. Doña Paca, strongly supported now by Juliana, is afraid of infection, and, at the end, she concludes that the best solution is to put Almudena into a hospital; the common-sense solution, even though, typically, she stumbles over the correct phrase: «Coloca a ese desdichado en una buena fonda... no ¡qué disparate! en el Hospital» (365; *OC,* V, 1982). Paca has indeed come to think with the Trujillos of this world, and with the Julianas, for that is Juliana's solution also. Paca has charitable instincts, and often reacts at first in a charitable way, but her instincts are contaminated by self-interest and, with the possession of moderate affluence, «reason» comes to dominate.

Obdulia lives in a dream-world throughout the novel, and hence hardly notices the poverty and misery of others. When she day-dreams about the future, she decides that when she is rich she will be charitable:

> Pero crea usted una cosa, y se la digo con el corazón. En medio de todo ese barullo, yo gozaría extremadamente en repartir muchas limosnas; iría yo en busca de los pobres más desamparados, para socorrerles y... En fin, que yo no quiero que haya pobres... ¿Verdad, Frasquito, que no debe haberlos? (163; *OC,* V, 1923).

What is significant here is that Obdulia wants to abolish poverty because she cannot stand the idea of it; she is acting, or planning to act, in her own interest and not in that of the people she is assisting. And when she does come into money, and has the possibility of being charitable in her own house, she does not live up to her promises.

Galdós cannot approve of Obdulia's ostensible desire to practise charity because it is not based on a genuine wish to improve the lot of the recipient. It is for this reason that he rejects the unthinking giving of alms, which not only does no good to the giver, but at the same time debases the recipient. Trujillo, ironically called «aquel santo varón» (13; OC, V, 1879), is a man of rigid routine, in his almsgiving as well as in his religious observances:

> Tal era su previsión que rara vez dejaba de llevar la cantidad necesaria para los pobres de uno y otro costado: como aconteciera el caso inaudito de faltarle una pieza, ya sabía el mendigo que la tenía segura al día siguiente; y si sobraba, se corría el buen señor al oratorio de la calle del Olivar en busca de una mano desdichada en que ponerla (14; *OC,* V, 1880).

Having received the daily ration, the beggars in the porch of San Sebastián begin to gossip about Trujillo: «Otro más cristiano — says one of the women — sin agraviar, no lo hay en Madrid» (15; *OC,* V, 1880). But another answers that «sé que el don Carlos, cuando se le hace mucho lo que nos da, se pone malo por ahorrarse algunos días...» (16; *OC,* V, 1880). Gossip is a means whereby the beggars are able to «engañar su inanición y sus tristes horas, regalándose con la comidilla que nada les cuesta» (15; OC, V, 1880), and it is equally available to rich and poor alike. Such charity benefits the recipient on a purely worldly level, but morally it tends to debase him. The malicious and spiteful la Burlada points out the advantage of having a child or children to loosen the purse-strings of the almsgiver:

> No hay como andar con dos o tres criaturas a cuestas para sacar tajada. Y no miran a la decencia, porque estas holgazanotas, como Demetria, sobre ser unas grandísimas pendonazas, hacen luego del vicio su comercio. Ya ves: cada año se trae una lechigada, y criando a uno, ya tiene en el buche los huesos del año que viene... Esta dice que tiene el marido en *Celiplinas,* y será que desde allá le hace los chiquillos... por carta... ¡Ay, qué mundo! Te digo que sin criaturas no se saca nada: los señores no miran a la *dinidá* de una, sino a si da el pecho o no da el pecho (30-31; *OC,* V, 1884).

Later in the novel she finds a suitable *arreglo,* receiving food every day from the servant of a banker. She has found a way to «*chincharse* en las ricas*» (249; *OC,* V, 1948).

This attitude is fostered by the unthinking giving of alms. A funeral and a wedding party are occasions when the beggars might expect to benefit; but those who are present at the funeral give very little, and the wedding guests are almost assaulted by the beggars, until the *padrino* throws a handful of coins in the middle of the patio to distract them. In the ensuing scramble, all dignity is lost, and the beggars are reduced to the level of animals:

> Al fin los del funeral no repartieron cosa mayor; y si los del bodorrio se corrieron algo más, acudió tanta pobretería de otros cuadrantes, y se armó tal barullo y confusión, que unos cogieron por cinco, y otros se quedaron *in albis.* Al ver salir a la novia, tan emperifollada, y a las señoras y caballeros de su compañía, cayeron sobre ellos como nube de langosta, y al padrino le estrujaron el gabán, y hasta le chafaron el sombrero. Trabajo le costó al buen señor sacudirse la terrible plaga, y no

171

tuvo más remedio que arrojar un puñado de calderilla en medio del patio. Los más ágiles hicieron su agosto; los más torpes gatearon inútilmente. La *Caporala* y Eliseo trataban de poner orden, y cuando los novios y todo el acompañamiento se metieron en los coches, quedó en las inmediaciones de la iglesia la turbamulta mísera, gruñendo y pataleando. Se dispersaba, y otra vez se reunía con remolinos zumbadores. Era como un motín, vencido por su propio cansancio. Los últimos disparos eran: «*Tú cogiste más... me han quitado lo mío... aquí no hay decencia... cuánto pillo...*» (184-185; *OC,* V, 1929).

It is significant that Galdós should describe the beggars as a society within a society, a microcosm with its hierarchies and classes:

Como en toda región del mundo hay clases, sin que se exceptúen de esta division capital las más ínfimas jerarquías, allí no eran todos los pobres lo mismo (18; *OC,* V, 1881).

The leader is Casiana with her «carácter duro, dominante, de un egoísmo elemental» (19; *OC,* V, 1881). Seniority is usually respected:

En las limosnas colectivas y en los repartos de bonos, llevaban preferencia las *antiguas;* y cuando algún parroquiano daba una cantidad cualquiera para que fuese distribuida entre todos, la antigüedad reclamaba el derecho a la repartición, apropiándose la cifra mayor, si la cantidad no era fácilmente divisible en partes iguales. Fuera de esto, existían la preponderancia moral, la autoridad tácita adquirida por el largo dominio, la fuerza invisible de la anterioridad (19; *OC,* V, 1881).

But authority and hierarchy are easily upset by the unthinking giving of alms, just as in the macrocosm of human society the quest for easy wealth will help to overthrow the old social order.

Further, it is ironic that doña Paca, ignorant of the fact that her servant supports her by begging at a church door, counsels her: «Yo que tú, rechazaría la limosna. Mientras tengamos a nuestro don Romualdo, podemos permitirnos un poquito de dignidad» (98; *OC,* V, 1904). But her dignity is supported by Benina's begging: «No hay más don Romualdo que el pordioseo bendito» (184; *OC,* V, 1929). «Don Romualdo», the symbol and not the flesh-and-blood priest, is the equivalent of money which is not earned, whether it be the coppers begged at the church door or the unexpected windfall of the legacy. The legacy may make the way of life of doña Paca more tolerable but, in the long run, it is clearly going to bring her much unhappiness; similarly, the money received by the beggars is evidently essential to their physical survival, but it does them no kind of moral good, and the unthinking throwing of copper coins as practised by the *padrino* at the wedding can serve actively to debase and dehumanise the individual.

This type of unthinking charity may be contrasted with the active philanthropy of doña Guillermina Pacheco, the character from *Fortunata y Jacinta* who does not personally intervene in this novel (for she is said to have died some years before the action takes place), but for whom Benina is at one stage mistaken. At this point in the novel, Benina has many cares: she is looking after Frasquito Ponte and at the same time endeavouring to find Almudena. She helps a ragged old man carrying a child whom she meets on the way to the Puente de Toledo (259; *OC*, V, 1951), and she feeds not only him and his family, but other beggars, including «un lisiado sin piernas» (263; *OC*, V, 1952), who gives her the whereabouts of Almudena. On the following day she goes again to visit Almudena on the outskirts of Madrid and is met by the old man, Silverio, and the legless cripple, as well as by other beggars. The cripple asks,

> en nombre del gremio de pordioseros allí presente, que la señora debía distribuir sus beneficios entre todos sin distinción, pues todos eran igualmente acreedores a los frutos de su inmensa caridad (274; *OC*, V, 1955).

Benina replies that she is as poor as they, but her explanation is received with incredulity, and Silverio claims

> que bien a la vista estaba que la señora no era lo que parecía, sino una *dama disfrazada,* que, con trazas y pingajos de *mendiga de punto,* se iba por aquellos sitios para *desaminar* la verdadera pobreza y remediarla. Tocante a esto del disfraz no había duda, porque ellos la conocían de años atrás. ¡Ah!, y cuando vino, *la otra vez,* la *señora disfrazada,* a todos les había socorrido igualmente (274; *OC*, V, 1955).

Benina disclaims all connections with the previous distributor of charity, the late doña Guillermina Pacheco, «corazón hermoso, espíritu grande, la cual andaba por el mundo repartiendo los dones de la caridad, y vestía humilde traje, sin faltar a la decencia, revelando en su modestia soberana la clase a que pertenecía» (275; *OC,* V, 1955). Benina, on the other hand, was a poor woman, as poor as her listeners, one who lived on the charity of others.

> Habíala hecho Dios generosa, eso sí; y si algo poseía, y encontraba personas más necesitadas que ella, le faltaba tiempo para desprenderse de todo... y tan contenta (276; *OC,* V, 1956).

But her explanations are received with incredulity, and ragged children surround her, asking for bread. She takes pity on them, buys bread and distributes it between them. But her charitable act brings the same consequences as the scattering of coins at the wedding:

> La operación se dificultó en extremo, porque todos se abalanzaban a ella con furia, cada uno quería recibir su parte antes que los demás, y alguien intentó apandar dos raciones. Diríase que se duplicaban las manos en el momento de mayor barullo, o que salían otras de debajo de la tierra. Sofocada, la buena mujer tuvo que comprar más libretas, porque dos o tres viejas a quienes no tocó nada, ponían el grito en el cielo, y alborotaban el barrio con sus discordes y lastimeros chillidos (277; *OC,* V, 1956).

Benina is then recognised by Basilisa, a beggar whom she had seen previously in the company of *la Burlada,* and is taken by her to see a family reduced to appalling circumstances. Deeply moved, she is however unable to help them financially, and although Basilisa and the mother of the family express their gratitude, «bien se conocía que algún reconcomio se les quedaba dentro del cuerpo por no haber recibido el socorro que esperaban» (279; *OC,* V, 1957). Two old women then compare her unfavourably with doña Guillermina; by comparison, she is a *tía ordinaria.* And as she goes out into the street, she is surrounded by a swarm of beggars who ask for money or for bread. She is forced to part with another peseta before she can leave and seek Almudena. When she finds him, they sit down to eat as on the previous day, but are immediately surrounded by «gitanillos maleantes, alguno que otro lisiado de mala estampa, y dos o tres viejas desarrapadas y furibundas» (280; *OC,* V, 1957), who shout insults and finally hurl stones at the pair, calling Benina «una ladrona que se fingía beata para robar mejor... una lame-cirios y chupa-lámparas...» (281; *OC,* V, 1957).

This episode must clearly be related to the charitable works of doña Guillermina which play an important part in *Fortunata y Jacinta,* and the episode has been studied in that sense by Professor Brooks.[2] But its importance in *Misericordia* is to suggest that indiscriminate charity, even when given out of a sense of pity and with no intention of self-aggrandisement, can still produce ill effects on the recipients. The squabbling children, the malicious old women and the final assault on Benina and Almudena signify the brutalising effect of poverty and the irrelevance of indiscriminate alms-giving. The comparison with doña Guillermina serves, in this novel, to suggest that such charity is bound to some extent to be affected, not genuine, just as the «humilde traje» of the *dama disfrazada* failed to hide her superiority of birth, «revelando en su modestia soberana la clase a que pertenecía». Benina calls this «vestirse de máscara» (275-276; *OC,* V, 1955-56). Benina is not, of course, herself «vestida de máscara» in this episode, but the beggars have been conditioned to expect a certain type of condescending alms-giving, and can not conceive that a woman of their own class, and as poor as they, can be giving all that she has. They take what she has to offer, with little sense of genuine gratitude, and are infuriated to find that her funds are very limited, disregarding the generous impulse which moves her heart.

A solution which is urged by various characters in the novel for the predicament in which Almudena finds himself is that whose name is echoed in the title of the novel, La Misericordia, or the work-house. This is the «rational» solution; the solution of society, based on money and balance-sheets, where an equivalent amount of charity is offered to those who can produce in return an equivalent amount of work. An institution is urged on Benina as a possible solution by the priest who is a friend of don Romualdo (and who gives Almudena charity in return for Arabic conversation lessons) (291; *OC,* V, 1960), and it is also urged by the *guarda-agujas* (284; *OC,* V, 1958), by doña Paca (365; OC, V, 1982) and by Juliana (367; *OC,* V, 1983). *El Comadreja* suggests earlier in the novel that Frasquito Ponte be taken to the hospital when he has fallen ill of a fit (200; *OC,* V, 1934). Don Romualdo

---

[2] J. L. Brooks, «The Character of Doña Guillermina Pacheco in Galdós's Novel, *Fortunata y Jacinta*», BHS, XXXVIII (1961), 86-94. It is difficult to agree with Gustavo Correa, *El simbolismo religioso en las novelas de Pérez Galdós* (Madrid, 1962), 207, that the beggars of las Cambroneras genuinely appreciate the saintliness of Benina in this episode.

has offered to put the two grand-children of Silverio into an Asilo, and for this he is called «un alma caritativa» (260; *OC,* V, 1951). But it is ironic that the poor cannot expect to gain entry to such an establishment without «recomendaciones y tarjetas de personajes» (284; *OC,* V, 1958). Don Romualdo is «patrono y mayordomo mayor» of La Misericordia itself,

> y como a él se dirigían las solicitudes de ingreso, no daba un paso por la calle sin que le acometieran mendigos importunos, y se veía continuamente asediado de recomendaciones y tarjetazos pidiendo la admisión (317-318; *OC,* V, 1968).

Spain is fast becoming the work-house of Europe, he adds, so great is the number of those in need.

La Misericordia as an institution clearly has its good points, and it is not wholly to be despised. But it is nevertheless not the solution which Galdós favours. It is necessary to cast one's mind back to the previous works in which Galdós had explored the possibility of the institution as one answer to the ills of society and as an outlet for charitable instincts: the *asilo* of *Angel Guerra,* the City of God (or Isle of Barataria) of *Halma.* In *Halma* the institution is finally rejected in favour of the family unit: charity must literally begin at home. It is therefore not surprising that in *Misericordia* the institution of that name is not the final solution; it is the solution of society, a rational solution, not to be despised, but not that which Galdós wishes to put forward for the ills from which an emerging nineteenth-century capitalist society is suffering.

* * *

Almudena, on his first appearance in the novel, makes an obvious contrast with the figure of Trujillo. Whilst the latter lectures Benina, for the benefit of her mistress, and gives her an account-book and pencil, Almudena quickly comes to her aid. As they sit at the feet of the statue of Mendizábal — significantly enough — Benina thinks of all the money which is available in the world: she is in need of a *duro,* the *átomo inmenso;* if a *duro* were to change hands, then the financial balance of society would hardly be imperilled. But it is the mendicant Arab who comes to her aid, and not one of the passers-by, the «gentes presurosas o indolentes» (41; *OC,* V, 1887). He offers to pawn his clothes, which will raise half the required sum, and takes another peseta from the clothes of *la Petra* as she lies in a drunken stupor in his lodging. To this he adds «una monedita de dos reales, nueva y reluciente», and the desired sum is almost realised. « ¡Ay, hijo, qué bueno eres! » cries Benina (47-48; *OC*, V, 1889). Another aspect of Almudena's charity is also apparent in this scene for he gives shelter and sympathy to *la Petra*. She is a girl of 22, but sodden with drink, befriended by the Moor out of the generosity of his heart:

> Almudena la trataba, con buen fin, desde que se quedó huér-fana, y al verla tan arrastrada, dábale de tres cosas un poco: consejos, limosna y algún palo (120; *OC*, V, 1911).

But she cannot control her desire for drink, and Almudena laments: «No poder mí con ella. *B'rracha* siempre. Es un dolor... un dolor. Yo estar ella amigo por lástima...» (121; *OC*, V, 1911). His pity is a re-lative matter: when *la Petra* awakens from her drunken stupor, he intends to beat her with his staff, «como infalible remedio de la embriaguez», but on this occasion pity overcomes him, and he mutters to himself: «Pegar ti otro día» (50; *OC*, V, 1890).

La Petra herself, despite her alcoholism, is not without generous impulses. If she had been sober when Almudena was searching for the coin, she would have offered it willingly herself. When she comes to her senses and finds the coin gone, her reactions confirm Almude-na's assertion: «Pero di, gorrón, me has quitado la peseta. No me im-porta. *Pa* ti era» (50; *OC*, V, 1890). Another female who turns out to have unexpected charitable impulses is *La Bernarda*, the keeper of the lodging-house, who once lent doña Paca eight *duros*. And even though, as doña Paca recalls, «venía todos los días a reclamar la deu-da y nos freía la sangre», Benina is convinced that «es buena mujer. No nos hubiera reclamado *por justicia*, aunque nos amenazaba. Otras son peores» (90; *OC*, V, 1902). *El Comadreja* shows himself to be «*caritativo él, buen cristiano él*» when he takes in Frasquito Ponte after the latter has fallen ill in a fit in the street (196; *OC*, V, 1933). And *La Pitusa*, Teresa Cornejo the brothel-keeper, is a woman who, for all that she appears superficially unattractive, «de todas estas exterioridades desapacibles se desprendía un cierto airecillo de afabilidad, un moral atractivo» (193; *OC*, V, 1932); she agrees to take in Ponte, and, on being reminded of a good turn done to her by Benina on a previous occasion, willingly lends her jewels which Benina can pawn in order to raise the vast sum of ten *duros.* She gives the jewelry to her without requiring more than a «palabra formal» (199; *OC,* V, 1934). The *lecheros,* «gente buena y humilde», also show practical charity when they allow Pulido, one of the blind beggars, to lodge in their stable (214; *OC,* V, 1938).

But the clearest case of active charity among the minor characters in the novel is that provided by the crossing-keeper and his wife. When Almudena and Benina have been stoned by the angry beggars in las Cambroneras,

> un guarda-agujas, que vivía en una caseta próxima al lugar del siniestro, hombre reposado y pío que, demostrando tener en poco a las víctimas del atentado, las acogió como buen cristiano en su vivienda humilde, compadecido de su desgracia. A poco llegó la guardesa, que también era compasiva, y lo primero que hicieron fue dar agua a Benina para que le lavase la herida a su compañero, y de añadidura sacaron vinagre, y trapos para hacer vendas (282; *OC,* V, 1957).

The crossing-keeper and his wife act as true Samaritans. They bind up the wounds of Almudena, and offer the pair sardines and *churros,* whilst Benina offers to share the rest of their unfinished meal: «Hubo por una y otra parte ofrecimientos, finuras y delicadezas, y cada cual, al fin, se quedó con lo suyo» (283; *OC,* V, 1958). Benina, seeing their evident generosity, decides to ask them if Almudena can remain with them for a few days. The crossing-keeper and his wife accept: «después de corta vacilación», and advise the pair that they should each enter an *asilo.* Benina gives them what money she has, and they promise to look after Almudena as though he were their own child. Although they are paid for this particular service, the first actions of the *guarda-agujas* and his wife are motivated by pure compassion, and as examples of generosity, they vie with Benina herself, the character in the novel who demonstrates most clearly that active, selfless charity which was Galdós's ideal.

* * *

It might be thought, from the enumeration of the examples given above, that the split between those of whom Galdós approves and those of whom he disapproves is made along the lines of class cleavage. But whilst it is true that all the characters of whom he most approves are from the lower class—and many of them live on the edge of extreme poverty—the activities of doña Guillermina are not to be despised, nor are the impulses, advice and actions of the priests treated with disdain. Doña Paca has a generous instinct, even though her wilful foolishness prevents her from doing any positive good. And by no means all the poor characters are generous and open-hearted: poverty breeds violence and suspicion, as well as offering the opportunity for actions so generous as to be almost saint-like.

The novel, then, is not clearly split on the lines suggested by the opening description of the church of San Sebastián, a church which stands between the «barrios bajos» and the «señorío mercantil de la Plaza del Angel». The novel concerns itself largely with the lowest of the «barrios bajos», with people living a marginal existence, where a *duro* is a fortune, as Casalduero points out, and not with the world of high finance —as in the later novels of the Torquemada series— where money is so easily come by as almost to lose its significance. Galdós has often shown one of the connections between these two worlds, the fall from the high or moderate estate, and the equivalent rise from rags to riches: «Ejemplos sin número de estas caídas nos ofrecen las poblaciones grandes, más que ninguna ésta de Madrid, en que apenas existen hábitos de orden» (60; *OC,* V, 1893). Doña Francisca Juárez de Zapata, the *rondeña,* has fallen from her moderate middle-class state (as people in Ronda are said to be attracted by the great gulfs which surround them) and has become doña Paca. But at the end of the novel she has risen again to comparative affluence. A better representative of the middle class is Trujillo, and, as we have seen, there is an implied contrast early in the novel between the moderate ease and soulless routine of Trujillo's life, and the extreme poverty and genuine compassion which characterise Almudena.

Another look at the opening description of the church of San Sebastián suggests that the life of Madrid is not going to be treated in this novel with the desperate seriousness of a Zola:

> En ninguna parte como aquí advertiréis el encanto, la simpatía, el *ángel,* dicho sea en andaluz, que despiden de sí, como tenue fragancia, las cosas vulgares, o algunas de las infinitas cosas vulgares que hay en el mundo. Feo y pedestre como un pliego de aleluyas o como los romances de ciego, el edificio bifronte, con su torre *barbiana,* el cupulín de la capilla de la Novena, los irregulares techos y cortados muros, con su afei-

te barato de ocre, sus patios floridos, sus hierros mohosos en la calle y en el alto campanario, ofrece un conjunto gracioso, picante, *majo,* por decirlo de una vez. Es un rinconcito de Madrid que debemos conservar cariñosamente, como anticuarios coleccionistas, porque la caricatura monumental también es un arte. Admiremos en este San Sebastián, heredado de los tiempos viejos, la estampa ridícula y tosca, y guardémoslo como un lindo mamarracho (6; *OC,* V, 1877).

It has the charm of popular art, and the passage reminds the reader that Galdós precedes Unamuno and Azorín in their descriptions of the charm of the everyday, and that he anticipates Baroja's «extraña poesía de las cosas vulgares». [3]

The world in which most of the characters live is harsh enough — like the subjects of Darwin's observations they experience the «rudo luchar por la pícara existencia» (8; *OC,* V, 1878)— and it is not surprising that they should seek some compensation, or endeavour to escape from their marginal existence. *La Petra* seeks an escape in the traditional way of the naturalists' characters; she escapes by way of the bottle, drinking herself into merciful oblivion. But not all seek the dram-shop. The *lecheros* pin their faith on the magic number of the lottery, and are ironically compared to their *pollinas* and *burras,* as they enlist the aid of the blind Pulido so that they may see the more clearly:

Tuvo Benina la suerte de encontrar a toda la familia reunida, ya de regreso las pollinas de su excursión matinal. Mientras éstas devoraban el pienso de salvado, los racionales se entretenían en hacer cálculos de probabilidades, y en aquilatar las razones en que se podía fundar la certidumbre de que saliese premiado al día siguiente el 5.005, del cual poseían un décimo. Pulido, examinando el caso con su poderosa vista interior, que por la ceguera de los ojos corporales prodigiosamente se le aumentaba, remachó en convencimiento de los burreros, y en tono profético les dijo que tan cierto era que saldría premiado el 5.005, como que hay Dios en el Cielo y Diablo en los Infiernos (214-215; *OC,* V, 1938). [4]

---

[3] Compare Joaquín Casalduero, «Significado y forma de *Misericordia*», reprinted in *Vida y obra de Galdós: 1843-1920* (Madrid, 1951), 249-250.

[4] Almudena «sees» the truth about Benina: *«¡B'nina!... Tú vinir cielo»* (265; V, 1952). Galdós uses the blind in other novels also to indicate an ability to «see» or perceive the truth; compare the blind girl at the end of *Angel Guerra.* Here the same device is used for a comic purpose.

La Diega also plays the lottery, and, buying a *décimo,* exclaims: «Seremos ricas, ricachonas en *efetivo...* Yo, si me la saco, San Antonio me oiga, volveré a establecerme en la calle de la Sierpe» (123; *OC,* V, 1911). Of such stuff dreams are made, and the fortunes of football-pools promoters.

Almudena, the blind beggar, has several avenues of escape. His religious rites and his prayers, ambiguously reported as being Mohammedan and Jewish, are «su consuelo, su placer más vivo» (49; *OC,* V, 1890). [5] His physical blindness is not quite absolute, and like other blind characters in the novels of Galdós he believes he can «see» the truth:

> Explicó que distinguía las masas de obscuridad en medio de la luz: esto por lo tocante a las cosas del mundo acá. Pero en lo de los mundos misteriosos que se extienden encima y debajo, delante y detrás, fuera y dentro del nuestro, sus ojos veían claro, cuando veían, *mismo como vosotros ver migo* (126-127; *OC,* V, 1912).

Almudena's beliefs are by no means rational: he assures Benina that all the wealth of Trujillo could be his, if only he had the faculty of sight, and he offers to explain his secrets to Benina. Benina is superstitious, and moreover «la miseria despertaba en ella el respeto de las cosas inverosímiles y maravillosas, y aunque no había visto ningún milagro, esperaba verlo el mejor día». Almudena explains how to ask for one's desires from *Samdai,* «el Rey de *baixo terra*» (111-112; *OC,* V, 1908). Benina, on hearing the details of the necessary rites, is only half convinced of its feasibility, but «si a pie juntillas no le creía, se dejaba ganar y seducir de la ingenua poesía del relato, pensando que si aquello no era verdad, debía serlo» (117; *OC,* V, 1910). The world is full of mysteries. When Almudena goes on to describe an experience to Benina, la Petra and la Diega,

> Oían esto las tres mujeres embobadas, mudas, fijos los ojos en la cara del ciego, entreabiertas las bocas. Al comienzo de la relación, no se hallaban dispuestas a creer, y acabaron

---

[5] On the significance of Almudena as a synthesis of religious faiths, see Casalduero, 252; Robert Ricard, «Sur le personnage d'Almudena dans *Misericordia*», *BH,* LXI (1959), 12-15; Vernon A. Chamberlin, «The Significance of the Name Almudena in Galdós's *Misericordia*», *HBalt,* CLVII (1964), 491-496; and Denah Lida, «De Almudena y su lenguaje», *NRFH,* XV (1961), 297-308.

13

creyendo, por estímulo de sus almas, ávidas de cosas gratas
y placenteras, como compensación de la miseria bochornosa
en que vivían (129-130; *OC,* V, 1913).

The «poetry» of Almudena's tale takes them out of their narrow
surroundings. The King tells Almudena that he would not bestow
upon him both riches and a wife; that he would have to choose:

que optase entre las pedrerías de gran valor que delante
miraba, y con las cuales gozaría de una fortuna superior a la
de todos los soberanos de la tierra, y una mujer buena, bella
y laboriosa, joya sin duda tan rara que no se podía encontrar
sino revolviendo toda la tierra (130; *OC,* V, 1913).

It is out of these simple desires for wealth and affection that Almudena's greatest compensation and escape rises: his love for Benina.
At first the vague desire for companionship and affection had been
centred on la Nicolasa, whom he had met in Valencia and with
whom he had lived for three years. But during the course of the
novel his desire becomes centred on Benina. He tells how he had
unavailingly followed a mysterious figure:

Mas él caminaba, más adelante iba la mujer, sin poder alcan-
zarla nunca. Andando el tiempo, creyó que la fugitiva era
Nicolasa, que con él vivió tres años en vida errante. Pero
no era; pronto vio que no era. La suya delante, siempre delante, entapujadita y sin dejarse ver la cara... Claro, que él
veía la figura con los ojos del alma... (224; *OC,* V, 1941).

It is, then, with «los ojos del alma» that he sees Benina as the object
of his search, so reminiscent of the unavailing endeavour of Romantic
heroes to capture the elusive, mysterious figures which ever beckon
them on. Almudena is jealous of Ponte, as jealous as a young and
sprightly lover might be of a pretty, fresh girl. His love could appear
to be ridiculous, but never does so, despite the implied comparison
to and contrast with the Romantic hero, because his love is sincere
and genuine. There are reminiscences here of the burning love of
«la insignificante» Abelarda in *Miau,* and of the love of the blind
Pablo for the heroine of *Marianela.* Almudena never finds his earthly
treasure, but he does find spiritual riches in the person of Benina,
and at the end of the novel he has a further compensation, for he
now speaks of going on a pilgrimage to Jerusalem, an idea which has
supplanted his earlier desire to return to his native Sus. Almudena

is, as we have seen, a genuinely charitable man, and the misery in which he lives and in particular the physical darkness which his blindness entails, whilst encouraging him to indulge in escapist fantasies, does not prevent him from showing himself to be a shining example of the ability of the individual to throw off the constricting influences of environment and to escape out of physical, financial and social frustration to a higher plane of true charity and compassion.

Obdulia, the daughter of doña Paca, suffers from epileptic fits, and has a semi-ridiculous love affair with the son of an undertaker. She has a great facility for day-dreaming, and she indulges in long bouts of wishful thinking in the company of Frasquito Ponte Delgado, the decayed gentleman, the dandy gone to seed, whose greatest experience was enshrined in a visit to Paris at the time of the Exhibition. Like Obdulia, Frasquito has a great ability to escape from his surroundings, and Obdulia adores hearing him speak of vanished and imagined delights: «Con las cosas bonitas que cuenta me entretiene», she says, «y casi no me acuerdo de que no hay en casa más que dos onzas de chocolate, media docena de dátiles, y algunos mendrugos de pan». They exchange polite courtesies until Benina breaks in on their conversation with brutal directness: «¿Tienes carbón? —preguntó Benina bruscamente, como quien arroja una piedra en un macizo de flores» (139-131; OC, V, 1916-1917). But they are able to shrug off such trivia: «En tanto el lánguido Frasquito y la esmirriada Obdulia platicaban gozosos de cosas gratas, harto distantes de la triste realidad» (142; OC, V, 1917). Frasquito is «aniñado», a useless individual, who lives in the past, is of necessity antiquated in dress, but also in thoughts and expressions. [6] His language is a series of outdated clichés. As a young man he acted in private theatricals, and it was the great care which he bestowed upon his person which cost him his first job. Whilst one may laugh at the lengths to which Ponte now has to go in order to keep up appearances, we realise that it is his pride which keeps him going: «Antes se muriera de hambre Frasquito, que hacer cosa alguna sin dignidad» (148-149; OC, V, 1919).

In their Romantically-inspired day-dreams, Obdulia and Ponte conjure up a never-never world for themselves. Obdulia cries:

---

[6] Michael Nimetz, *Humor in Galdós. A Study of the «Novelas contemporáneas»* (New Haven and London, 1968), 40-42, 64-65, 76, in an acute characterisation, says of Ponte that «like his beloved Gaul, he is tripartite: señorito, romántico, and cursi».

> Yo sueño con tener un magnífico jardín y una estufa... ¡Ay!
> esas estufas con plantas tropicales y flores rarísimas, quisiera
> verlas yo. Me las figuro; las estoy viendo..., me muero de
> pena por no poder poseerlas (161-162; *OC*, V, 1922-1923).

And in their longing for such a life, «soñando, soñando, y viendo
cosas que no existen, es decir, que existen en otra parte» (162; *OC*, V,
1923), she asks herself whether some day she will not indeed have
a magnificent, elegant house, with its drawing-room and conservatory.
This type of day-dream is identical in kind with the wishful-thinking
of Benina as she watches the passers-by and wonders who will give
her the money she so desperately needs. As we have seen, Obdulia's
dreams include the possibility of being charitable to the poor, but her
motives are by no means pure, for she wishes to abolish poverty in
order to save herself from the disagreeable spectacle of its existence.
We note, too, that she expresses a longing to go more often to the
theatre.

Ponte's day-dreams are centred round the possibility once again of
riding on horseback, as he had done in his youth. But as they luxu-
riate in such pleasant fantasies, «hízoles caer de bruces sobre la realidad la brusca entrada de Benina» (169; *OC*, V, 1925). Ponte realises
that he must go to his work —for it is not beneath his dignity to work
in his present indigence— and Obdulia is left alone:

> mostrándose pesarosa de la soledad en que hasta el próximo día
> quedaba en sus palacios, habitados por sombras de chambe-
> lanes y otros guapísimos palaciegos. Que éstos, ante los ojos
> de los demás mortales, tomaran forma de gatos mayadores, a
> ella no le importaba. En su soledad, se recrearía discurriendo
> muy a sus anchas por la estufa, admirando las galanas flores
> tropicales, y aspirando sus embriagadoras fragancias (169-170;
> *OC*, V, 1925).

The wheel of fortune turns and, unexpectedly, the rosy imaginings
are able to be realised. Don Romualdo appears in the unlikely
disguise of fairy god-mother before the astonished eyes of Ponte,
Obdulia and doña Paca. After he has learnt the news of his inheritance, Ponte walks about the city with head held high, «haciendo
risueños cálculos». Then reality intrudes as he suddenly realises he
is hungry: «no se vive sólo de ilusiones» (237; *OC*, V, 1971). His first
care is for his appearance, but he retains generous impulses. When

asked on what he would spend the first fruits of his inheritance, he replies: «Le compraré unas botas a Benina cuando parezca, si parece, y un traje nuevo» (338; *OC*, V, 1974). Again, however, his generosity, although genuine, is concerned with providing Benina with suitable clothes, with externals. He does not spend his money wisely and, although repeatedly asked by doña Paca to bring her the account-book which she has improbably sworn to use, he always forgets the errand. Eventually we see him on horseback again, ridiculous in a way he never was when poor. Like a Calderonian figure, he falls from his horse: a second fall, and this time a literal one, paralleling the previous fall of doña Paca, *la rondeña,* from moderate estate. His fall disturbs his mental balance and he becomes the «innocent» and is thus able to give a «true» judgment of Nina. Already at an earlier stage, he has flattered Benina with his sentimental, out-of-date expressions:

> —Señora Nina..., yo aseguro, bajo mi palabra de honor, que es usted un ángel; yo *me inclino a creer* que en el cuerpo de usted se ha encarnado un ser benéfico y misterioso, un ser que es *mera* personificación de la Providencia, según la entendían y entienden los pueblos antiguos y modernos (160; *OC,* V, 1922).

But although he recognises at this point the worth of Nina, his views are veiled and clouded by his superficial vanities of expression and pose. At the end of the novel, we see him suffering the after-effects of a stroke and in a state bordering on madness. But what he says is indeed the truth as far as it concerns Benina: «...La Nina no es de este mundo..., la Nina pertenece al cielo...» (389; *OC,* V, 1989). Once again the child-like «innocent» is used by Galdós to present a «true» picture of reality.

Ponte's riches only serve to make him ridiculous, bring about a physical fall and, finally, lead to his death; the fantasies of Obdulia turn out to be no more productive of happiness. She does indeed fill the house with flowers, as she had long wished to do, but fantasy, in the shape of Obdulia, comes up against reason, in the person of Juliana. The flowers —symbol of her dreams— are banished. When we hear Juliana counselling doña Paca: «Múdese a un cuarto baratito, y viva como una pensionista de circunstancias, sin echar humos ni ponerse a farolear» (347; *OC,* V, 1977), we can sympathise with the advice to some extent. Common-sense spells the death-knell of the day-dreams of Obdulia. Her escape, like that of Ponte, is unproductive and in effect dangerous. The human being must come to terms with reality, and cannot live a life of rose-coloured dreams.

When we first see doña Paca, she appears to be permanently disillusioned by her social and financial fall:

> Tras un día malo, viene otro peor. Pasan años aguardando el remedio, y no hay ilusión que no se me convierta en desengaño. Me canso de sufrir, me canso también de esperar. Mi esperanza es traidora, y como me engaña siempre, ya no quiero esperar cosas buenas, y las espero malas para que vengan... siquiera regulares (56; *OC*, V, 1892).

But this is in reality a superficial pose, and we are reminded of the self-deception practised by Villaamil in *Miau*. Doña Paca is quick to catch at straws; she has plenty of bounce. She claims dignity and decorum —attributes which in her view are lacking in Benina and in Juliana— but in her turn lacks common-sense. Her fall from affluence is the result of her own temperament. Attracted by the abyss, as a good daughter of Ronda «instintivamente se despeñaba» (60-61; *OC*, V, 1893). Like Mr. Micawber, she now sits waiting for something to turn up:

> Dime, Nina, entre tantas cosas raras, incomprensibles, que hay en el mundo, ¿no habría un medio, una forma..., no sé cómo decirlo, un sortilegio por el cual nosotras pudiéramos pasar de la escasez a la abundancia...? (180; *OC*, V, 1928).

The reference to the «sortilegio» suggests to Benina the spells of Almudena, and this wishful-thinking is as ridiculous as the magic of the Moor. The miracle does indeed happen, however, although not in the way in which doña Paca imagines. Doña Paca lives an illogical life of fantasy in the midst of her dismal surroundings: «Doña Paca no admitía razonamientos, por juiciosos que fuesen. Cuanto más lógicas y justas eran las aclaraciones del contrario, más se enfurruñaba ella» (174; *OC*, V, 1926). It is for this reason that the cold-hearted reception of Benina by Trujillo particularly infuriates her, and it is also for this reason that she dreams so vividly. She dreams that two of her fellow *rondeños* come to visit her and inform her that don Pedro José García de los Antrines has left his property to Ponte and herself, as his only surviving relatives: «...todo ha sido obra de un sueño; pero tan a lo vivo que aún me parece que les estoy mirando» (209; *OC,* V, 1936). In rational terms, she recognises that this was indeed a dream, but her fantasy dominates her reason: «Otros puede que vengan con la misma música el mejor día» (246; *OC,* V, 1947). At this point in the narrative, Benina disappears, having been forced to invent a priest, don Romualdo, as the source of the money which she has collected by begging, for she knows that doña Paca would not tolerate the idea that she was living on charity. On her return, she is astonished to hear that don Romualdo has been to visit doña Paca, and not only has her invented figure acquired life, but the dream of doña Paca has become reality: the son of Antrines has died, and doña Paca and Ponte have indeed inherited a part of his fortune, sufficient to keep them in comfort for the rest of their lives. «¿Estaremos soñando?» asks Ponte (319; *OC,* V, 1969). Doña Paca and Ponte hear the details of the will «con la religiosa atención que fácilmente se supone»; doña Paca «creía soñar» (311; *OC,* V, 1966). After hearing details of the inheritance, doña Paca not unnaturally asks for news of Benina, who has disappeared again, and is astonished to hear from don Romualdo that she is to be seen begging in the company of the blind Almudena. Doña Paca hastily rejects the idea that Benina should be a beggar —for it does not accord with her view of her own dignity— but Ponte interjects timidly, «Pida o no pida limosna, y esto yo no lo sé, es un ángel, palabra de honor» (315-316; *OC,* V, 1968).

Doña Paca is now plunged into mental confusion:

> El aturdimiento, el vértigo mental de doña Paca fueron tan grandes, que su alegría se trocó súbitamente en tristeza, y dio en creer que cuanto decían allí era ilusión de sus oídos; ficticios los seres con quienes hablaba, y mentira todo, empezando por la herencia (316; *OC,* V, 1968).

Illusion and reality have changed places. The dream of the inheritance is now true; what appeared to be the solid reality of her faithful servant, working in the house of don Romualdo to keep her mistress alive, is seen to be based on a fiction. As we have seen, doña Paca's first reaction is a generous one: «Vuelva a casa», she says, «aunque se traiga al africano metido en la cesta» (316; *OC,* V, 1968). But from now on her outlook is in the process of changing; the inheritance

produces a strange psychological effect: «Se le anubló la inteligencia... Quiso hablar de su Niña, y dijo mil disparates» (321; *OC,* V,
1969). The inheritance places her on a different economic level, where
Benina is no longer a necessity and could be an embarrassment. This
is pointed out later by Juliana, but that the idea has already occurred
to doña Paca is shown by her inability to think clearly about Benina.
Whilst on the one hand feeling a genuine regret that her servant is
not at hand to share her prosperity, doña Paca makes an effort to be
«reasonable». She vows to keep an account-book, as counselled by
Trujillo, although as we have seen, Ponte always forgets to buy it
and doña Paca never goes out to buy one herself. Despite the apparent
acceptance of the ideas of Trujillo, she buys absurdities, such as the
chandelier which is so large as almost to reach the table beneath it.
When Benina finally comes home and sees the chandelier, she thinks
for a moment that Almudena's irrational beliefs have come true and
that the shining pendants of the chandelier poised just above the table
are the heap of jewels which he had promised her. This irrational
reaction is not without its significance; doña Paca has achieved the
treasure on earth which she sought, but it does her little good, just as
the inheritance is the indirect cause of the death of Ponte. The fact
of the inheritance brings Juliana on to the scene: Reason comes to the
aid of Fantasy, as Casalduero points out,[7] but doña Paca, although
she may live a life of material ease under the thumb of Juliana, has
lost her freedom.

Benina sees her being taken to the new flat which Juliana has
arranged for her:

> ¡Qué desmejorada encontró a doña Francisca! Llevaba un
> vestido nuevo; pero de tan nefanda hechura, como cortado
> y cosido de prisa, que parecía la pobre señora vestida de li-
> mosna. Cubría su cabeza con un manto, y Obdulia ostentaba
> un sombrerote con disformes ringorrangos y plumas. Andaba
> doña Paca lentamente, la vista fija en el suelo, abrumada,
> melancólica, como si la llevaran entre guardias civiles (382-
> 383; *OC,* V, 1987).

There is a clear comparison here with the arrest and imprisonment of
Benina, which has occurred just before in the novel. Behind them

---

[7] P. 255.

walks Juliana, urging them on like the shepherd taking his flock to the slaughter-house. Juliana is one of those human beings intended by nature as a leader. She acts competently and governs with a firm hand:

> En la ínsula de doña Francisca estableció con mano firme la normalidad al mes de haber empuñado las riendas, y todos allí andaban derechos, y nadie se rebullía ni osaba poner en tela de juicio sus irrevocables mandatos. Verdad que para obtener este resultado precioso empleaba el absolutismo puro, el régimen de terror; su genio no admitía ni aun observaciones tímidas: su ley era su santísima voluntad; su lógica, el palo (391; OC, V, 1990).

The *ínsula* of doña Paca is to be no Isle of Barataria, nor is it to be the happy family home which Galdós offers in *Halma* as the final solution to the desire to be charitable to others. Juliana, like Casiana, the beggar in the church of San Sebastián, has come out on top by a process, we might say, of natural selection, and the microcosm represented by Doña Paca and her circle parallels the microcosm of the beggars at the beginning of the novel, and reflects the society in which all are destined to live.

* * *

As we have seen, Ponte compares Benina to a saint at the end of the novel, thus echoing the earlier ironic presentation of the character by the novelist (51; OC, V, 1890). But when we first see Benina with our own eyes, as it were, she is introduced as an ordinary servant who has worked for the family on two previous occasions, and who does not desert doña Paca when she has fallen on bad times. Benina has a tendency to be a «sisona», to take a cut for herself from all that passes through her hands. In the novel this suggests a feeling of insecurity rather than deliberate dishonesty. «Tenía el vicio del descuento, que en cierto modo, por otro lado, era la virtud del ahorro» (66; OC, V, 1895). In much the same way, she deliberately lies to doña Paca about the real source of her income, in order to save the latter's feelings. She invents the figure of don Romualdo, and when she is forced to give details of his house and way of life, these are the «simulacro perfecto de la verdad» (85; OC, V, 1900). Despite the

189

measures which she is forced to adopt, and despite the poverty in which she and her mistress live, Benina retains a firm trust in the goodness of God: «Dios es bueno... Pues yo que la señora, tendría confianza en Dios, y estaría contenta... Ya ve que yo lo estoy..., ¿no me ve?» (56; *OC*, V, 1892). She is indeed happy in the responsibilities she has assumed, although the burden becomes progressively heavier: «Cada cual, en esta vida, se defiende como puede... Los gorriones, un suponer, ¿tienen vergüenza?» (57-58; *OC*, V, 1892). She is somewhat superstitious, and very ready to give some credence to the wild beliefs of Almudena: «La miseria despertaba en ella el respeto de las cosas inverosímiles y maravillosas, y aunque no había visto ningún milagro, esperaba verlo el mejor día» (111; *OC*, V, 1908); in this we can of course compare her to her mistress. She listens in awe to Almudena, and half believes:

> Lo que contaba Almudena era de lo que *no se sabe*. ¿Y no puede suceder que alguno sepa lo que no sabemos los demás? ¿Pues cuántas cosas se tuvieron por mentira y luego salieron verdades?... (117; *OC*, V, 1910).

But whilst she herself, impelled by her desire to escape from her sordid surroundings, lends herself to these fantasies —«¡Señor, qué cosas, qué cosas se van viendo cada día en este mundo tan grande de la miseria!» (142; *OC*, V, 1917)—, at the same time she represents the brusque, cold reality which from time to time confronts Obdulia and Ponte, although she fails to shock them out of their day-dreams.

At this point she takes pity on Ponte, and gives him a peseta, an immense gift. Later she finds him ill and brings him home, tends him and gives up her bed to him: the act of a true Samaritana. As a result of a good turn done in the past, she is able to borrow ten *duros,* a considerable sum, which in effect sinks her financially. Up to this point, she has been able to repay her small debts, but this sum, incurred in order to be charitable to Ponte, is too much for her; in a worldly sense, Trujillo was right and she should have looked more closely at her «balance».[8] This good action arouses the jealousy of Almudena and the spite of doña Paca, who both become convinced that Benina wishes to marry Ponte. Benina is not roused by the

---

[8] Compare the way in which Rosalía Bringas finally loses her financial equilibrium in *La de Bringas,* as a result of the loan to Milagros.

insinuations of doña Paca, and that night puts her to bed as usual. She is long inured to doña Paca's hard tongue.

Doña Paca now tells Benina that don Romualdo has visited her. She forgets this, «por tener cosas de más importancia en que ocupar su entendimiento» (257-258; OC, V, 1950), but the next day she meets a beggar who also knows don Romualdo, and Benina is «confusa, sintiendo que lo real y lo imaginario se revolvían y entrelazaban en su cerebro» (260; OC, V, 1951). Having practised charity towards Ponte, she now goes looking for Almudena, who has disappeared from his usual haunts. She finds him on the outskirts of Madrid. She has by now lost all faith in his spells, and in the possibility of an easy escape from her troubles: «No, no; aquí no hay salvación para el pobre; y eso de sacar tesoros, o de que le traigan a uno las carretadas de piedras preciosas, me parece a mí que es conversación» (271-272; OC, V, 1954). Although her money is running short, she is charitable towards Silverio and his family, but is mistaken for the late doña Guillermina and she and Almudena are stoned. They are given shelter by the guarda-agujas and his wife, who also mention don Romualdo. Benina is now at the end of her tether: «Las necesidades aumentaban, imponíase la dura realidad...» (290; OC, V, 1960). She and Almudena begin to beg again in San Andrés, and she is thinking of giving up the struggle: «Perdía la fe en la Providencia, y formaba opinión poco lisonjera de la caridad humana» (293; OC, V, 1961). The last blow falls when she is arrested as a vagrant. Her reaction is to wonder what will happen to doña Paca, and she resolves that when she is freed she will tell Paca the truth, and «sea lo que Dios quiera» (298; OC, V, 1962). She has decided to confront reality face to face, without evasions.

But it is here that the fortunes of doña Paca and Benina diverge. As Benina is imprisoned, doña Paca is freed from her narrow world by the news of the inheritance. Doña Paca goes up in worldly fortune, but loses her former freedom; Benina declines in worldly fortune but becomes more saint-like. When Benina is freed, she does not yet know the details of the inheritance, but she has been pondering for some time on the nature of reality:

> ...Ya no se apartó de su mente la idea de que el benéfico sacerdote alcarreño no era invención suya, de que todo lo que soñamos tiene su existencia propia, y de que las mentiras entrañan verdades (293; OC, V, 1961).

¡Vaya con don Romualdo! Le había inventado ella, y de los senos obscuros de la invención salía persona de verdad, haciendo milagros, trayendo riquezas, y convirtiendo en realidades los soñados dones del Rey *Samdai* (359; *OC,* V, 1980).

Juliana argues doña Paca out of the idea of receiving Benina again in her flat; she will be given money and food, but there will no longer be a home for her. Benina refuses to abandon Almudena, and asks doña Paca if charity is dependent on the social rank of the recipient. She is firmly put in her place by Juliana, and weeps for the ingratitude of doña Paca.

Almudena's reaction is another flight of fancy, the pilgrimage to Jerusalem. But Benina is now unable to banish reality by wishful-thinking: «Muy bonito», she says, «pero ahora caigo en la cuenta de que tú y yo tenemos hambre» (370; *OC,* V, 1984). Almudena reveals the signs of leprosy, and thus Juliana is, in a worldly sense, justified in her refusal to have him in the house. Her charity —and Galdós does not refuse her this: «no carecía de amor al prójimo» (372; *OC,* V, 1984)— cannot stand up to this trial. But Benina's reaction is the opposite: «Con miradas no más expresó Nina su lástima del pobre ciego, su decisión de no abandonarle, y su conformidad con todas las calamidades que quisiera enviarle Dios» (374; *OC,* V, 1985). She is bitterly disappointed by doña Paca's treatment of her, but her decision to meet adversity face to face allows her to see her troubles in perspective:

> Su conciencia le dio inefables consuelos: miró la vida desde la altura en que su desprecio de la humana vanidad la ponía: vio en ridícula pequeñez a los seres que la rodeaban, y su espíritu se hizo fuerte y grande. Había alcanzado glorioso triunfo; sentíase victoriosa, después de haber perdido la batalla en el terreno material (379; *OC,* V, 1986).

And, in the end, the rational Juliana has to recognise the spiritual victory of Benina.

* * *

What, then, is the nature of true charity? In this novel, Galdós presents charity from many angles. He shows us charity in terms of social realities, and in terms of the microcosm of the society of the

beggars. He looks at the New Testament virtues, and, as in *Nazarín*
and *Halma,* sets the lessons of the New Testament against the background of the class situation and of the social evils of nineteenth-
century Madrid. *Misericordia* here differs from the two preceding novels, in that the Christian virtues are suggested directly —by reference, for instance, to the parable of the Good Samaritan— and are not
seen reflected in the deforming mirror of the novels and works of
Tolstoy. Galdós further recalls the parable of the Widow's Mite,
teaching us that terrestrial values are relative, whilst spiritual values
are eternal. And he shows us how charity can enable man to survive,
and to overcome, the despairs and frustrations engendered by modern
society.

Clearly the foolish impulses of doña Paca are of no utility as a guide
to conduct, nor are the rose-coloured illusions of Ponte, the flower-
filled dreams of Obdulia. Rather let *la razón* predominate over *la
insensatez.* Eyes must be opened, and reality must be confronted face
to face, as Benina herself learns in the course of the novel. But *la
razón* alone is not sufficient. This is no longer the world of the
determinist novelist, the so-called scientist endeavouring to work out
his formulae (by methods so blatantly unscientific). This is the new
novel, the novel of the turn of the century, the novel of will : contem-
poraneous with Ganivet's Pío Cid, and forerunner of Unamuno's men
of will. The epilogue shows us reason succumbing before intuition,
before pure charity. Juliana falls ill and suffers «embelecos nerviosos
y ráfagas de histerismo, afecciones de que Juliana se había reído más
de una vez...» (393; *OC,* V, 1990). She becomes convinced that her
children are ill and in mortal danger, and on a sudden impulse —so foreign to her calculating nature— she goes to visit Benina, whom she
finds on the outskirts of Madrid in the company of Almudena. Benina
tells her that she has at last met don Romualdo, and that she is sure,

> después de mucho cavilar, que no es el don Romualdo que yo
> inventé, sino otro que se parece a él como se parecen dos
> gotas de agua. Inventa una cosas que luego salen verdad, o
> las verdades, antes de ser verdaderas, un suponer, han sido
> mentiras muy gordas... (396; *OC,* V, 1991).

Juliana offers her money and tells her of her fears for her children.
On the next day, she visits Benina again. Benina, for the first time,
speaks to her familiarly in the second person, whilst Juliana still uses

usted. She asks Benina as a favour to command her not to believe that her children are in danger: «Si usted me lo afirma, lo creeré, y me curaré de esta maldita idea... Porque... lo digo claro: yo he pecado, yo soy mala...» Benina pardons her and, in words which recall those of Christ, tells her: «No llores ...y ahora vete a tu casa, y no vuelvas a pecar» (398; *OC,* V, 1992). Reason is overcome by intuition, by faith, by charity. [9] The novel which began as though it were to be another *L'Assommoir,* ends as an irrational statement of faith in the positive good to which the human being can attain.

Man can escape from his surroundings; he is not inevitably conditioned by his heredity and his environment, nor by any other external force. And true charity, pure charity, will enable man to face all adversities. Charity is more than the giving of alms, the unthinking scattering of a handful of coins, the calculated bribery of Saint Peter: charity is a state of mind, a way of life which enables the human being to escape from his own troubles because it allows him to escape into the troubles of others. In the words of Benina,

Cada uno, por el aquel de no sufrir, se emborracha con lo que puede: ésta con el aguardentazo, otros con otra cosa. Yo también las cojo; pero no así: las mías son de cosa de más adentro... Ya te contaré, ya te contaré (48; *OC,* 1889).

Benina's compensation is a life of true, active charity.

Westfield College,
London.

---

⁹ I can not share the view of Rupert C. Allen, «Pobreza y neurosis en *Misericordia,* de Pérez Galdós», *HispI,* no. 33 (1968), 46 who asks if Benina at this point «no ha quedado contagiado del desorden espiritual que reina a través de la novela...»

V. A. SMITH and J. E. VAREY

«Esperpento»:
*Some Early Usages in the Novels of Galdós**

The earliest usage of the word *esperpento* hitherto recorded is to be found in Juan Valera's «*Pequeñeces.* Currita Albornoz, al Padre Luis Coloma», which is dated Madrid, 1891. Currita, protesting at the treatment meted out to her by her literary creator, complains that «en las últimas páginas de *Pequeñeces* me presenta usted tan ajada y marchita, que parezco un esperpento». [1] This usage is noted by Joan Corominas, who gives as the first definition of *esperpento:* «Persona o cosa muy fea.» Martín Alonso's first definition is very similar: «Persona o cosa notable por su fealdad o mala traza.» Both philologists give also a second definition. Alonso: «Desatino, absurdo»; Corominas: «Desatino literario.» [2]

Corominas also refers to usages recorded by philologists in Spain and Spanish-America. Feliz Ramos y Duarte noted the word in 1895 in Veracruz, México, and defined it as follows: «Estantigua, endriago, cosa ridícula, papasal, pamema, centón, etc.» He quotes an undated leaflet of José Miguel Macías in which the word occurs twice:

> De los preceptos de los PP. de Port Royal no se infiere que se articule un disparate, para que la escritura reproduzca semejante barbarismo, ni que se escriba al capricho, para que se pronuncia en armonía dicho esperpento (p. 23).

---

* Page and volume references are to the first edition of each work by Galdós quoted; these are immediately followed by a second reference to the Aguilar edition of the *Obras completas,* ed. F. C. Sáinz de Robles, vols. IV (3rd. ed., Madrid, 1954), V (2nd. ed., Madrid, 1950) and VI (2nd. ed., Madrid, 1951). Accentuation has been modernised.

[1] Jun Valera, *Obras completas,* 2nd. ed., (Madrid, 1949), II, 862.

[2] Joan Corominas, *Diccionario crítico etimológico de la lengua castellana* (Berne, 1954), II, 389; Corominas, *Breve diccionario etimológico de la lengua castellana* (Madrid, 1961), 244; Martín Alonso, *Enciclopedia del idioma* (Madrid, 1958), II, 1854.

The second example is as follows:

> Pruébanlo, entre otros *esperpentos,* la ya olvidada regla sobre
> el uso de la g en las sílabas *je, jí* (p. 52).

Ramos y Duarte concludes that the use of the word can be equated
with that of barbarisms such as *presupuestar, dictaminar* and *etique-
ta.* [3] In 1908 Roberto Pastor y Molina notes the word in a list of
madrileñismos, and defines it as «persona muy fea». In an introductory note to his study, he claims that «no he adoptado otras acepciones
que aquellas que he recogido de la boca del mismo pueblo». [4] Manuel Antonio Román gives two definitions:

> Usado en España, en Méjico, en Chile y quizás en toda la
> América Latina por obra intelectual o literaria mal pergeñada
> o extravagante; persona o cosa que de fea causa espanto.

As an example of the second usage he quotes Valera's *Carta.* [5] Lisandro Segovia lists *esperpento* as both a *castellanismo y neologismo:*
«Persona fea, extravagante y de aspecto ridículo»; and as an *argenti-
nismo:* «Escuerzo, basilisco, *escracho,* harpía, hablando de una mujer
horrorosa, especialmente si es vieja.» [6]

* * *

The first usage which we have found in the novels of Benito Pérez
Galdós occurs in Part I of *La desheredada,* published in 1881. Don
José de Relimpio is defending Isidora against the attacks and imputa-
tions of his wife and, stressing her beauty, exclaims: «¡Y qué guapa
es...!» Whereupon Doña Laura retorts: «Quita allá, quita, esperpento.
Contenta me tienes...» (138; *OC,* IV, 1019). Relimpio, the sixty-year-
old book-keeper, has already been described by the author:

---

[3] Feliz Ramos y Duarte, *Diccionario de mejicanismos* (México, 1895), 246.
[4] Roberto Pastor y Molina, «Vocabulario de madrileñismos (Primera serie)»,
BH, XVIII (1908), 51, 59.
[5] Manuel Antonio Román, *Diccionario de chilenismos y de otras voces y lo-
cuciones viciosas* (Santiago de Chile, 1901-1918), II, 292; vol. II is dated 1908-
1911.
[6] Lisandro Segovia, *Diccionario de argentinismos, neologismos y barbaris-
mos. Con un apéndice sobre voces extranjeras interesantes* (Buenos Aires, 1911),
208-209.

> El bigotito de cabello de ángel, de un dorado claro y húmedo;
> los ojos como dos uvas, blandos y amorosos; la cara arrebo-
> lada, fresca y risueña, con dos pómulos teñidos de color rosa-
> ajada; el mirar complaciente, la actitud complaciente, y todo
> él labrado en la pasta misma de la complacencia (barro huma-
> no, del cual no hace ya mucho uso el Creador) formaban aquel
> conjunto de dulzura e inutilidad, aquel ramillete de confitería,
> que llevaba entre los hombres el letrero de José de Relimpio
> y Sastre, natural de Muchamiel, provincia de Alicante. Rema-
> temos este retrato con dos brochazos. Era el hombre mejor
> del mundo. Era un hombre que no servía para nada (126;
> OC, IV, 1013-1014).

He is further characterised as a feeble and timid would-be womaniser:

> D. José había sido un galanteador de primera. No lo podía
> remediar: estaba en su naturaleza, en su doble condición de
> tenedor de libros y de galán joven, y así, ya casado y viejo, no
> veía mujer bonita en la calle sin que la siguiera y aun se pro-
> pasase a decirle alguna palabreja. Entre sus amigos, solía llevar
> la conversación desde los temas trillados a los motivos de
> amor y aventuras; y todo se volvía almíbar, hablando de pies
> pequeños, de tal pantorrilla hermosa, vista al subir de un co-
> che, de una mirada, de un gesto. Las aventuras no pasaban
> generalmente de aquí y eran pura charla, porque su timidez
> le ponía grillos para pasar a cosas mayores (129; OC, IV, 1015).

Relimpio is now old and decrepit and Doña Laura lashes him with her tongue, calling him «hombre inútil, hombre-muñeco...» (127; OC, IV, 1014). «¡Lástima que no vengan los pintores a sacar tu figura de gorrión mojado!» she cries (128; OC, IV, 1014).

The use of esperpento in La desheredada must be looked at in the light of the description of the character and of the other epithets applied to him. It suggests that the man so described is decrepit and ridiculous, a figure of fun, but one who is largely responsible for the fact that others consider him comic.

In La de Bringas (1884) the term esperpento is applied both to the famous trabajo de pelo and to its destined recipient, Carolina Pez. Don José María del Pez, speaking to himself, shows that he despises the artist (Francisco Bringas), the work and the recipient:

> Vaya una mamarrachada... Es como salida de esa cabeza de
> corcho. Sólo tú, grandísimo tonto, haces tales esperpentos, y
> sólo a mi mujer le gustan... Sois el uno para el otro (102;
> OC, IV, 1602).

197

13

Later in the novel, Rosalía Bringas blames Carolina Pez for the loss of sight which her husband suffers as a result of the close work entailed in the making of the hair-picture:

¡Ah!, ella tiene la culpa, con sus obras de pelo. ¡Qué esperpento de mujer!... (132; *OC,* IV, 1611).

Again, one must look at the object and at the person to whom the epithet is applied. The *obra de pelo* is described by Galdós as composed of various old-fashioned motifs, both eighteenth-century and Romantic (16; *OC,* V, 1576); as a work of art it is out of date, ridiculous and futile. No less ridiculous is the proviso laid down by Carolina Pez that the hair-picture, a *delicado obsequio* in memory of a dead child, should be entirely piscine:

Lo que sí espero de la rectitud de usted —dijo Carolina, disimulando la desconfianza con la cortesía—, es que por ningún caso introduzca en la obra cabello que no sea nuestro. Todo se ha de hacer con pelo de la familia.
—Señora ¡por los clavos de Cristo!... ¿Me cree usted capaz de adulterar...?
—No... no..., si no digo... Es que los artistas, cuando se dejan llevar de la inspiración (*Riendo.*) pierden toda idea de moralidad, y con tal de lograr un efecto...
—¡Carolina!... (13-14; *OC,* IV, 1575).

Carolina, influenced by her cousin Serafinita de Lantigua, becomes infected with *misticismo,* and the peace of the family is shattered (76-80; *OC,* 1594-1595); we must, however, take this with a pinch of salt, for we hear it from Pez, engaged in trying to win Rosalía's sympathy for himself. But Rosalía is taken in, refers to Carolina as a *mula rezona* (99; *OC,* IV, 1601) and dreams of the wife who would be worthy of a Pez:

Para tal hombre, una mujer de principios, de mucha labia, señora de finísimos modales, y que supiera honrar a su marido honrándose a sí propia; que supiera darle lucimiento luciéndose ella misma; una dama que se creciera cada día haciéndole crecer, porque el secreto de las brillantes carreras de algunos hombres está en el talento de sus mujeres. Paquito decía ayer que Napoleón no hubiera sido nada sin Josefina. Si en vez de esa beata viviera al lado de Pez una dama que reuniera en sus salones lo más selecto de la política, ya Pez sería ministro... De veras... si yo tuviera a mi lado un sujeto semejante...! (100; *OC,* IV, 1601).

This interior monologue reveals Rosalía's character to us, but also implies that she looks down upon Carolina as unworthy of her polished consort, the female equivalent of that *pisa-hormigas,* Francisco Bringas.

In the Second Part of *Lo prohibido* (1885), the term is applied to the Marqués de Fúcar, when it is related that in Paris Eloísa had left him for a Frenchman:

> En París había desplumado a un francés, dando un lindo esquinazo a aquel esperpento de Fúcar (II, 115; *OC,* IV, 1805).

The Marqués de Fúcar is described for the first time in *La familia de León Roch:*

> El Marqués de Fúcar andaba lentamente a causa de su obesidad. Había en su paso algo de la marcha majestuosa de un navío o galeón antiguo, cargado de pingüe esquilmo de las Indias. También él parecía llevar encima el peso de su inmensa fortuna, amasada en veinte años, de esa prosperidad fulminante que la sociedad contemplaba pasmada y temerosa (*OC,* IV, 766).

He is strongly characterised in Chapter X of Part I of the same novel:

> Era de cuerpo pequeño, rostro fino y afeminado, al cual daba, por cálculo, trocado al fin en costumbre, una gravedad pegadiza, semejante a un cosmético que empleara diariamente metiendo el dedo en los botes de su tocador de viejo florido. Ojo, nariz y boca eran en él, como los de su hija, de una corrección admirable; mas lo que en ella cautivaba, en él hacía reír, y lo serio se mudaba en cómico, porque nada es tan horriblemente bufón como la fisonomía de una mujer hermosa colgada como de espetera en las facciones de un viejo mezquino.
>
> Su vestir correctísimo y elegante, sus ademanes desembarazados, su cortesía refinada y desabrida, que encubría una falta absoluta de benevolencia, de caridad, de ingenio, adornaban su persona, brillando como la encuadernación lujosa de un libro sin ideas. No era un hombre perverso, no era capaz de maldad declarada, ni de bien; era un compuesto insípido de debilidad y disipación, corrompido más por contacto que por malicia propia; uno de tantos; un individuo que difícilmente podría diferenciarse de otro de su misma jerarquía, porque la falta de caracteres, salvas notabilísimas excepciones, ha hecho de ciertas clases altas, como de las bajas, una colecti-

199

vidad que no podría calificarse bien hasta que los progresos del neologismo no permitan decir *las masas aristocráticas*.

Y aquel ser vacío y sin luz tenía palabras abundantes no exentas de expresión, y manejaba a maravilla todos los lugares comunes de la Prensa y de la tribuna, sin añadirles nada, pero tampoco sin quitarles nada. Era, pues, un propagandista diligente de ese tesoro de frases hechas, que para muchas personas es compendio y cifra de la sabiduría (*OC*, IV, 785).

The Marqués de Fúcar is clearly intended as a typical member of the moneyed classes of Madrid, a hollow man. In *Lo prohibido* he appears as lover of Eloísa, and cuts a ridiculous figure:

Era Fúcar bastante viejo; pero se defendía bien de los años y los disimulaba con todo el arte posible. Era abotargado, patilludo, de cuello corto, y parecía un cuerpo relleno de paja por su tiesura y la rigidez de sus movimientos. Se teñía las barbas; y como los tiempos no consienten la ridiculez de la peluca, lucía una calva pontifical (I, 177; *OC*, IV, 1727).

María Juana says that she can not understand how there could exist a woman

capaz de echarse a pechos (textual) el carcamal asqueroso del marqués de Fúcar, sólo por estar forrado de oro; un adefesio que había sido negrero en Cuba y contrabandista por alto en España, y que, por añadidura, se teñía la barba (II, 93; *OC*, IV, 1798).

The term is also used in the same novel by Camila, when she asks the narrator:

¿Nos prestas tu coche, esperpento? (II, 234; *OC*, IV, 1841).

This usage should be equated with the many epithets applied by Camila to the narrator throughout the course of the novel: *majadero, grandísimo soso* and, more particularly, *tísico*. *Esperpento* suggests that the narrator cuts, as does Fúcar in another context, a ridiculous figure.

In *Torquemada en la hoguera* (1889), the money-lender screams at Tía Roma:

El demonio está contigo, y maldita tú eres entre todas las brujas y esperpentos que hay en el cielo... digo, en el infierno (103; *OC*, V, 933).

200

The slip of the tongue reveals Torquemada's state of mind, and in this context *esperpento* suggests the *fealdad* to be found in many of the definitions quoted above.

The usage in Part Three of *Angel Guerra* (1891) is more revealing in that it describes a Carnival-like figure :

> Un poco más allá, a la entrada de la calle de San Marcos, vio a un tío muy sucio, cubierto con una estera vieja, la cara y las manos pintadas de hollín, el cual llevaba una especie de caña de pescar, con cuerda de la cual pendía un higo. En derredor suyo, un apretado cerco de chicuelos, cuya algazara se oía en toda la plaza y calles adyacentes. Empujábanse unos a otros para acercarse, y con la boca abierta daban brincos pretendiendo coger el deseado *higui,* que saltaba en el aire con las sacudidas de la cuerda, a los golpes dados en la caña por el horrible esperpento, que tan estrafalariamente se divertía. La bulliciosa inquietud de los muchachos contrastaba con la estúpida seriedad del tiznado personaje (III, 8; *OC,* V, 1424).

* * *

As we have seen, Valera in 1891, Ramos y Duarte in 1895, Pastor y Molina in 1908, Román in 1908-1911 and Segovia in 1911 all indicate that the word *esperpento* is to be found applied to a «persona fea, extravagante y de aspecto ridículo», to quote the definition of the last-named lexicographer. Valera's use of the term suggests that the person to whom it is applied is a faded shadow of her former self. José Miguel Macías, quoted by Ramos y Duarte, gives the term a literary or philological usage, whilst Román indicates that it is applied to a crude or ridiculous literary production.

Galdós's use of the term is not incompatible with these definitions. In *La desheredada,* José de Relimpio is a ridiculous figure, faded («con dos pómulos teñidos de color rosa-ajada»), complacent, and utterly useless.[7] Once a womaniser, his present pretensions contrast unfavourably with past performances. Carolina Pez is a silly woman, lacking completely in taste, and, it is implied by Rosalía in her interior monologue, a frumpish, dowdy figure given over to vapid moralising and

---

[7] It is interesting to note that José F. Montesinos, *Galdós* (Madrid, 1969), II, 14, characterises Relimpio as «claramente en la españolísima tradición del esperpento».

tedious and superficial religious observances. The Marqués de Fúcar is a moneyed man, his wealth acquired in dubious circumstances. His facial contortions are a mask, and in no way indicative of his true sentiments. Indeed, Galdós gives us to believe that he is not troubled either by sentiments or by ideas. He is a purely artificial, exterior figure, a hollow man, and ridiculous as the lover of the charming and beautiful, if morally reprehensible, Eloísa. The narrator of *Lo prohibido* is also seen in the novel as a ridiculous lover, harbouring a passion for his cousin Camila and incapable of seeing the true state of her feelings towards him, or towards her husband. The usages to be found in *Torquemada en la hoguera* and in *Angel Guerra* are of slighter interest: both suggest an ugly and repulsive figure. In *Torquemada en la hoguera* the word implies a witch or demon-like figure; in *Angel Guerra* a black-faced clown, diverting children with «estúpida seriedad». Again the note of ridicule is struck.

Perhaps of more interest, in view of the later development of the word at the hands of Valle-Inclán, is the suggestion that the characters to whom the term *esperpento* is applied are puppet-like. The black-faced clown of *Angel Guerra,* Don José Relimpio and the Marqués de Fúcar may appear to have little in common as far as their physical descriptions are concerned, but it is worthy of note that the effect of the descriptions, although differing widely in detail, is to suggest that their faces do not reflect ordinary human emotions: that they are, in effect, masks. The man described in *Angel Guerra* has a black mask of soot; Relimpio's face is characterless, «los ojos como dos uvas, blandos y amorosos», with faded roses on his cheeks and a complacent, gentle, useless look about him; the Marqués de Fúcar's face displays «una gravedad pegadiza», a cosmetic smile, a facial contortion which is so false as to give his very seriousness a comic effect. Apart from their mask-like features, Relimpio and Fúcar are puppet-like in their movements. Doña Laura calls her husband an *hombre-muñeco,* and Fúcar «parecía un cuerpo relleno de paja por su tiesura y la rigidez de sus movimientos».

Such figures as the Marqués de Fúcar are ridiculous not only because of their outward appearance, but because they belong to a hollow, vicious and ridiculous society. Just as Relimpio apes the lady-killer, so Fúcar gives the outward appearance of wisdom and sententious morality which he is far from possessing. If Relimpio is «un hombre que no servía para nada», Fúcar is «uno de tantos», one of the *masas aristocráticas,* or, as Ortega would have classified him, an *hombre-masa:* a vulgar, pretentious nonentity.

These men, then, together wtih Carolina Pez and the narrator of *Lo prohibido,* could well be figures from the *esperpento* world later to be conceived by Ramón del Valle-Inclán. Their values are inverted; they are formed by their world, and they are ridiculous because they try to give the appearance of being what they are not. It is therefore interesting to note that Galdós also applies the term *esperpento* to a pseudo-work of art, the *trabajo de pelo* which causes Francisco Bringas to lose his sight. [8] The work is intended to commemorate the death of a child; even Carolina Pez must have felt genuinely enough the death of her fifteen-year-old daughter, but the genuine emotion is entombed beneath layer upon layer of false artistic expression, and of vapid sentimentality. Again, the artistic clichés employed by Francisco Bringas —the willow, the tomb, the angel, the moonlight— although by his time outdated, had once meant something to their original creators. But the artistic coinage has worn smooth and the sharp outline blurred. As a work of art, the *obra de pelo* suffers from being second-hand, ridiculously antiquated, *mal pergeñada* and *extravagante,* to quote the definition of Román. [9] But Galdós does not condemn it only for being a *mamarrachada;* he condemns it because the *delicado obsequio* is also a token of Francisco Bringas's gratitude for the sinecure which his son has received, thanks to the manipulations of Pez. As a work of art it is useless and tasteless; as a token of gratitude, it celebrates yet another act of corruption by a prominent member of the bureaucracy. It might well be said to be an ordinary, every-day act of social intercourse seen in the distorting mirror of Galdós's social criticism.

A usage linking the word *esperpento* with a play is to be found in the prologue which Galdós wrote for his play *Los condenados,* dated December, 1894. On its first performance on 11 December, *Los condenados* had failed to find favour with the public. Defending his work, Galdós complains about the shallowness of much of the newspaper criticism devoted to his play:

---

[8] On the significance of the blindness of Francisco Bringas, see J. E. Varey, «Francisco Bringas: *nuestro buen Thiers*», *Anales galdosianos,* I (1966), 63-69.

[9] Valle-Inclán likewise parodies the clichés of the debased Romanticism of this period; for instance, in the graveyard scenes of *Las galas del difunto* and *Los cuernos de don Friolera.*

Algún crítico, que goza fama de mordaz, se mostraba duro con la obra, con su autor, considerado y respetuoso. Otros, en cambio, salieron tan desmandados, como si se tratara del último esperpento de los teatros por horas, de una de esas efímeras piezas, cuya crítica suele hacer el aburrido público con las extremidades inferiores (x; *OC,* VI, 697).

Here the term is applied in a theatrical context, and clearly defined.

* * *

This brief note is not intended to be exhaustive, We have not, for this purpose, examined all the novels of Galdós, and it may well be that other early usages of *esperpento* will be found in Galdós and in other contemporary writers. Nor do our findings shed light on the etymology of the word, a problem concerning which Corominas has rightly remarked that «todo... es problemático». But we have indicated a usage ten years earlier than the earliest hitherto recorded, and our study of the contexts in which it occurs may perhaps shed light on the pre-history of the word which Ramón del Valle-Inclán was, many years later, to universalise.

Westfield College,
London.

COLECCION TAMESIS

SERIE A - MONOGRAFIAS

EDWARD M. WILSON and JACK SAGE: *Poesías líricas en las obras dramáticas de Calderón*, pp. xix + 165.

PHILIP SILVER: *'Et in Arcadia ego': A Study of the Poetry of Luis Cernuda*, pp. xv + 211.

KEITH WHINNOM: *A Glossary of Spanish Bird-Names*, pp. 157.

BRIAN DUTTON: *La 'Vida de San Millán de la Cogolla' de Gonzalo de Berceo. Estudio y edición crítica*. El tomo I.º de las *Obras completas* de Gonzalo de Berceo, pp. xiv + 248.

A. D. DEYERMOND: *Epic Poetry and the Clergy: Studies on the 'Mocedades de Rodrigo'*, pp. xix + 312, with two maps.

ABDÓN M. SALAZAR: *El escudo de armas de Juan Luis Vives*, pp. viii + 136.

P. GALLAGHER: *The Life and Works of Garci Sánchez de Badajoz*, pp. x + 296.

CARLOS P. OTERO: *Letras, I*, pp. xviii + 202.

EMMA SUSANA SPERATTI-PIÑERO: *De 'Sonata de otoño' al esperpento (Aspectos del arte de Valle-Inclán)*, pp. viii + 341.

'Libro de buen amor' Studies. Edited by G. B. Gybbon-Monypenny, pp. xiii + 256.

Galdós Studies. Edited by J. E. Varey, pp. XII + 204.

SERIE B - TEXTOS

LOPE DE VEGA: *Triunfo de la fee en los reynos del Japón*. Edited by J. S. Cummins, pp. xlix + 116, with seven illustrations and one map.

FERNÁN PÉREZ DE GUZMÁN: *Generaciones y semblanzas*. Edición crítica con prólogo, apéndices y notas de R. B. Tate, pp. xxvii + 112.

El sufrimiento premiado. Comedia famosa, atribuida en esta edición, por primera vez, a Lope de Vega Carpio. Introducción y notas de V. F. Dixon, pp. xxvii + 177.

José de Cadalso: *Cartas marruecas.* Prólogo, edición y notas de Lucien Dupuis y Nigel Glendinning, pp. lxiii + 211.

Virgilio Malvezzi: *Historia de los primeros años del reinado de Felipe IV.* Edición y estudio preliminar por D. L. Shaw, pp. liv + 206, with 3 illustrations and 3 maps.

La comedia Thebaida. Edited by G. D. Trotter and Keith Whinnom, pp. lxi + 270.

Juan Vélez de Guevara: *Los celos hacen estrellas.* Editada por J. E. Varey y N. D. Shergold, con una edición de la música por Jack Sage, pp. cxxvii+273.

SERIE D - REPRODUCCIONES EN FACSIMIL

Cayetano Alberto de la Barrera y Leirado: *Catálogo bibliográfico y biográfico del teatro antiguo español, desde sus orígenes hasta mediados del siglo XVIII (Madrid, 1860),* pp. xi + 727.